The psychology of
deductive reasoning

International Library of Psychology

General Editor: Max Coltheart
Professor of Psychology, University of London

The psychology of
deductive reasoning

Jonathan St. B. T. Evans

Routledge & Kegan Paul
London, Boston and Henley

First published in 1982
by Routledge & Kegan Paul Ltd
39 Store Street,
London WC1E 7DD,
9 Park Street,
Boston, Mass. 02108, USA, and
Broadway House,
Newtown Road,
Henley-on-Thames,
Oxon RG9 1BN
Set in Baskerville by
Input Typesetting Ltd, London
and printed in Great Britain by
The Thetford Press Ltd
Thetford, Norfolk

Library of Congress Cataloging in Publication Data

Evans, Jonathan St. B. T., 1948–
The psychology of deductive reasoning.

(International library of psychology)
Includes bibliographical references.
1. Thought and thinking. 2. Logic.
3. Reasoning (Psychology) I. Title. II. Series.
BF455.E93 1982   153.4'33   81–13991

ISBN 0-7100-0923-2   AACR2

Contents

Acknowledgments

It is not possible to identify everyone who has influenced my thinking about the psychology of reasoning, and thus contributed indirectly to the writing of this book. There is no doubt, however, that without Peter Wason, who stimulated and nurtured my early interest in the field, the book would never have been written. My ideas owe much to the many discussions I have had with him over the years, and also to the colleagues and research students who have shared my interest in reasoning research at Plymouth Polytechnic. I would especially wish to acknowledge the contributions of Paul Pollard, Steve Newstead, Ken Manktelow and Phil Brooks.

Few persons care to study logic, because everyone conceives himself to be proficient enough in the art of reasoning already.

(Charles Sanders Peirce)

Men may argue badly but they reason well, that is, their professed grounds are no sufficient measure of their real ones.

(Cardinal Newman)

I'd be a donkey, a monkey or a bear, or anything but that vain animal who is so proud of being rational.

(John Wilmot, Earl of Rochester)

1 Introduction

In one sense this book is only about deductive reasoning. In another sense it is about language comprehension, mental imagery, learning processes, memory organisation and the nature of human thought. The first sense is defined by the *paradigms* employed; the second by nature of the psychological *processes* which the paradigms evoke.

We will start with a brief consideration of the notion of deductive reasoning as a philosophical concept, and then proceed to psychological issues. One rough definition of deductive thought is that it leads from the general to the particular, e.g.

All swans are white,
This bird is a swan
Therefore, this bird is white.

An *inductive* inference, on the other hand, leads from the particular to the general:

All the swans I have ever seen are white,
Therefore all swans are white.

This inference is not valid, nor is any other inductive inference. An argument is valid if assumptions which are true cannot lead to conclusions which are false. However many white swans I have seen, there may be some black ones around.

The validity of a logical argument is not affected by whether its premises and conclusions are, in fact, true or false. The following argument is valid, even though its conclusion is obviously false:

All cats are fish,
All fish have gills,
Therefore, all cats have gills.

This valid argument permits a false conclusion because one of its assumptions is false. Invalid arguments may also lead to true conclusions:

If $2 + 2 = 4$ then dogs chase cats,
Dogs chase cats,
Therefore, $2 + 2 = 4$.

Deductive reasoning is tautological. It adds no new knowledge, but states necessary consequences of that which is already assumed. However, logical systems adopt certain principles as axiomatic, such as the law of non-contradiction. A contradiction is the simultaneous assertion that some proposition *p* and its negation *not p* are both true. The avoidance of such contradictions is fundamental to most systems of logic.

A logical system normally has a set of principles or *rules of inference* which provide techniques for making valid deductions of conclusions from assumptions or premises. Mathematics can be regarded as a set of logical systems, in which symbols are manipulated. For example, the solution of simultaneous equations starts with the equations (premises) and, by application of rules, deduces the necessary numerical values of the algebraic variables as the conclusion. A good example of a set of logical arguments is Euclid's geometry, in which a set of *theorems* (conclusions) are deduced from a set of *axioms* (premises).

We are not concerned in this book with mathematical logic, but rather with the deduction of conclusions stated as verbal propositions. A number of philosophers, from Aristotle onwards, have been concerned with devising systems of logic to achieve this. Assuming that it is possible to analyse the logical structure of natural language arguments, we might ask why it is necessary to do so. One area in which logical argument seems to be essential is in the construction and testing of scientific theories. Logic facilitates this process in two ways. Firstly, it provides a check on the internal consistency of a theory; it should not be possible to deduce a contradiction from the assumptions of the theory. Secondly, deductive logic is involved in testing empirical predictions of scientific theories.

Philosophers of science traditionally viewed science as a process of making *inductive generalisations* from experimental observations. However, as observed earlier, such inductive inferences can never be valid, so is it not unsatisfactory for science to be based on an invalid type of logic? The modern philosopher Karl Popper (e.g. 1959) has resolved this dilemma by asserting that the purpose of science is not the verification but the *falsification* of theories. Falsification can be achieved by deductive logic. I can never prove the statement 'All swans are white' to be true, but I only need to observe one black swan to prove that it is false. The logical nature of scientific theory testing is as follows:

1   State theory.
2   Deduce logically necessary and empirically testable predictions.
3   Test predictions by experiment or observation.
4   Re-evaluate theory.

If a theory's predictions fail, i.e. are not borne out by empirical observation, then we have a contradiction between prediction and observation. Assuming the experiment was properly conducted, this means that at least one assumption of the original theory must have been incorrect. Consequently, the theory must be either revised or abandoned. If the prediction is confirmed, this does not necessarily mean that the theory is correct. Popper argues that a theory must be open to empirical falsification in order to be called a scientific theory, and that a good theory will make risky predictions, i.e. predict things that would not be likely *a priori*.

Science, as Popper sees it, consists of alternating conjectures and refutations. Bad theories are weeded out, and good ones survive by a kind of natural selection. We may agree with Popper, then, that deductive logic is fundamental in science. We must be able to deduce conclusions and to eliminate contradictions. Is deductive logic a necessary and natural part of human thought, however? The answer depends upon whether or not one adopts a *rationalist* view of man.

In the rationalist approach (e.g. Kelly, 1955) man is seen as a kind of scientist in his everyday life. According to this model, people are continually involved in constructing theories, deriving predictions, collecting evidence and the like in all aspects of life, including, for example, the development of interpersonal relationships. A rational man would need, and be expected to possess, some system of deductive logic. The *behaviourist* view (e.g. Skinner, 1972), on the other hand, sees man's behaviour as under the control of his environment, and determined by his personal history of reinforcement. This approach does not require the assumption of any internalised logical system. Behaviour will accord with logical principles if and only if the appropriate reinforcement contingencies have been applied.

There are, of course, many intermediate positions, but it will be useful to keep sight of these extremes. Rationalism, in particular, is manifest in many of the approaches to reasoning research that will be reviewed. This viewpoint has implications beyond the assumption of logical competence. For example, it may lead to the assumption that thought processes are available to introspection, an idea that will be critically examined in the later part of this book. It is even supposed by some that a system of logical thought is innately determined. Recent books on the psychology of reasoning have had a distinct bias towards the rationalist approach (Falmagne, 1975; Revlin and Mayer, 1978). In contrast, this book will emphasise non-rational aspects of human reasoning, in the context of a review of the recent literature in the field.

All the experimental research to be reviewed can be seen, in one sense, as assessing people's competence to solve logical tasks. Part I of the book is concerned with relatively simple tasks where error rates are generally low. In the more complex tasks involving syllogistic reasoning (Part II), and propositional reasoning (Part III), however, logical errors abound in all studies. This might, in itself, lead one to abandon rationalism; but rationalists are not so easily deterred.

Rationality is seen as subjective to the individual. In the field of decision-making, for example, rational man is supposed to choose in such a way as to maximise personal gain (see Lee, 1971). Objectively, many decisions appear 'irrational', but can be explained as rational by assuming subjective distortions in the assumptions which the decision-maker holds. Some discussion of decision research and its applicability in the explanation of reasoning data is given in Chapter 11. In reasoning, as in decision-making, 'rational' explanations can be offered for apparently irrational, i.e. illogical, performance. Henle (1962) proposed that subjects interpret the premises of reasoning arguments in a personal way. They may alter, add or drop premises. She contends, however, that subjects' conclusions follow logically from their reinterpreted version of the problem. This highly influential paper is discussed in detail in Chapter 5, and the merits of 'Henleism' are subsequently examined with reference to both syllogistic and propositional reasoning.

In this book, it will not be assumed, *a priori*, that 'reasoning' is necessarily going on in reasoning experiments. This brings us back to the point of the opening paragraph of this chapter. The book reviews research which has involved deductive reasoning paradigms. Our concern is with the psychological explanation of performance on such tasks, and the wider implications that follow. One disadvantage of the psychology of reasoning is the relative isolation of the field from other work in cognitive psychology. A further aim of the present book is to relate reasoning research to general issues in the study of cognition.

At this point, it would be helpful to define the criteria by which work has been included in the review that forms the major part of this book. A deductive reasoning task involves making an inference from information which is *given*. If the task requires access to memory of things which are not presented, then it is not simply a reasoning task. This means, for example, that problems which draw on semantic memory for their solution are inadmissible. For similar reasons, the interesting area of pragmatic inference (see, for example, Harris and Monaco, 1978) is not included. Many of the complex reasoning tasks discussed in Parts II and III employ abstract materials such as letters and numbers, although the use of thematic content in logically equivalent tasks is also considered in some detail. Even in the latter case, however, instructions to these tasks will always indicate that subjects should evaluate the validity of arguments on the basis of what is presented.

The limitation is, of course, one of paradigms not processes. Subjects may well be influenced by transfer of learning from other situations, and a number of the explanations to be considered are along these lines. Both rationalists and non-rationalists account for reasoning errors in terms of some learned tendencies, relating to the interpretation of sentences, or other factors. The non-rationalist, however, has both more to explain (right as well as wrong answers) and more devices with which to formulate explanations (e.g. response biases).

The tasks used do, of course, require some linguistic knowledge for their solution. For example, negation has the logical property of reversing truth value: if p is true then *not p* is false, and vice versa. Studies of sentence verification (Chapter 3) reveal that negation serves this function in language as well, but linguistic negation is more complicated. Other reasoning tasks involve sentences such as *All A are B*, *If p then q* and *Either p or q*. Obviously, subjects can only attempt to solve such tasks if they understand the meaning of connectives such as 'If . . . then . . .'. Again, we shall see that the linguistic interpretation of such connectives is a good deal more complicated than the corresponding relations in standard textbooks of logic.

The aims of the present book are twofold. The first aim is to provide a comprehensive review of research involving deductive reasoning tasks. The expansion of the field in recent years necessitates this arduous exercise. It is assumed that the reader is familiar with basic work in experimental and cognitive psychology, but the book is otherwise self-contained. In Part II, a chapter is devoted to discussion of basic issues in the study of language and imagery, which are necessary for understanding of the work reviewed in Chapters 3 and 4. Parts II and III each contain an introductory chapter which explains the basics of the logical systems used in the reasoning tasks with which they are concerned.

The second aim is to provide a viable theoretical alternative to rationalist theories of human reasoning, and to relate the study of logical reasoning performance to the main field of cognitive psychology. The Discussion is concerned with this latter objective. In Chapter 11 it will be argued that a major change of approach is needed to the psychology of reasoning. From consideration of the material reviewed in Parts I to III of this book, it appears that there is little evidence for the influence of a general system of logical competence, and that the thought processes involved are highly *content dependent*. It is also argued that reasoning experiments are best viewed as specialised problem-solving or decision-making tasks, and explanations for various phenomena are offered in line with these considerations. In Chapter 12, attention is focused on the dual process theory of reasoning (Wason and Evans, 1975) and its subsequent development. In this respect, reasoning phenomena are related to diverse work in social psychology, memory theory and the differential function of the two hemispheres of the brain. Whilst some of these later suggestions may be rather speculative, I would maintain that it is for its contribution to cognitive psychology that psychology of reasoning – and this book – must be judged.

Finally, a point about style is in order. Like all writers of the English language, I was confronted with the problem that there are no generic pronouns which are neutral with respect to sex. For stylistic reasons I have retained the old-fashioned 'he', 'his', etc., in preference to such devices as 'he/she', '(s)he', etc. This in no way implies that the people referred to (e.g. experimental subjects) are more likely to be male than female.

Part I

Elementary reasoning tasks

2 Theoretical background

In Part I the focus is on relatively simple tasks involving sentence verification (Chapter 3) and transitive inference (Chapter 4). These are considered first because of their comparative simplicity. Performance on the complex tasks discussed in Parts II and III is subject to high error rates which provide the main basis for statistical analysis. By contrast, performance on the tasks reviewed in Part I is generally subject to low error rates, so that the latency of response becomes the main measure of interest. These tasks are also thought to give relatively direct information about the manner in which simple sentences are comprehended or *represented* in memory.

In general, it is important in studying any problem-solving task to ask how the information given is represented internally by the subject. One must bear in mind that the subject responds to the problem as *he* understands it, which is not necessarily the way that the experimenter intends or a logic textbook instructs. However, an interest in the representation of sentences and other forms of information is also the concern of psycholinguists, memory researchers and other cognitive psychologists. It is, therefore, necessary to establish a general theoretical context within which to assess the research reviewed in the following two chapters. Particularly relevant is the debate about the relative status of theories proposing that sentences (and pictures) are represented by underlying abstract *propositions*, and those which postulate the use of *mental images*. We will first consider the nature and origin of these types of theory, and then attempt to identify the issues of conflict which arise.

Propositional representations

Propositional treatments of sentence comprehension assume that the underlying meaning is represented in an abstract semantic code, consisting of a set of propositions. The idea of such underlying representation owes much to the work of the linguist Noam Chomsky (1957, 1965, 1968). Chomsky argued that one's ability to produce and to understand utterances could not be acquired by the principles of learning theory (see Chomsky, 1959), but must be *generative* in nature, in order to account for a language user's potential to produce or understand an infinite number of different utterances. Specifically, he proposed that the *surface structure* of a sentence – as it actually appears – must be generated from an underlying *deep structure* by use of transformational rules. The deep structure consists of a set of base strings or propositions plus transformational markers. These markers can be regarded as instructions for generating the surface structure from the deep structure.

Take, for example, the sentence, 'The big boy did not hit the girl'. The elementary propositions of the deep structure correspond to simple assertions of fact:

The boy is big.
The boy hit the girl.

Both the combination of these propositions and the negation of the second proposition are achieved by 'transformations'. The idea that negative sentences (also passives, etc.) have greater transformational complexity than affirmatives has stimulated some psychological research (see Chapter 3). Early psychological interest in Chomsky's theories (e.g. Miller, Galanter and Pribram, 1960) were in fact, focused on the *syntactic* aspect of Chomsky's theories, e.g. transformational rules, rather than the *semantic* aspect of how meaning may be obtained from a deep structure representation. Indeed, in his original formulation Chomsky (1957) appeared to be mainly interested in syntactic mechanisms which he considered at that time to be independent of meaning.

Psychologists such as George Miller were, at one time, interested in testing the 'psychological reality' of Chomsky's 1957 theory. The question asked was, in effect, whether the psychological 'rules' of sentence comprehension correspond in some way to Chomsky's linguistic rules. The practical problem from the psychologist's point of view concerns testability, although there is the more general question of whether a theory can simultaneously function as both a linguistic and a psychological theory. One difficulty, discussed by Chomsky himself, lies in the distinction between linguistic *competence* and linguistic *performance*. A language user's competence is revealed by his intuitive ability to distinguish grammatically legal from illegal utterances. In practice such competence would always be subject to distortion by performance factors such as memory lapses, or a change of mind occurring halfway through uttering a sentence. Thus competence and performance would not correspond exactly; and Chomsky argued that the task of generative grammar is to describe competence, not performance. While linguistically necessary, the distinction between competence and performance severely restricts the empirical falsifiability of a linguistic theory. Any deviation from the theory's predictions might be attributed to some kind of performance factor.

In the revised version of his theory (1965), Chomsky introduced a semantic component, which operated on the deep structure representation to generate meaning. Subsequent trends in psycholinguistics have continued to show a change of emphasis from syntactic to semantic aspects of language. There has also been a trend towards consideration of connected prose rather than isolated sentences. Some of the modern work is based largely on theoretical analysis (e.g. Miller and Johnson-Laird, 1976) with a considerable interest in the formulation of language processing theories in the form of computer programs (e.g. Winograd, 1972; Shanck, 1972). We will, however, confine our interest to theories which lend themselves to ready empirical test.

The notion that language is understood by reference to underlying propositions is now widespread in both computer simulation models and in general psycholinguistic and memory theories. Modern propositional analysis is, however, quite detached from Chomsky's linguistic theories. This is illustrated by the remarkable absence of terms such as 'generative grammar' and 'transformation' in the subject index of the recent text on psycholinguistics by Clark and Clark (1977). There are now a number of formulations of propositional theories which differ with respect to how the propositions are written and the nature of the mechanisms proposed to underlie them. Kintsch's (1974) theory is primarily applied to semantic memory, while H. Clark (see, for example, Clark and Clark, 1977) has applied his propositional theory to verification and reasoning tasks. Clark's work in these areas will be considered in Chapters 3 and 4. Anderson's (1976) ACT simulation model, which operates on a propositional network, is applied to practically everything (for ACT's predecessor HAM see also Anderson and Bower, 1973).

Clark's theory is concerned with the manner in which people process the linguistic structure of individual sentences. He starts with the notion that sentences are broken down into *constituents*. His analysis of constituent structure is essentially similar to Chomsky's treatment of surface structure. He defines a constituent as ' . . . a group of words that can be replaced by a single word without a change in function and without doing violence to the rest of the sentence' (Clark and Clark, 1977, p. 48). The propositions underlie the constituents, and both have a hierarchical structure. Propositions themselves are written in the form of algebraic functions, in which a modifier is followed, in parentheses, by the object or objects it modifies, e.g. 'John walks' would be written: Walk (John). Clark is not, however, posing simply a linguistic structure, but also a psychological structure. For example, the listener is supposed to comprehend language by breaking sentences down, firstly into constituents, and secondly into underlying propositions.

Propositional theories, have, however, a much broader range of application than suggested by the examples given. A propositional analysis can be made of whole texts rather than individual sentences (see Kintsch, 1974). It can also be applied to knowledge acquired by non-linguistic means. We shall see later, for example, that propositional theories have been offered for the explanation of pictorial representations. In current usage propositions are regarded as *abstract* (hence not verbal). They also have a useful property of *truth value* – they may be true, false or indeterminate. It is argued by some that all knowledge can be represented as a set of verifiable propositions. Whether or not this is an adequate characterisation of human knowledge is, however, a matter for considerable debate. Many authors favour the view that some forms of representation are achieved in the form of mental images, a view that will now be examined.

Mental imagery

The topic of mental imagery has had an interesting history in psychology. A fashionable topic in the late nineteenth and early twentieth centuries when the introspective method was respectable, it was banished by the advent of Watson's behaviourism. In recent years, however, imagery has made a sensational comeback into psychological study, riding on the bandwagon of 'cognitive psychology'. Indeed, it is hard now to think of a trendier or more intensively researched aspect of cognition. However, there is some considerable confusion in the use of the term 'imagery'. For some it means a subjective experience of mental pictures, whereas others use it to designate an operationally defined cognitive process.

Galton (1883) is frequently cited as one of the earliest serious investigators of mental imagery. However, it should be pointed out that his study was entirely introspective in nature, and not necessarily connected with all current uses of the term imagery. The use of subjective report techniques implies that imagery is a mental experience. It might be defined as an experience which resembles that of a perception in the absence of an appropriate stimulus. Familiar examples would be visualising a face, or hearing a tune 'in your head'. Perky (1910) claimed that subjects could be tricked into confusing a perceptual experience with an imaginal one, and Segal has, under special conditions, been able to repeat this result in recent times (for a review see Segal, 1971).

Most people, however, would agree that the aim of cognitive psychology is not to study mental experience as such, but to investigate *processes* which mediate behaviour. Imagery has been claimed to constitute such a cognitive process, although, as we shall see, this viewpoint is highly controversial. A good example of the process approach occurs in 'mental rotation' studies (e.g. Shepard and Metzler, 1971; Cooper and Shepard, 1973; Cooper, 1975). In these studies subjects are required to make same/difference judgments about two figures which are rotated with respect to one another. The general finding is that on positive judgments (i.e. when the two figures match) the reaction time increases linearly with the degree of angular displacement of the figures. This finding is consistent with the notion that the subject mentally rotates one of the pictures, at a constant angular velocity, and then matches it against the other.

The introspective or experiential definition of imagery clearly has a strong influence on some cognitive psychologists. For example, one line of work is concerned with investigating the properties of visual images by asking subjects to 'scan' them. (e.g. Kosslyn, 1975; 1978). Although some objective behavioural measures such as re-action times are employed, this work rests upon the assumption that the subject perceives and responds to instructions about an inner mental picture, available only to his personal experience. In these experiments subjects are asked to describe and measure aspects of their images *as if* they were percepts. For example, Kos-slyn (1978) reports that after being asked to visualise an object, subjects, 'were requested to imagine that they were moving towards the object, and asked whether it seemed to loom larger as they moved closer'. A sceptic of the 'mental picture' approach might suggest that such instructions contain clear demand characteristics to evoke subjective reports in the terms favoured by the theoretical position of the experimenter.

Criticisms of the mental picture approach are not, however, re-stricted to the problems of introspective reports. The general prob-lem of introspective reports is discussed in Chapter 12. Several logical difficulties arise in such accounts as we shall see in the next section.

Images versus propositions

An important debate has developed recently about the status of mental imagery as an explanatory construct. The Kosslyn kind of approach is sometimes referred to as the 'imagery position'. This definition is not too helpful, since the term 'imagery' is not in practice restricted to the vocabulary of those adopting this ap-proach. As Anderson (1978) puts it, 'No one seems to deny that there is a phenomenon called *mental imagery*. On the other hand there is considerable debate over whether there is a useful repre-sentational construct called an *image*.' Pylyshyn (1973), a leading critic of the so-called 'imagery position' has characterised it as employing a *picture-metaphor* – subjects are supposed to 'see' an image *as if* it were a picture. Although imagery theorists have protested this to be a 'strawman' (Paivio, 1976, Kosslyn and Pom-eranz, 1977), it does seem a fair description. For example, Kosslyn and Pomeranz (1977) also assert that 'some of the operators . . . that are used in analysing percepts are also applied to images', and 'the question of how knowledge can be derived from imagery is quite similar to the question of how knowledge is derived from ongoing sensory activity.' Anderson (1978) has also concluded that, 'it seems the picture metaphor *is* the imagery theory.'

The critics of this approach generally prefer to account for the representation of all forms of knowledge in terms of propositions (e.g. Anderson and Bower, 1973; Pylyshyn, 1973). Pylyshyn, for example, regards mental imagery as an *epi-phenomenon*. He argues that it is not a process, but the result of a process. He proposes that neither the information capacity of the brain nor the problems of organising retrieval would permit information to be stored as visual images. Since they must be constructed from some underlying abstract (or propositional) representation, then it is the nature of these representations that should serve to explain the mediation of behaviour. Pylyshyn also attacks the use of the picture metaphor by imagery theorists on several grounds. For example,

1 The metaphor leads to a false analogy between perception and imagery. Thus the image which is the consequence of perceptual processing is treated as if it were a stimulus *to be* processed.

2 Advocates of the 'imagery position' are unduly influenced by introspective data. In line with considerations of our previous section, Pylyshyn points out that terms like 'image' are used in quite different senses when applied to information processing than when applied to conscious experience. He adds, 'The recent literature abounds in examples which reveal that the investigator tacitly assumes that what is functional in cognition is available to introspection.' Unfortunately, Pylyshyn's assertion is quite correct.

3 Imagery theorists make bogus use of operational definitions. Different converging operations to demonstrate the importance of imagery in, for example, verbal learning (Paivio, 1971) logically define different constructs. 'The unity of these constructs, and consequently, the notion of imagery, rests on a metatheoretical assumption. This assumption, in turn, rests on the persuasiveness of subjective experience and the ordinary informal meaning of the word *image*.'

While I think that these criticisms are sound and am not convinced by the attempts of Kosslyn and Pomeranz (1977) to refute them, I do not think that Pylyshyn's paper either destroys the imagery position entirely, or establishes the propositional position. While the malpractices he cites are certainly associated with many imagery theorists, they are not an inevitable consequence of assuming pictorial representation.

Anderson (1978) attempts to undermine much of the basis of the picture-proposition argument. He argues two essential points. He claims that no theory about the nature of the *representation* of knowledge can be assessed independently of assumptions about the *process*. Thus it is meaningless for people like Pylyshyn and Kosslyn to argue about whether representations are in the form of pictures or propositions, without also specifying process assumptions. Any cognitive theory must be specified as a *representation-process pair*. Secondly, he claims that any picture theory can be formulated as a propositional theory and vice versa. He argues, for example, that it is a simple matter to produce a propositional model to account for the mental rotation studies:

> The model would involve a propositional description of an object and its orientation in space. Just as Kosslyn and Schwartz (1977) compute a series of small changes in their image, so a series of small changes can be computed in the propositional representation.

The force of Anderson's argument is brought home by the consideration that if it were not possible to represent such a model in terms of propositions, then one could not write a computer program to simulate it.

Anderson's two points are not, of course, independent. The point about mental rotation is that it is a hypothesis about a *process* and not a representation. The only aspect that the picture representation might seem to add to that of the propositions is in its intuitive correspondence to our subjective experience. Anderson dismisses this consideration as follows:

> The introspective reports are data that require explanations like any other data. However, there is no reason to suppose that the best representation to account for verbal reports of picture-like properties is a picture. A computer program could be written to deliver such reports from a propositional data base.

Anderson's arguments have come under considerable criticism (e.g. Hayes-Roth, 1979; Pylyshyn, 1979; Johnson-Laird, 1979), although he has stuck resolutely to his position in replying to some of these papers (Anderson, 1979). In particular, his critics dispute the assertion that the postulated format of representation has no functional consequences. At the time of writing the images v. propositions debate is being conducted in a manner which is both philosophically deep and technically complex, and shows no immediate signs of resolution. I will simply offer some tentative conclusions:

1 Difficulties arise in the application of the imagery construct, especially when explicit or implicit reliance is placed upon the subjective experience of mental pictures.

2 Imagery representations may be viewed as a form of structural analogue of the external world. However, it is claimed by some that the information they contain can be entirely described by a propositional representation.

3 It is important to distinguish between the *format* of a representation (image versus proposition) and its information-processing structure. The relative value of either type of format, and even the possibility of distinguishing them is a matter of unresolved debate.

In view of this last conclusion, it is important to ask whether there are structural differences between the types of propositional and imagery theories that have been proposed, apart from the assumptions about format. There is, indeed, a general structural issue, which is of considerable relevance to the understanding of reasoning data in both this and later parts of the book. This issue is explained in the following section.

Dual coding versus central processing

Those favouring the notion of imaginal representation have tended to adopt multiple processing approaches to cognition, while propositional theorists have tended towards a single process position. For example, Paivio (1971) proposed a dual coding theory to account for verbal learning data. He argued that words may be entered into one of two codes which are *visual* and *verbal* in nature. He proposed that the long-established superiority of learning concrete over abstract words is due to the fact that while the latter have access only to the verbal code, the former also have access to the visual code which has strong mnemonic properties. Further evidence for the dual-code hypothesis is obtained through the use of various 'converging operation', such as instructions to adopt an imagery strategy, which facilitate the learning of concrete words. (For a recent example of the use of this technique see Richardson, 1978.)

Propositional theorists such Pylyshyn, on the other hand, have tended to a single coding approach. As Kieras (1978) puts it,

> Most of the debate on the nature of imagery has centered on an extreme form of the propositional position. The extreme position takes a cue from the abstract nature of propositions and insists that all human knowledge is itself abstract and retains no trace of its original source modality.

From the considerations of the previous section, there is obviously no reason why a propositional theory need be cast in this form, and Kieras himself goes on to consider propositional theories which do retain information about source modality.

What though of the evidence for dual versus single codes or processes? The mnemonic type evidence comes under fire from Pylyshyn's point 3. If there is no logical path from the various operational definitions to a unified imagery construct, then the results of each separate paradigm may be open to alternative explanations. Anderson (1978) suggests that such evidence is weakened by recent experimental findings, which demonstrate the importance of the type and level of semantic processing adopted with either type of material in establishing memory strength.

The notion of dual *codes* is rather static, and ostensibly more a hypothesis about representation than about process. Paivio (1975) has, however, extended the notion to thought processes. This extended theory will be discussed in Chapter 12, whereas the present discussion will focus on the argument for dual coding. Potentially the strongest evidence for such a position, and the work which causes most problems for propositional theorists, arises from the selective interference studies (Brooks, 1967; 1968; Atwood, 1971; Salthouse, 1974; 1975). What these studies appear to show is that if a subject is asked to carry out two concurrent tasks, one involving imagery and the other perception, then there is more interference if the two tasks involve the same modality. This evidence, if sound, refutes an extreme propositional theory in which it is assumed that all mental operations are performed on an abstract code which contains no reference to a perceptual modality.

Anderson (1978) has suggested that such results are an artifact, and that interference arises from similarity of *content* rather than modality. I do not think that all the evidence can be explained in this way, however, particularly that of Brooks. Consider, for example, one of the experiments in his 1967 paper. Subjects were required to learn a verbal list with either a clear visual-spatial reference or else a control 'nonsense' list. In the spatial list, sentences referred to a 4 × 4 grid of squares and contained instructions such as

In the starting square put a 1.
In the next square to the right put a 2.
In the next square up put a 3, etc., etc., etc.

With nonsense materials spatial adjectives such as 'up' and 'down' were replaced by adjectives such as 'quick' and 'slow', thus presumably precluding the possibility of constructing a spatial image as a mnemonic device. The tests were presented for learning either aurally, or else aurally *and* visually. The mean number of errors made in learning is shown in Table 2.1. We see that a cross-over interaction occurred. When subjects were reading, as well as listening, they did worse on the spatial than nonsense material; the reverse was true when they listened only. Brooks concludes that the use of the visual perception system interferes with imaginal coding of the same modality. He has also claimed interference with the perceptual modality used in response output, and further generalised his evidence to auditory as well as visual imagery (Brooks, 1968).

TABLE 2.1   *Results of Brooks (1967) Experiment I*
(Mean number of errors)

	Spatial material	Nonsense material
Listening	1.2	2.3
Listening and reading	2.8	1.3

Though widely accepted and quoted, Brooks's results have recently come under attack from Phillips and Christie (1977). They criticise Brooks for not using *blank controls*, i.e. conditions under which no interfering task is given. They also report experiments which fail to reproduce his modality related interference effects. It should be noted, however, that their 'imagery' task was very different from his. Phillips and Christie's subjects were asked to memorise a novel visual pattern. Equating this with Brooks's task of constructing spatial images is a good example of the overinclusive use of the term 'imagery' of which Pylyshyn complains. Nevertheless, Brooks's finding may have less generality than was once thought.

In conclusion, there may be some advantages in proposing that alternative forms of representation are available to the information processor. Is the issue really independent of assumed format, however? If modality specific interference effects are substantiated, then it is hard to reconcile them with a general propositional theory of memory. Even if input modality is included in the propositional representation, it is hard to see why such memory should suffer interference from a perceptual task. On the other hand, if an analogue (imagery) representation is proposed, it is perfectly reasonable to suggest that it would employ some of the mechanisms used in the perceptual system of the corresponding modality.

Conclusions

It should be clear from the work reviewed in this chapter that the study of language, memory and thought are becoming increasingly interconnected. Chomsky made an invaluable contribution to psychology by stimulating the development of psycholinguistics. The field of psycholinguistics has developed since towards a greater concern with how underlying meaning is represented and used. Memory research, always verbal in emphasis, has moved from the study of individual words to sentences and connected prose. Thus the two fields have firmly connected and the propositional theories arise at their intersection.

The use of the imagery construct gives rise to a number of theoretical problems, especially with regard to its association with subjective mental experience. Nevertheless, the construct has been used as a mnemonic device in verbal learning and memory, and as the basis of performance of various cognitive tasks. Anderson's view that the debate between imagery and propositional theorists has confused representation and process is accepted. It is a matter of current debate whether or not the format of representations (imaginal v. propositional) can be distinguished. An important structural issue concerns the distinction between the use of a single semantic code, and two (or more) types of code specialised for processing different types of information. With these conclusions in mind, we shall now consider the findings of experimenters on elementary verification and reasoning tasks.

3 Sentence verification

This chapter is concerned with the way in which people verify (decide the truth or falsity of) relatively simple sentences, in relation to a situation that they purport to describe. Many of the experiments involve sentence-picture comparison. For example, subjects may be told that 'The star is above the plus' and shown a picture of either a star above a plus or vice versa. The subjects are required to make a true/false judgment and their latency or response time is measured. Such tasks are frequently complicated by the introduction of negatives, e.g. 'The plus is not above the star.' Verification tasks involving logically complex sentences such as universals (*All A are B*) or conditionals (*If p then q*) will be considered in later sections of the book.

Although such verification tasks are often referred to as simple 'reasoning' problems, they do not actually require deductive reasoning as defined in Chapter 1. Subjects are not required to understand the concept of validity, i.e. that the truth of one or more statements logically necessitates the truth of another. They merely have to decide whether or not a description is accurate. It is, however, essential to review performance on such tasks in a book such as this. For one thing, the tasks provide information about people's ability to represent and process linguistic structures that are involved in *bona fide* deductive reasoning problems. Thus, the studies reviewed in this chapter tell us about people's ability to process negatives, which are frequently involved in complex reasoning tasks. Similarly, the manner in which people verify conditional sentences is of vital relevance to the understanding of conditional reasoning performance (see Chapter 8). It will also emerge that the types of theoretical model which can be proposed to account for subjects' strategies on verification tasks are of essentially similar structure to those applicable to tasks involving genuine deduction. In a deductive task one must compare the representation of two (or more) premises and deduce a conclusion. In a verification task one compares the representations of a sentence and (say) a picture and decides whether or not they match.

Before considering particular experiments an arbitrary but necessary limitation must be placed on the material to be discussed. It was indicated in Chapter 1 that only tasks in which all the information required for their solution is presented to the subject would be considered. There are many studies of sentence verification where this is not the case. In such experiments the subject verifies a sentence not against a picture or some other presented material, but against his own knowledge or semantic memory (e.g. 'A canary is yellow – true or false?'). Consideration of such studies and their attendant theories would be an interesting but unjustifiable diversion from the purpose of this volume.

We will consider the literature in historical order. Early experiments were concerned with investigating the effect of syntactic variables, particularly negation. As research developed people became increasingly aware of the importance of semantic factors. In the early 1970s information-processing models based on propositional representation were developed, and have tended to dominate the subsequent literature.

Syntactic factors in sentence verification

The earliest systematic studies of the processing of positive and negative statements were carried out by Wason (1959, 1961). The basic syntactic function of the negative with which he was concerned is its reversal of truth value. Essentially, if any proposition p is true, then it follows that *not* p is false; similarly if *not* p is true then p must be false. This essential property of negation makes it fundamental to any system of formal logic, and hence of considerable relevance to the study of reasoning. Wason set out to investigate this property by considering four types of statement in which truth value (true/false) and polarity (affirmative/negative) were both varied. The following examples illustrate the four statements.

True affirmative	(TA)	4 is an even number
False affirmative	(FA)	6 is an odd number
True negative	(TN)	4 is not an odd number
False negative	(FN)	6 is not an even number

Wason (1961) carried out two experiments using materials of the sort illustrated. Strictly speaking subjects are verifying the sentences against their semantic memory, but the evenness and oddness of numbers is highly overlearnt and thus immediately available for all subjects. The results did, in any event, prove reasonably comparable with later sentence-picture verification tasks and will serve to illustrate the usual findings. In one of the experiments subjects were given a *verification task* in which one of the four types of sentence would be presented and the subject required to make a true/false judgment as quickly as possible. The other experiment, however, involved a *construction task* on which there has been little subsequent work. In this task the subject was given an incomplete sentence with or without a negative, ' . . . is (not) an even number', and instructed to fill in a number either to make the sentence true or to make it false. Thus, in a rather different sense, we again have the four categories, TA, FA, TN, FN.

The construction task results showed that both falsity and negation slowed latencies in additive fashion, the overall order being TA<FA<TN<FN. On the verification task latencies, however, there was no clear effect of falsity, only of negation. Error scores suggested that the TN was *harder* than the FN. Many subsequent experiments have, however, confirmed that such an *interaction* between polarity and truth values occurs reliably on the verification latencies. A later experiment by Wason and Jones (1963) included a repetition of this condition with automatic timing (a stop-watch was used in the original study). While false affirmatives were considerably slower to process than true affirmatives, the false negative was actually slightly *quicker* than the true negative. This interaction has been consistently found in subsequent sentence-picture verification tasks provided that (a) the sentences are presented before the pictures and (b) the negated values are not converted by the subject into an equivalent affirmative form (see Trabasso, 1970). Subsequent studies have usually found a significantly faster judgment on the FN than the TN (e.g. Clark and Chase, 1972; Just and Carpenter, 1971, but *not* Gough, 1966). This may be less clear on

the Wason studies because the negatives *are* recodable (e.g. 'not even' = 'odd').

The additive and interactive effects are shown schematically in Figure 3.1. Note that in either case both negative conditions are slower than both affirmative conditions.

Wason (1961) accounts for the discrepancy between construction and evaluation tasks as follows. On the construction task one first of all thinks of a number which will make the statement true, and then reverses it if the instruction is to make the rule false. Thus on both affirmative and negative problems the false task takes longer.

FIGURE 3.1 Schematic representations of additive and interactive effects in response latencies, for different types of sequence

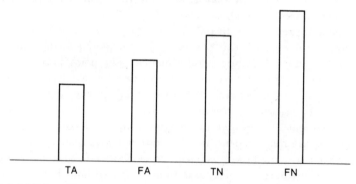

(a) Additive effect

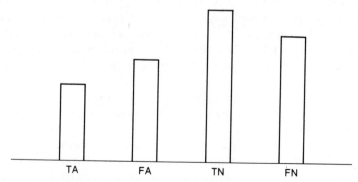

(b) Interactive effect

On the verification task, however, it is the TN rather than the FN which involves a double negative. The four types of sentence can be defined as follows (Wason, 1980).

True affirmative – a fact
False affirmative – a falsehood
True negative – a denial of a falsehood
False negative – denial of a fact

The FN, e.g. '6 is not an even number' is easily perceived since it is evident that 6 *is* an even number, so the negative makes it false. The TN, e.g. '7 is not an even number' is harder since one must delete the negative, decide the sentence is false, then bring the negative back to decide that is, after all, true. Thus an extra step of processing is required.

The interpretation of the polarity/truth value interaction, and the conditions under which it occurs, will be explored further in the section on information-processing models. The point to note here is that the verification task does not provide a 'pure' measure of the difficulty of comprehending the negative. The latency depends not only on the presence of the negative, but also on the nature of the task that one is required to perform with it. If comprehension processes are not independent of operational requirements on such a simple reasoning task, it is hardly to be expected that they would be so on the more complex tasks to be discussed later in the book.

Wason's original intention was to investigate the ways in which positive and negative *information* could best be communicated (see Wason, 1980). He was not, as is often supposed, concerned with 'transformational complexity', for Chomsky's theories had had little impact on British psychology at this time. An American literature concerned with Chomsky's (1957) theory did, however, develop in parallel, and should also be considered as part of the 'syntactic' approach.

This line of work was initiated by George Miller. The basic idea was that if Chomsky's theory had 'psychological reality' then transformational complexity – presence of negatives, passives etc. – should require additional cognitive space and processing time. In the early experiments (Miller, 1962; Miller and McKean, 1964) he tried to measure 'transformation time' by a subtraction method. Subjects were shown a sentence in either kernel (a sentence without transformations – simple, active, affirmative, declarative), negative, passive, or passive negative form and asked to find a 'match' in a list of sentences, either in the same form, or in one of the others. Transformation time was taken to be the difference between the time taken to match a sentence to itself, and to a transformationally different version. For example, the difference between the time taken to match a kernel to its negative and to match a kernel to itself was taken as the negation time. If the passive and passive negative times are computed similarly, then the differences between those should also equal the same negation time.

The results using this odd technique were quite encouraging, but the early optimism was soon to be discouraged. Studies by Gough (1965, 1966) and Slobin (1966) were among the first to use the sentence-picture verification task which subsequently became so popular. In line with Miller, these studies found that both negatives and passives slowed down processing time, but that the effect was much stronger for negatives. This in itself is awkward for the linguistic theory since the passive involves far more complex rearrangement of the kernel, and hence suggests that some additional *semantic* difficulty was also associated with the negative. Gough (1966) also introduced a three-second delay between the sentence and the picture to allow transformational decoding to be complete. The effect of negatives and passives did *not*, however, disappear from the verification latencies. Some evidence for the transformational complexity hypothesis was also claimed on the basis of memory tasks (e.g. Savin and Perchoneck, 1965; Mèhler, 1963), but subsequent research suggested that errors in recall are better explained in terms of subjects' retaining the essential *meaning* of what is presented, irrespective of its grammatical form (e.g. Fillenbaum, 1966; Johnson-Laird and Stevenson, 1970).

A powerful critique of all these kinds of experiment was made by Goldman-Eisler and Cohen (1970), who point out that sentences containing negatives and passives occur far more infrequently in everyday language than ones which are affirmative and active. Thus a sentence-frequency effect, analogous to the well-known word-frequency effect, could be an artifactual cause of the observed comprehension and memory deficits associated with transformationally complex sentences. This type of research was, in any case, set back by Chomsky's (1965) revision of his original theory, in which the theoretical basis for the transformational complexity hypothesis is far less clear (see Greene, 1972).

The one undisputed result that all these experiments (and similar subsequent ones) have in common is that negatives are reliably more difficult to process than affirmatives. It seems to me that one powerful argument against a syntactic explanation of this is that the difficulty of negation seems to be a characteristic of *thought* rather than language. The difficulty of utilising negative *information* has been demonstrated across a wide variety of paradigms. For example, on concept-identification tasks, subjects find it harder to learn from negative as opposed to positive instances (e.g. Smoke, 1932; Hovland and Weiss, 1953; Bruner, Goodnow and Austin, 1956). Subjects find it hard to construct or solve coding problems where they have to make use of negative information (Whitfield, 1951; Donaldson, 1959, Campbell, 1965). Subjects also find it difficult to refute hypotheses on tasks where they need to generate negative instances in order to do so (see Wason and Johnson-Laird, 1972, and also Miller, 1967, Mynatt, Doherty and Tweney, 1977) and so on.

We will now consider studies that while investigating negatives and passives in a linguistic context, recognised that they may serve a semantic function.

Semantic factors in sentence verification

Wason (1959) suggested a semantic aspect of negatives, in that they might evoke unpleasant emotional connotations due to association with prohibition in childhood. The evidence claimed in support for this hypothesis has, however, been most tenuous and unsatisfactory. For example, Eifermann (1961) repeated Wason's (1961) experiments in Hebrew using one of two negatives 'lo' and 'enyo', the latter of which is never used in a prohibitive context. As predicted, there was some evidence that 'enyo' was processed faster, but there is no way of determining what aspect of the linguistic difference between the two words is responsible.

The other type of evidence that has been offered for the emotionality hypothesis is that implicit negatives are faster to process than explicit negatives. The idea is that the implicit negative carries the same logical function and information-processing requirements (see

Carpenter and Just, 1975) but lacks the emotional connotations. Wason and Jones (1963) showed the negation difficulty was reduced by training subjects to use a nonsense word to serve as a negative (DAX = 'isn't'). Their claim that this was due to lack of emotional connotation has subsequently been withdrawn on the grounds that the result could be an artifact of special strategies adopted (see Wason and Johnson-Laird, 1972; Wason, 1980).

Further evidence for the hypothesis was claimed by Jones (1966a; 1966b; 1968) using not a verification task but a digit-cancelling task. Her basic finding was that instructions such as 'Do not mark 3, 5, 7, mark all the rest', took longer to carry out than instructions of the form 'Mark all numbers except 3, 5, 7'. One difficulty of interpreting Jones's results is that one cannot tell whether the extra difficulty of the explicit negative lies in comprehending it, or com-plying with it. A recent experiment run by Philip Brooks, in my own department, used a sentence-picture verification task and sep-arated comprehension times (CT) from verification times (VT) – the former measured the time that subject used to read and under-stand the instruction before the picture was presented. Explicit negatives such as 'Respond true to all shapes which are not green ones' were compared with implicits such as 'Respond true to all shapes except those which are green'. The results were complicated by interactions with the order of presenting tasks. However, where differences between the two types of negative emerged, they were different in the two analyses. On VT our subjects, like Jones's, tended to be slower in carrying out an explicitly negative instruc-tion. However, on CT subjects appeared to understand the explicit form more quickly. Jones's digit-cancelling task would be heavily loaded on VT, of course. It is not clear why these discrepancies should arise, but the result of our CT analyses might indicate an additional linguistic complexity of the implicit form, and an emo-tionality effect cannot be ruled out.

In my view, the most important semantic characteristic of ne-gation lies in the pragmatic aspect first discussed by Wason (1965). He points out that a statement such as 'The train was not late this morning' implies that the train normally *is* late. Further, it is anom-alous to say that 'A horse is not a fish' but sensible to say that 'A whale is not a fish'. In the 1965 paper Wason was mainly concerned with the idea that a negative is normally used to deny something

which is exceptional in its context (like whales and fish), and produced experimental evidence on an artificial task to support this.

Subjects were shown a display of numbered coloured lights in
which (say) seven were red and one was blue. Wason argued that
a negative of the form 'No 3 is not red' was more 'natural' than one
of the form 'No 5 is not blue'. Since the general context is red, then
it is only natural to use a negative to indicate an exception. The
latency analysis supported this 'exceptionality hypothesis' but not
an alternative 'ratio hypothesis'. However, Wason no longer considers the latter to be a correctly derived prediction from the pragmatic argument (see Wason, 1980).

A more general form of this argument discussed by Wason (1972),
is that the negative is normally used to deny a prior belief. We do
not use a negative to assert new information, and as mentioned
earlier, performance on a variety of cognitive tasks is impeded by
such 'unnatural' usage. We use a negative to say something about
a prior or *presupposed* affirmative, namely that it is false.

Greene (1970a, 1970b) similarly argued that a negative has a
semantic function of 'signalling a change in meaning'. For example,
given the sentence:

x exceeds y

it is 'natural' to deny this by a negative such as:

x does not exceed y

but 'unnatural' to affirm it by a negative such as

y does not exceed x

In her experiment she measured subjects' latencies to decide if
two sentences mean the same thing or not. With passive sentences
she argued that the opposite effect should occur: a passive which
retains meaning (y is exceeded by x) is more 'natural' than one that
differs (x is exceeded by y). As predicted, the 'natural' sentence
pairs were processed faster in each case. Whether this is due to
'semantic function' of the sentence forms is, however, debatable. So
far as the negatives are concerned, Greene was effectively replicating
the general finding that a false negative is processed faster than a

true negative: a point to which we shall return in the next section. The finding that True Passives are processed faster than False Passives might also be accountable in terms of information-processing differences. With the benefit of the hindsight achieved by consideration of the information-processing models developed later, Greene's papers seem somewhat naïve. She assumes, in effect, that performance on a verification task is a direct function of comprehension processes, without reference to reasoning operations. Nevertheless, no one seems to doubt that negatives *do* naturally seem to deny presuppositions, including the leading advocate of the information-processing approach, H. Clark (see Clark and Clark, 1977).

Before examining these models, let us consider briefly the semantic function of the passive. If we accept Greene's argument that it is not to alter meaning, then why should the passive voice exist at all? A more reasonable view is that while the passive does not *drastically* alter the meaning, as the negative does, it makes a subtle change. Johnson-Laird (1968a; 1968b) suggested that the passive is used to emphasise the logical object of the sentence. If we take a simple active sentence as follows:

The boy hit the girl

'Boy' is both the grammatical (surface structure) and logical (deep structure) subject, while 'girl' is the grammatical and logical object. In the passive form:

The girl was hit by the boy

the logical object is now the grammatical subject and vice versa. Johnson-Laird's assumption that the passive is used to emphasise the logical object is supported by a rather odd experimental technique. Subjects were required to decide which of various coloured strips were better described by sentences such as 'Red is followed by Blue', on the assumption that a larger area of colour would be matched to the more 'important' part of the sentence. This assumption, and consequently Johnson-Laird's conclusion, has been recently challenged by Costermans and Hupet (1977); and Johnson-Laird (1977) has replied.

In conclusion to this section, it should be seen that while arguments for the semantic function of negatives and passives seem plausible and have, in fact, gained wide accceptance, the experimental evidence on which they rest is rather weak. The main problem with the studies considered is a failure to consider the operations required for the solution of the experimental tasks. We now look at attempts to deal with this latter problem.

The information-processing models

Information-processing models of sentence verification first appeared in conference papers by Trabasso (1970) and Clark (1970). The two authors appeared independently to have devised logically equivalent modes. Trabasso's paper is more complete in that he deals with Wason's construction-task data as well as the verification task. He was also the first to point out that the order of presenting the picture and sentence was important. Clark's model was more precisely formulated, however, and after its subsequent publication in an expanded form by Clark and Chase (1972), it became the best-known and most widely cited model of this kind. Their paper will be described in some detail to illustrate this type of approach.

Clark and Chase present two models: Model A to account for experiments where the sentence is processed before the picture, and Model B to account for the reverse situation. Both models, however, incorporate a general notion of a sequential strategy moving through a series of fixed stages, and make the strong assumption that the total response time is the simple addition of the time taken at each stage. This general model which is also applicable to deductive tasks is illustrated in Figure 3.2. They further assume that representation of both pictures and sentences takes place by encoding the stimulus into a common, abstract propositional code. After this encoding has been completed, comparisons are then made on the propositional representations. Thus their paper constitutes a direct application of propositional theory (discussed in Chapter 2) to a reasoning task.

The actual formulation of their models is very specific to their paradigm, which must be explained. Subjects in the first experiment were shown a display which had a sentence on the left and a picture on the right. There were two types of picture showing either a star

FIGURE 3.2 A general sequential strategy which is implied by various models of sentence verification and reasoning

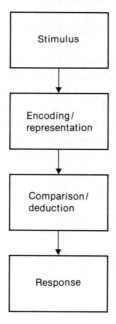

above a plus or vice versa. Sentences were either affirmative e.g. 'star is above plus' or negative e.g. 'plus isn't below star'. Subjects were required to decide as quickly as possible whether or not the display was 'true' (sentence matches the picture) or 'false' (sentence doesn't match the picture). Model A assumed that the sentence was processed first, and has the following 'additive' stages.

Stage 1 – Representation of sentences

It is assumed that affirmatives are encoded as elementary propositions, and negatives are encoded as false affirmatives. Assuming a picture showing A above B the four logical possibilities are as follows:

	Sentence	Representation
TA	A is above B	(A above B)*
FA	A is below B	(B below A)
TN	A isn't below B	(false (A below B))
FN	A isn't above B	(false (A above B))

These representations consist of an inner string (A above B), etc., plus an outer string, which contains a marker for falsity in the case of negatives, and is implicit in the case of affirmatives. Clark and Chase assume that encoding a negative will take longer than encoding an affirmative by a constant amount. They also assume that 'above' is a more natural way of encoding verticality than 'below' and consequently assume that an additional increment will be required for the latter stage.

Stage 2 – Representation of pictures

It is assumed that the picture is encoded as either (A above B) or (B below A) according to the comparative used in the sentence representation. Clark and Chase comment

> As for latency predictions one might assume *a priori* that the *above* representation should be faster to construct than the *below* representation just as in Stage 1. But since the two codes have been found empirically to take approximately equal amounts of time to construct (cf. Experiment II and Clark and Chase, in preparation) Model A makes no provision for the different encoding latencies of *above* and *below* in Stage 2.

This rather extraordinary remark reveals the fact that while the models are *presented* prior to the experiment data, they were clearly constructed on a *post hoc* basis.

Stage 3 – Comparison of sentence and picture representations

Clark and Chase propose two substages, involving comparison of the inner strings followed by comparison of the outer strings. The

---

* Clark's current notation gives ABOVE (A,B), etc.

subject is supposed to have a 'truth index' set initially to the value True. Every time a mismatch is found the value of the index is reversed from True to False or from False back to True. The operations at this stage can be described as follows:

Operation 1
Compare inner strings. If they match proceed to Operation 2. If not proceed to Operation 1a.

Operation 1a
Reverse truth index. Proceed to Operation 2.

Operation 2
Compare outer strings. If they match proceed to response stage. If not proceed to Operation 2a.

Operation 2a
Reverse truth index. Proceed to response stage.

The operations described lead to prediction of the interaction between truth value and polarity normally observed on the verification task (cf. the earlier section on syntactic factors). This is illustrated in Table 3.2. It can be seen that the TA is quicker than the FA because both operations 1 and 2 lead to matches, and so neither reversal of the truth index 1a or 2a is necessary. FA, on the other hand, mismatches at operation 1 so requires the additional time for 1a. The FN is quicker than the TN because it matches at stage 2 when the additional 'false' in the outer string of the sentence representation is detected.

The comparison stage thus predicts the normally observed inter-

TABLE 3.2 *Operations required at the comparison stage in Clark and Chase's (1972) Model A, for the different logical types of problem*

	Sentence representation	Picture representation	Operations
TA	(A above B)	(A above B)	1,2
FA	(A below B)	(B below A)	1,1a,2
TN	(false (A below B))	(B below A)	1,1a,2,2a
FN	(false (A above B))	(A above B)	1,2,2a

action, and processes on encoding and comparison stages predict the additional finding that negatives are slower than affirmatives. It should be noted that the explanation of why the FN is easier than the TN is no more than a formalisation of the explanation of Wason (1961) described earlier in this chapter. It does, however, make a more specific prediction. All else being equal the difference in processing time between FA and TA should be equal to the difference between TN and FN (i.e. the time taken to execute operation 1a).

Stage 4 – Response production

The truth index is converted into a response True or False. This stage is supposed to add a constant increment to the total response time.

The model described (Model A) makes very specific predictions. To a general processing time t_0, a number of increments may be added at either the Representation or Comparison stage. Clark and Chase assign parameters to these time components and estimate them by subtraction of total processing time of various sentences. The results of their experiments seem to provide fairly good evidence for their predictions, and the parameters do seem to be additive, rather than interactive.

One of the problems of formulating a model in such precise terms is that it is very paradigm specific. As soon as slight alterations of the paradigm are introduced, the model has to be revised. We will consider two examples. The first relates to reversing the order of presenting the sentence and the picture. As Clark and Chase (1972) comment 'Model A cannot apply to the picture-first task without modification, because it assumes that the coding of the picture is contingent on the coding of the sentence'. Thus they develop Model B to cope with this other situation. In Model B it is assumed that the picture is always encoded in terms of *above* due to linguistic preference (direct evidence for this assumption is provided by Clark and Chase, 1974). The artificiality of the models is illustrated by the fact that Clark and Chase are also forced to modify the *comparison* stage. To determine a match or mismatch of the inner strings in Model A they suggested that subjects compare only the subject of the inner string. This is because the comparative *above* or *below* is guaranteed by the model to be identical in each representation. In

Model B this is not necessarily the case, so a modified comparison rule is introduced. Evidence for Model B is produced both in the original paper and a later study (Clark and Chase, 1974).

A second example of how paradigm specific the models are is illustrated by the explanation offered for the finding that sometimes the order of difficulty on the verification task is not interactive but additive (cf. Figure 3.1). This additive result is, for example, obtained by highly practised subjects in the study of Trabasso, Rollins and Shaughnessy, (1971). Trabasso and Clark are both in agreement that this is due to *conversion* of the negative. Where a negative refers to a binary dimension, it may be recoded, e.g. not even = odd. We have already noted that this might have accounted for the weaker than normal interaction observed in the Wason and Jones (1963) study. It is quite simple to see how, for example, Clark and Chase's Model A would predict an additive result if the negative is converted. Instead of representing the sentence 'A isn't above B' as (false (A above B)), it would be represented as (A below B) or (B above A). This means that at the comparison stage the subject is dealing, in effect, with affirmative representations only, so that the *false* statement will always take longer than the *true* irrespective of whether the original sentence was affirmative or negative. The additional processing time of the negative would now be explained as the time taken to convert it into an affirmative form. Evidence that data conform to this modified Model A when subjects are *instructed* to make conversions was produced in a study by Young and Chase (1971), described by Clark and Chase (1972). More recently, Just and Carpenter (1976a) have shown that types of negatives whose verification data are consistent with conversion tend to be subsequently recalled in a converted form.

It was observed that some of the earlier studies of verification tasks assumed that processing time is a direct function of comprehension processes. The Clark and Chase model accounts for the data with a mixture of comprehension and verification parameters. The model of Carpenter and Just (1975) attempts to account for results in terms of reasoning operations alone. Their model is similar to that of Clark and Chase in assuming a representational stage with a propositional format, followed by comparison and response stages. The notion of truth index is also incorporated. However, the model accounts for differences between conditions with respect to a single parameter, which is the number of operations required at the comparison stage. In this model it is assumed that whenever a mismatch is found in either the inner or outer strings, the truth index is reversed, the mismatching strings 'tagged' and recompared. In the further comparison the constituents now match owing to the tags. This model makes the very specific prediction that response latencies will increase *linearly* from TA to FA to FN to TN, since each successive case requires exactly one additional comparison operation to the one before. This result is found in various experiments which Carpenter and Just themselves have carried out, and a number of other studies which they cite. Discrepant findings of some other studies are accounted for in terms of partial conversion of the negative at the encoding stage, which leads to a different number of comparison operations.

Carpenter and Just's (1975) model has led to a certain amount of controversy. There have been criticisms published by Tanenhaus, Carroll and Bever (1976) and Catlin and Jones (1976), with replies by Carpenter and Just (1976) and Shoben (1978). The model has been criticised with respect to its ability to account for particular experimental results, and also on the grounds that it is paradigm specific, and thus of little general theoretical interest.

Perhaps the strongest evidence produced in favour of the Carpenter and Just model is that of Just and Carpenter (1976b). They employed the rather ingenious technique of measuring the latency of eye-fixations on the sentence and the picture. For example, they take the initial fixation period on the sentence as a measure of comprehension time. Here they found a slight increment for negative sentences, suggesting some extra encoding time in line with Clark and Chase. However, they also find that the time subsequently spent gazing at the location mentioned in the sentence was linearly related to the number of mental operations postulated to occur at the comparison stage of their own model (in the order TA, FA, FN, TN).

However, this result was not repeated in experiments which instructed subjects to comprehend the rule before pressing a key to receive the instance. The experiment run by Brooks, described earlier, found no clear pattern in the VT analysis corresponding to Carpenter and Just's prediction. Also in a study by Glushko and Cooper (1978) – which is described in more detail in a later section – the authors failed to find any effect of linguistic complexity, including negation, at the VT stage. More complex evidence is offered by Carr and Bacharach (1977) who compared simultaneous presentation of sentence and picture, with a condition where the picture was delayed 4–5 seconds (subjects counted in the interval to prevent rehearsal). After a detailed analysis of the effect of response requirements in the delay condition, the authors conclude that the surface structure of the sentence has no effect on the comparison stage of the task. The validity of the Carpenter and Just model must, then, be seriously questioned.

This account of the information-processing models allows one to form precise criticisms of Greene's (1970a; 1970b) conclusion that her results indicated an effect arising at a comprehension stage. Consider one of her sentence pairs containing a 'natural' negative:

x exceeds y
x does not exceed y

In terms of Clark and Chase these would be encoded as:

(x exceeds y)
(false (x exceeds y))

Thus the comparison here is that of the FN with only one mismatch arising. With an 'unnatural' pair such as:

x exceeds y
y does not exceed x

the encoding would be:

(x exceeds y)
(false (y exceeds x))

The comparison here is as for TN, with mismatches arising in both inner and outer strings.

In the case of the passives, presumably their deep structure (propositional) representation would contain the logical relationship plus a transformational marker. E.g. 'x is exceeded by y' might be coded as (PASS (y exceeds x)). Since the two sentences to be compared would be encoded separately, and since both her 'natural' and 'unnatural' pairs contain one affirmative and one passive, then the encoding time would be the same. Again, the difference can be explained at the comparison stage. Since the passive marker has no logical effect on truth value, it can be ignored at this stage. Hence, the 'natural' passive pair is, in effect, a TA and the 'unnatural' an FA. Thus Greene's result could be a simple consequence of the reasoning operations required, and her negativity effect due not to the semantic function of a negative being 'to signal a change in meaning', but instead to the fact that a negative transformation reverses truth values, whereas a passive does not.

Encoding and comparison models have in fact been applied to results obtained with passive sentences (see, for example, Olson and Filby, 1972; Wannemacher, 1976), but space considerations preclude their discussion here. It is more important, for our purposes, to examine the general assumptions about language and thought that underlie such models, than to pursue details of the various examples proliferating in the literature. Before doing so, a few remarks are in order with respect to the criticism that the models are paradigm specific.

Some of the earlier studies of sentence verification were criticised for making inferences about comprehension in the absence of a theory of how the tasks are performed. On the other hand, the models which specify the strategies in detail *do* seem to be rather artificial and task specific. My objection to the models arises from the fact that they are devised in too precise a manner, to predict data in far too limited situations. Popper (1959) has pointed out that theories are more falsifiable, and hence of more scientific value, when their assumptions are very general and their predictions very specific. The Carpenter and Just model is superior to that of Clark and Chase in this respect, since it assumes less and predicts more. However, both models were constructed *post hoc* to fit a particular set of results, and thus the specific nature of their predictions is not over-impressive, even when applied to new variations within the same paradigm. What the authors of such models do *not* seem to do is to formulate a general theoretical framework, of which their model is a particular application, and assess its validity across a wide variety of experimental paradigms.

Wider implications of the information-processing models

Two important general assumptions seem to underlie the use of the information-processing models. The first, illustrated by Figure 3.2. is the supposition of sequential strategies. As we shall see, this conception is highly popular with many theorists who apply themselves to the various reasoning paradigms described throughout this book. The general notion is that reasoning tasks have two main stages. The first, comprehension (representation, encoding), stage, requires a representation of the information presented. The second, reasoning (processing, operating), stage, involves operations being carried out on the representation arrived at in the first stage. This fundamental notion about the nature of reasoning is intuitively appealing. As Neisser (1963) points out, the thinking that we are conscious of appears to be intrinsically sequential. Reasoning may not, however, be a conscious process, and evidence will be presented later in the book to suggest that it is not (cf. Chapters 9 and 12). Another reason why the sequential model might appeal is that it conforms to the general theoretical conventions of cognitive psychology, in which the cybernetic analogy of information flow has been greatly adopted. When memory models are so often presented in flow-chart form, it would be surprising if the same were not attempted by reasoning theorists.

The sequential model would seem to have its best chance of fitting data on comparatively simple tasks such as we have been considering here. As long as people get the problems *right*, by and large, one can add up the time taken at each postulated 'stage'. Such models are much harder to formulate when predictions of differences in *errors* are required, as we shall see later. Even within the verification-task literature, however, the notion of additive stages has been criticised. Seymour (1975) reviews evidence against the additive stage model of location judgment presented by Chase and Clark (1971). In one experiment, Seymour asked subjects in one condition to invert their response, saying 'yes' when they meant 'no' and vice versa. In the normal condition the difference between various conditions was as predicted by the Chase and Clark model. In the inverted response condition *all* problems were equally difficult. Seymour claims that his manipulation should only have affected the response stage, and should have done so by a constant amount. Hence, if the additive stage model is correct, the difference between conditions should have been unaffected. This result seems to cause difficulty for *any* additive stage model of this task, not just Chase and Clark's.

The second basic assumption underlying the models is that reasoning is accomplished by reference to propositional representations, which are abstract codes into which sentences and pictures alike are put during comprehension. From the discussion in Chapter 2, the reader will be aware that we can characterise two possible alternative positions to the propositional one: imagery and dual coding. An imagery theory would postulate that the problem information would be represented, and compared, as visual images rather than as propositions. As Clark and Chase (1972) point out, such an approach has a fundamental difficulty in that one cannot directly encode a negative. Given a sentence 'A isn't above B', one could only represent this visually by converting it into an affirmative form, e.g. as 'A is below B'. The latency data are, however, generally incompatible with the assumption of conversion except under special conditions. People can, in any case, perform verification tasks when the dimensions are non-binary and therefore not convertible. No one seems to have pursued an extreme imagery explanation of these tasks, though this approach has been popular on the more complex problems involving transitive inference (see Chapter 4).

A dual-coding approach (e.g. Neilsen and Smith, 1973) is far more feasible. Here, one would argue that sentences naturally go into a verbal code and pictures into a visual code. In order to make a comparison one must either convert the visual representation to a verbal form or vice versa. In view of the difficulty of encoding a negative visually one might expect that pictures are encoded verbally and comparisons made in the verbal code. Before considering this hypothesis, however, we will look further at the claims for the propositional point of view.

Clark, Carpenter and Just (1973) observe 'in the present paper, we will continue to assume that perceptual events are coded in an abstract, propositional format and will add weight to this assumption with new evidence we will present'. The evidence that they produce is similar to other experiments of these authors already referred to. In other words, because information-processing models can be made to fit (frequently *post hoc*) on the basis of assuming propositional representation, then this provides evidence that pictures are normally encoded in this way. I do not find this too convincing, and neither does Allport (1975). Allport alleges a weakness in the use of such tasks to argue for a semantic, propositional basis for perception; 'The trouble is that the task they employ for their demonstrations – matching a picture to a prior linguistic description – *requires* that the picture be represented in some format compatible with the description.' There are really two problems here: (1) just because sentences and pictures can be coded in a common form on these tasks does not mean that this would always be true, and (2) the common code used need not be propositional, it could be verbal or visual.

It was argued in Chapter 2 that the difference between propositional and dual-code theories is not really to do with the mode of representation used, but with the type of processing that is proposed. I agree with Anderson that explanations may be formulated in either manner. Take, for example, a study by Seymour (1974). He used simple affirmative descriptions (D) such as 'circle inside square' which subjects had to match against corresponding pictures (P). There were four conditions. Subjects either matched a description against a picture (DP) or two pictures to each other (PP). Presentation was either simultaneous or successive, with a two-second gap between the onset of the initial D (or P) and the subsequent P. The results showed that on simultaneous presentation DP verifications took longer than PP verifications, while on successive presentation there was no difference. A dual-coding explanation of this result would postulate that in the PP condition comparisons are made in the visual code irrespective of a delay. In the DP condition the description can be converted to a picture to make a similar comparison, but this takes time. Hence, in the delay condition the description is recoded *prior* to the presentation of the picture and so the comparison no longer takes additional time.

A propositional account of the same result would have to admit some kind of duality between visual and verbal processes, if only with respect to the initial procedure of converting information from a pictorial or verbal form of input into a common abstract form. Specifically, to account for Seymour's result a propositional theorist would have to suppose that verbal encoding takes longer than pictorial encoding. The real argument, then, is about the form of representation in which the comparison takes place.

In a second experiment Seymour (1974) compared a successive

PD condition to a successive DP condition and found the former to take more time. Linguistic complexity was also manipulated and found to influence PD but not the DP conditions. The propositional theory handles this result as follows: in this paradigm processing time is determined by what is presented second. Thus the DP condition should be faster than PD because we have already assumed that pictures are encoded faster. Linguistic complexity affects only PD, because its effects on the description of DP are lost in the interval. However, a dual-coding model could equally account for the same data on the assumption that comparisons in either case are made in the pictorial code, and that converting the description takes longer if it is more complex. DP is faster, and the effects of complexity unmeasurable, because in this condition the process takes place in the interval.

This example shows how propositional and dual-coding explanations can both be applied to the same effect. Can they, however, be distinguished? Seymour (1975), in a detailed, technical and difficult review of his many experiments on such matters, eventually concludes that 'No compelling reason to divide the memory system into verbal and pictorial elements was found . . . It seemed convenient, therefore, to retain Clark and Chase's (1972) notion of a single abstract (propositional) code . . .' This conclusion is phrased in an interesting manner with respect to the discussion in Chapter 2. There, it was concluded that propositional and imagery theories may not be easy to distinguish in terms of the format of representation proposed. The fact that Seymour finds the semantic code a more *convenient* assumption for explaining this kind of task, might tell us something more about the task than the structure of memory. The fact that Seymour also *rejects* Clark and Chase's notion of additive stages underlines the distinction between the representational and process aspects of a theory.

The Glushko and Cooper (1978) study also investigated DP and PP tasks but improved on the methodology of Seymour. In Experiment I, the subject took as long as he needed on the item presented first so that comprehension and verification time could be measured separately. The authors call these encoding and comparison times respectively, which seems a bit misleading to me. The 'encoding time' (ET) may be a reasonable measure of the time to encode the description in the DP condition, and the picture on the PP condition. However, the 'comparison time' (CT) must also contain a (presumably constant) time to encode the picture presented for comparison, as well as the comparison time itself. One interesting result is that ET for descriptions increases as a function of linguistic complexity, while ET for pictures is independent of their complexity. This qualitative difference supports a dual-coding model, and is particularly in line with a hypothesis of Paivio (1975) that while the verbal system of cognition is intrinsically sequential in nature, the visual system is capable of parallel processing (cf. Chapter 12). If features of pictures are encoded in parallel, then complexity need not increase latency.

Other results of this experiment, which were replicated in a second more complex experiment, were also out of line with the propositional models. It was mentioned in the previous section that Glushko and Cooper found no effect of linguistic complexity at the VT stage, thus failing to support the Carpenter and Just model. The Clark and Chase model also suffers, however, in that the effects of lexical marking did not occur, as predicted by their model, at the CT stage. This study is, then, altogether inconvenient for the propositional models.

Despite the emphasis on propositional models in recent studies of the verification task, the studies reviewed in this section suggest that an explanation in terms of dual coding is very much an open possibility. Conclusions about the studies discussed in this section will be given with the conclusions for the chapter as a whole.

Conclusions

We have seen that the verification task was devised by Wason as a way of investigating the processing of positive and negative information, and by early psycholinguists as a way of investigating transformational complexity. It was soon realised that the information processing requirements of the particular paradigm were important, and it was also suggested by Wason, in particular, that the negative had semantic effects. Recent developments have focused principally on the construction, testing and application of information-processing models. The semantic aspect seems to have been rather overlooked in this recent work. Although Greene's work on semantic function may be an artifact of processing demands, the pragmatic aspect of negation, identified by Wason, still seems to be important, and there is an unresolved literature on the emotionality hypothesis.

Wason (1972; 1980) claims that verification-task studies of negation have low external validity. He points out that in real life negatives are always used to deny presuppositions, and claims that few experiments provide any appropriate context for the negative statements they present. Wason's criticism is sound in so far as any extrapolation about the nature of *language* is concerned. Verification tasks are still, however, simple problem-solving experiments in their own right and may be expected to tell us something about cognitive processing.

The information-processing models have been based on an assumption that all 'reasoning' takes place with reference to propositional representation of sentences and pictures. We have seen, in the last section, that a dual-coding approach could also be applied to the same sort of tasks, and that there is some evidence that sentences and pictures are processed rather differently on these tasks. The use of theories based on imagery rather than propositional representation will be discussed in detail in the following chapter on transitive reasoning.

As stated earlier, the verification task does not require deductive reasoning. There is, however, no reason to suppose that the strategies applied to it would differ very much from those applicable to genuine deductive tasks. If, for example, one believes that people apply sequential strategies based on propositional representations to one sort of task, then it would be surprising if one did not expect to find the same to be true of the other. On the other hand, if Allport's (1975) contention that such models are task specific is correct, then they may not generalise. It will, therefore, be of interest to discover whether the features of information processing suggested by the successful models of the verification task correspond to those apparent on other reasoning tasks to be considered in this book.

4 Transitive inference

The study of transitive inference involves genuine deductive reasoning tasks, in which subjects are asked to put together two separate assertions in order to deduce a new assertion as a necessary consequence. Transitivity is a property of any scale or dimension on which objects can be compared and ordered. Such scales are usually defined by the adjectives describing their opposite poles, e.g. good – bad, tall – short, dark – light, etc. In general, if a relation r is transitive, then given that A r B and B r C it follows that A r C. For example:

> John is taller than Bill.
> Bill is taller than Jim.
> Therefore, John is taller than Jim.

It is usually possible to express the transitive relation in a negative or reverse form. For example, in the above argument, the second premise could be replaced by 'Jim is shorter than Bill' without altering the logical necessity of the inference. Whether such an alteration affects the psychological difficulty is, of course, a separate question.

Problems with two premises and a conclusion, as in the above example, are known as *linear syllogisms* or *three-term series problems*. The latter description arises from the consideration that three terms are related by the two premises (John, Bill and Jim). In order to define the general structure of these problems, let us define a transitive scale on which A is the most positively placed item, C the most negatively placed, and B the middle term. Let us, in general, call the relation '>' when expressed positively, and '<' when expressed negatively. By definition then A>B>C, or to put it another way, C<B<A.

TABLE 4.1   *Sixteen possible valid linear syllogisms*

		1	2	3	4
Premise pairs:		A>B	A>B	B<A	B<A
		B>C	C<B	B>C	C<B
Conclusion	(a)	A>C	A>C	A>C	A>C
	(b)	C<A	C<A	C<A	C<A
		1'	2'	3'	4'
Premise pairs:		B>C	C<B	B>C	C<B
		A>B	A>B	B<A	B<A
Conclusion	(a)	A>C	A>C	A>C	A>C
	(b)	C<A	C<A	C<A	C<A

There are sixteen possible *valid* linear syllogisms that can be constructed about 3 items, which are expressed in these general terms in Table 4.1. The conclusion always states the relationship between the two end terms, A and C, and may be expressed (a) positively, A>C, or (b) negatively, C<A. There are eight possible premise pairs, 1' – 4' being the same as 1 – 4 except that they are in the reverse order. However, most experiments on transitive inference reasoning present only premise pairs with a question rather than a conclusion to be evaluated. For example:

Jane is worse than Jill.
Mary is better than Jill.
Who is worst?

In this paradigm the two possible conclusions shown in Table 4.1 are replaced by two possible questions. In the above example, it could have been asked 'Who is best?'.

The research on transitive reasoning is highly relevant to issues discussed in the last two chapters. The major theoretical approaches all assume the general linear model of reasoning in which a comprehension stage precedes a reasoning stage (cf. Figure 3.2, p. 35). However, the theories differ with respect to the *mode* of representation postulated – propositional or imaginal, the *structure* of the representation, and the type of processing proposed. Before looking at experimental evidence, we will look closely at the theories.

Theories

Johnson-Laird (1972) refers to three major theoretical accounts of transitive inference as Operational, Imagery and Linguistic theories. I will adopt the same terminology, although I find it somewhat unsatisfactory, particularly in the case of the Imagery theory, for reasons that will become clear.

The Operational theory, proposed by Hunter (1957), will be described briefly for completeness, but it has had little impact on recent research and theoretical discussion in this field.

Hunter's argument is that problems are solved most easily when they are in a 'natural order'. Of the eight premise pairs shown in Table 4.1 only numbers 1 and 4' are of this form. Given A>B, B>C, it is easy to 'expunge' the middle term and see that A>C follows. Presumably conclusion type (a) should be more natural than (b). Similarly, the syllogism 4'(b) is entirely 'natural'.

When the premises are not in natural order the subject is supposed to convert them into a natural order by carrying out certain operations. E.g. problem 2 can be solved by converting the second premise C<B into B>C (problem 2' is similar). Problems 4 and 1' can be put into natural order by re-ordering the two premises. The most complex problems, according to Hunter, are 3 and 3' which require both conversion of the second premise, *and* re-ordering of the two premises.

Hunter's theory thus makes clear predictions about the relative difficulty of the different problem types shown in Table 4.1 and its fit to experimental data will be considered in due course.

Next, we consider the Imagery theory, although this term is misleading for two reasons. Although the proponents of this viewpoint have supposed that visual imagery is used in solving the problems, the predictions of the theory do not seem to depend on this assumption. The important feature of the theory is that it proposes that subjects solve the problems by constructing a linear ordering of the three items during comprehension of the premises, and then draw the conclusion (or answer the question) by reference to this linear representation. The supposition that this is achieved by constructing a visual image is not necessary. It is also misleading to talk of *the* Imagery theory since there are several variations.

The original theory was proposed by De Soto, London and Handel (1965). They proposed that the evaluative dimension 'good–bad' is imagined as a vertical spatial array, in which 'good' is assigned to the top and 'bad' to the bottom. This has subsequently been generalised to other dimensions which have a clear positive and negative end, with the assumption that the positive end is assigned to the top (e.g. tall, heavy) and the negative end to the bottom (e.g. short, light). The notion of the spatial array was derived from introspective reports, but validated by a direct experimental test to be described later.

De Soto *et al.* proposed two principles which affect the ease of constructing the mental representation and thus the difficulty of solving the problem. The first principle, *direction of working*, asserts that there is a preference for working from top to bottom of the spatial array. The second principle, *end-anchoring*, asserts that it is easier to construct a representation from a premise whose first item refers to an end item (A or C). Thus A>B or C<B should be easier to construct than B<A or B>C.

Let us examine the problems in Table 4.1 taking '>' to represent 'better' and '<' to represent 'worse'. Problems which use the same relational term (better or worse) in both premises, i.e. 1, 1', 4, 4', all contain one premise which is not end-anchored (starts with B). The principle of direction of working is applied both between and within premises. For example, 1 should be easier than 4' since the first premise refers to the top of the array in 1, and to the bottom in 4'. Within premises, top–bottom working is also preferred, implying that 'better' should be easier than 'worse'. On the problems which mix the relational terms, i.e. 2,2'; 3,3', some are to be preferred to others on the basis of end-anchoring in 2 and 2' and neither in 3 and 3'.

Deriving predictions from the two principles together is somewhat complex and unclear. Johnson-Laird (1972), in attempting to present the theory in a flow-chart form, decided that the two principles were not independent. He modified the theory to overcome this problem, and thus must be regarded as the author of an alternative version. In Johnson-Laird's account the subject is supposed to inspect each premise in turn to see whether or not it is end-anchored.

If it is not, the subject is supposed to convert it. The direction of working principle is then applied not to the premise presented, but to the premise the subject ends up with, which may or may not be converted. Consider the following problem:

B is worse than A
C is worse than B
Who is best?

In Johnson-Laird's version, the subject would study the first premise and note that it was not end-anchored. The model is rather artificial here, in that the subject can only arrive at this conclusion by *studying the second premise as well*. He then knows that B is the middle term rather than A, because it appears in both premises. The subject now converts the first premise into 'A is better than B', and places A and B in the array working downwards. In this problem the second premise is end-anchored, so does not need conversion. Johnson-Laird assumes that difficulty is a function of three things, (1) the need to convert the first premise, (2) the need to convert the second premise, (3) the direction of working in placing the items referred to *in the first premise only*. The last prediction is based on the assumption that the first premise 'sets' the direction of working. Since de Soto's theory proposed direction of working both between and within each premise, and based on the original premises without conversion, Johnson-Laird's model appears to be substantially different.

The best-known version of the Imagery theory is that of Hutten-locher (1968) which is similar to the original version of De Soto *et al*. Huttenlocher's theory is much influenced by introspections of adult subjects on linear syllogisms, and an analogy to the placement of actual physical objects into arrays by young children. In either case she supposes that on receiving the first premise (or instruction) the subject places one item above the other in the array (imagined or real). On receiving the second instruction the subject must now place the third item with respect to the first two. She proposes that this is more easily accomplished if the third item is the grammatical subject of the second premise. This is equivalent to predicting an end-anchoring effect for the second premise. The theory differs from De Soto's in not making a general end-anchoring prediction for the first premise. For dimensions with clearly preferred direction of working such as good–bad, the item placed first will be the 'better' one. For unclear dimensions such as 'light-hair–dark-hair' the item placed first will be the one mentioned first in the premise.

Thus it appears that there are three distinct versions of the Imagery theory.

Clark (1969) proposed what has become known as the Linguistic theory of transitive inference, which incorporates the notion that reasoning operations are performed not on the sentences themselves, but on their underlying propositional representation. This was asserted in the first of his three principles, which he terms *primacy of functional relationships*. At this time his terminology was influenced by that of Chomsky (1965), so that he refers to 'base strings' in the deep structure. The base strings can, however, be considered equivalent to underlying propositions. The essential argument is that a comparative sentence, such as 'John is better than Peter' is encoded as indicating that both John and Peter are good, but John is more so. Thus the underlying representation is 'John is good+*, Peter is good'. On the other hand 'Peter is worse than John' would be encoded as 'Peter is bad+, John is bad'.

The second principle, *lexical marking*, relates to the fact that many pairs of bi-polar adjectives are asymmetrical. One adjective may have a neutral unmarked sense, while the other has only a contrastive marked sense. If I ask 'How good if John?', I am asking only for his placement on the good–bad scale. If I ask 'How bad is John?', I am implying that I think he *is* bad. This unmarked–marked relationship occurs for many, but not all, bi-polar pairs, e.g. tall–short, heavy–light. Clark's lexical marking principle asserts that it should be easier to retrieve information from semantic memory if the underlying representation is of unmarked rather than marked adjectives. For example, 'A is better than B' should be processed faster than 'B is worse than A'.

The third principle, *congruence*, asserts that problems may be more simply solved if the question is congruent with the representation of the premises. The three principles can be most simply illustrated with reference to what Clark calls two-term series problems (Table 4.2). Premises in the form 'A is not as bad as B' are called *negative equatives* and were introduced by Clark to distinguish his predictions from Imagery theory – a point which will be discussed later. On

---

* In Clark's current notation, these would be written 'Good (John)', etc.

the principle of lexical marking he predicts that problem I will be more rapidly solved than II, but problem I′ more slowly than II′. This is because 'good' representations are unmarked. 'Best?' is assumed congruent with 'good' representations and 'Worst?' with 'bad' representations. Hence he predicts that the question 'Best?' will be answered more rapidly on problems I and II′, and 'Worst?' more rapidly on II and I′. Clark presents data which conform nicely to these predictions.

TABLE 4.2   *Two-term series problems for the 'good–bad' dimension*

	Premise	Analysis*	Question
I	A better than B	A is good B is good	(a) Best? (b) Worst?
II	B worse than A	A is bad B is bad	(a) Best? (b) Worst?
I′	A not as bad as B	A is bad B is bad	(a) Best? (b) Worst?
II′	B not as good as A	A is good B is good	(a) Best? (b) Worst?

* According to the Linguistic theory of Clark (1969)

The application to three-term series is more complex. Refer to Table 4.1 and take > to represent 'better than' and < to represent 'worse than'. Problems 1, 1′, 4, 4′ are homogeneous, i.e. use the same adjective. He would thus predict 1 and 1′ to be more quickly processed since they contain the unmarked adjective 'good' in their underlying representation. Congruence of the question 'best?/worst?' can be applied to these problems in a similar manner to the two term series.

The heterogeneous problems 2, 2′, 3, 3′ are more complicated. Neither has 'internal congruence', since the two premises are represented with reference to different adjectives. However, problems 2 and 2′ are predicted to be easier since they will be congruent with the question asked. If the question is 'Who is best?' the answer will be 'A' which is congruent with the premise in which A appears (A better than B). If the question is 'Who is worst?' then the answer 'C' appears in the premise 'C is worse than B' so that too is congruent. By contrast on problems 3 and 3' the question always turns out to be incongruent.

The reader may well have noticed that the predictions of the Linguistic theory are rather similar to the original Imagery theory. Firstly, if the unmarked adjective is the one placed at the 'top' of the array, the lexical marking and 'direction-of-working' make the same predictions for homogeneous syllogisms. Secondly, it also happens that the prediction that problems 2 and 2' are easier on heterogeneous syllogisms than problems 3 and 3' on the basis of congruence coincides with the prediction based on end-anchoring. Consequently, as we shall see in the next section, it is no easy matter to distinguish the theories in terms of their predictions of problem difficulty.

The original aim of all the transitive reasoning theorists was to predict the relative difficulty of the various problems. We will examine evidence of this sort, but for reasons indicated above it is unlikely to be conclusive. We will also examine evidence for the other issues arising from these theories. Firstly, what *direct* evidence is there that performance is mediated by mental images? Secondly, what evidence is there that a linear order is constructed at the time of comprehension? Recent work on the development of transitive reasoning, and studies of memory for inference shed light on the last question. First, however, let us consider the question of problem difficulty.

Predictions about problem difficulty

In presenting the various theories it was pointed out how they predicted the relative difficulty of the problems shown in Table 4.1. We shall now look at some data. Table 4.3 shows data for positive comparative problems in three studies, where asymmetrical adjective pairs are employed. Neither Huttenlocher (1968) nor De Soto *et al.* (1965) report data separately by question asked, so the evidence for congruence rests on the Clark (1969) data. First of all look at the percentage correct data of De Soto *et al.*, and the mean latency, averaged over question type, of Clark's study. For homogeneous syllogisms both direction-of-working and lexical marking predict that problems 1 and 1' will be easier than problems 4 and 4'. On average this is true for both data sets. For heterogeneous problems both end-anchoring (De Soto) and congruence predict that 2 and 2' will be easier than 3 and 3' – which is again supported in both sets of data.

TABLE 4.3 *Relative difficulty of linear syllogisms in three studies*

Problem	Comparative:	De Soto *et al.* (1965) better-worse	Huttenlocher (1968) taller-shorter	Clark (1969) good-bad		
				Best?	Worst?	M
1 A>B B>C		60.5	155	542	610	575
1' B>C A>B		52.8	135	498	552	525
2 A>B C<B		61.8	141	535	534	534
2' C<B A>B		57.0	142	484	584	532
3 B<A B>C		41.5	157	500	602	549
3' B>C B<A		38.3	157	612	545	577
4 B<A C<B		50.0	142	593	504	547
4' C<B B<A		42.5	161	627	653	640
		% correct	Latencies in centiseconds			

Now, the order of presenting premise pairs should make no difference according to Clark's three principles, so that 1 and 1' etc. should be equivalent. The other theories make various predictions shown in Table 4.4. Huttenlocher's (1968) data fit well to her prediction based on end-anchoring in the second premise. It should be noted, however, that her latencies were only measured from the presentation of the second premise, and do not include the time taken to read and understand the first premise.

TABLE 4.4 *Predicted effect of reversing premise order by various theories*

	Hunter	De Soto	Huttenlocher	Johnson-Laird	Clark
1 v. 1'	1 easier	1 easier	1' easier	1 easier	No difference
2 v. 2'	No difference	2 easier	No difference	2 easier	No difference
3 v. 3'	No difference	3 easier	No difference	3 easier	No difference
4 v. 4'	4' easier	4 easier	4 easier	4 easier	No difference

It is interesting that Johnson-Laird's restructured Imagery theory makes identical predictions to De Soto *et al.* in these comparisons. Both theories fit well to the percentage correct data of De Soto *et al.*, but less well to the mean latencies of Clark (1969); only the comparisons of 3 to 3' and 4 to 4' fit the predictions. That there are significant effects of premise order at all is beyond Clark's (1969) theory to explain, as he admits in the paper. Hunter's Operational theory does not fit any of the experiments very well.

Both Imagery theorists and Clark have pointed to variables which affect problem difficulty and apparently favour one theory or the other. In the case of Imagery theory the type of comparative used should affect the reasoning, according to its imageability. Clark (1969) claims, on the other hand, that responses to negative equatives and the effects of congruence on the question asked distinguish the superiority of his theory. We will examine some of the arguments.

The predictions specified for Imagery theories above were qualified as applying only to dimensions which had a clear spatial reference with a preferred direction of working. De Soto *et al.* (1965) produced evidence of people's preferred direction for evaluation (good–bad) and hair colour (lighter–darker) by asking people to place the comparatives in vertically or horizontally opposite boxes. The results suggested that better–worse has a vertical representation with the 'good' end at the top, but that there was no clear spatial reference for 'lighter–darker'. In a subsequent experiment they showed, as predicted, that the differences based on preferred direction of working disappeared for subjects reasoning with 'darker–lighter'. On these problems, subjects also did much better if the two premises contained the same relational term rather than a mixture of the two. Similar results were obtained by Shaver, Pierson and Lang (1975).

While these results seem to support the Imagery prediction, they are not inconsistent with the Linguistic theory. As we have seen, direction-of-working predictions coincide with lexical marking predictions, and 'lighter–darker' does not seem to have a lexically unmarked pole. Lexical marking does, in fact, appear to affect spatial assignment in just such a way that two theories will coincide. Jones (1970) presented subjects with three-term series problems and asked them to write down the three terms and nothing else. Subjects did arrange them in an appropriate linear order, usually vertically but sometimes horizontally. Jones examined preferences for placing one adjective or its opposite at the top of the vertical arrangements. With unmarked–marked pairs she found a bias to place the unmarked adjective at the top, e.g. good above bad, and a weaker tendency to place the term mentioned first at the top. For marked–marked pairs (e.g. light–dark) the second factor dominated. Thus spatial preference does seem to coincide with lexical marking, at least for the adjectives she investigated.

Clark (1969) claimed that negative equative problems distinguished the two theories, and the results he obtained certainly supported his own predictions very well. But do they refute the Imagery theory? His claim is based on the assumption that, for example, 'x is not as good as y' had bottom–top directionality. However, Huttenlocher, Higgins, Milligan and Kaufman (1970) have pointed out that there are various ways of interpreting the sentence. If the subject reads it as 'x is worse than y', then Clark is correct, but in that case the lexical marking prediction would alter also. The subject might, quite easily, read the sentence as 'y is better than x' thus leading to top–bottom directionality and again coincidence with the lexical marking predictions.

Thus negative equatives cannot be considered the decisive test claimed by Clark. The congruence predictions for two-term series and homogeneous three-term series *are* beyond the scope of the basic Imagery theory. This, however, is balanced by the observation that the effect of premise order is beyond the Linguistic theory. On balance, the two theories fit most of the data quite well and coincide in most of their predictions. Clark and Huttenlocher conducted a rather heated debate in which they each tried to argue that their own theory was superior to that of the other (Huttenlocher and Higgins, 1971; Clark, 1971; Huttenlocher and Higgins, 1972; Clark, 1972). I am in agreement with others (Johnson-Laird, 1972; Shaver *et al.*, 1975) in thinking that the issue was not satisfactorily resolved. Indeed I do not think it *can* be resolved on the basis of measures of problem difficulty. It is for this reason that I turn to other forms of data.

Direct evidence for the presence of imagery

The dispute between Clark and Huttenlocher should be placed in the context of the current debate about propositional v. imagery representations, which was considered in some detail in Chapter 2. One conclusion of that discussion was that arguments about the *format* of representation (abstract, propositional v. analogue, imagery) tend to be confused with arguments about the information-processing structure of rival theories. In this section we shall focus on the format question. The questions asked are (i) what evidence is there that 'imagery' is involved in the solution of transitive inference problems and (ii) does this imagery involve a cognitive process with functional significance, or simply a mental experience that could be regarded as an epi-phenomenon (cf. Pylyshyn, 1973; Chapter 2 of this book)?

A number of different types of evidence have been offered in support of the claim that imagery is involved. The first type of evidence is introspective. Subjects frequently report constructing visual arrays. De Soto *et al.* (1965) and Huttenlocher (1968) were clearly influenced by such reports in constructing their theories. There are logical difficulties here. If such evidence is used to construct the theory, it can hardly be claimed subsequently as evidence for it. Also, the mere existence of such phenomenal reports does not prove that imagery has any functional significance.

Two studies have concerned themselves with individual differences in subjective reports. Shaver *et al.* (1975) classified such reports into those indicating an 'imagery strategy' and those indicating other types of strategy. In their experiment, problems were presented either visually or aurally, and following Brooks (1967; 1968) they expected that an imagery strategy would be harder to apply to visually presented problems. For some extraordinary reason, they tested this not by correlating reports with *performance*, but with the subjects' reports of 'which mode of presentation . . . seemed most difficult'. Quinton and Fellows (1975) classified subjects as using different strategies by introspective report, and did in fact find significant differences in behaviour associated with these. These authors make the strong and unwarranted conclusion that the reports reflected a *causal* strategy. The correlation between reports and behaviour can, of course, be interpreted in different ways. The report could be constructed *post hoc* and be determined, to some extent, by the success of the performance.

Introspective reports of imagery are important if you feel *by definition* that imagery is a mental experience, but are of little relevance to an information-processing conception of imagery (see Chapter 2). In the latter terms it is more relevant to ask whether there is evidence of a mode of representation linked to that of visual perception.

Evidence for this has been claimed by Shaver *et al.* (1975) on the basis of 'converging operations' analogous to those employed by Brooks and Paivio (cf. Chapter 2). The authors argue, in effect, for a dual-coding theory in which the use of imagery, while not essential, will facilitate performance when its use is permitted or encouraged. If Brooks's (1967; 1968) evidence is accepted as showing that there is a conflict between perceiving and imagining in the same modality, then it follows that *if* visual imagery is employed, it will compete with perceiving visually. As mentioned previously, Shaver *et al.* varied the mode of presentation between visual and auditory. They also manipulated the 'imageability' of the problems in the spirit of Paivio (1971). Following De Soto *et al.* (1965), they regarded 'above–below' as high on imageability, 'dark hair–light hair' as low on imageability, with 'good–bad' intermediate. ('Imageability' refers to the existence of a *spatial* representation of the adjective pair in this context.) Shaver *et al.* found that people did worse on visual than aural presentation, and also did worse on less imageable problems. Such main effects are, however, always open to other interpretations. The critical test is the interaction; there should be more interference of visual presentation on the more imageable problems, for it is here that an imagery strategy is more likely to be adopted. The interaction was in the right direction but not significant. Williams (1979) has also shown that syllogisms with higher *a priori* ratings of imageability are solved more quickly, but failed to control for or even consider alternative explanations of this main effect. If the subjects' ratings actually reflect say, ease of retrieval from semantic memory, then a linguistic theorist like Clark would expect faster latencies.

Shaver *et al.'s* marginal evidence for imagery is weakened by the results of a study by Mosenthal (1977). The author discusses his results solely in terms of the Linguistic theory, but inadvertently produces data of relevance to the Imagery theory. He gave two-

and three-term series problems on the 'good–bad' dimension to children of 7-8 years of age. He was actually interested in whether reading and listening involve access to the same system of linguistic competence. He found that children made more errors when reading aloud than when listening to the problems. However, *silent* reading produced no more errors than listening in two detailed experiments. This, in effect, is a failure to replicate Shaver *et al.'s* basic finding of a main effect of presentation modality.

Other claims of Shaver *et al.* are also suspect. For example, they found a significant correlation between a test of visual–spatial intelligence tests and reasoning performance. However, since both measures can be assumed to load on general IQ there is no reason to assume that this arises from an imagery component. Shaver *et al.* also showed that subjects' performance improved if instructed in the use of an imagery strategy. However, they did not instruct the use of any other strategy as a control, nor test for an interaction with the imageability of the problems.

Huttenlocher has also claimed as evidence for the use of imagery the fact that there is a close parallel between the data of children placing actual objects in arrays, and the data of adults reasoning 'in their heads' (e.g. Huttenlocher *et al.*, 1970). The suggestion is that adults are doing mentally what the children are doing physically. However, the parallels arise in the results of manipulating the linguistic structure of the problems. Since either task involves understanding the instructions or premises the similarities could arise from the comprehension process rather than subsequent solution strategies.

Finally, a recent study by H. van Duyne and Sass (1979) is of relevance. There is increasing evidence that visual–spatial functions are associated with the functioning of the right hemisphere of the brain, whereas verbal functions are normally associated with the left hemisphere (see Cohen, 1977). Van Duyne and Sass presented transitive inference problems to either left or right ears – which relay the information first to the opposite hemisphere. In general there was a right ear (i.e. left hemisphere) advantage in children's reasoning performance (frequency correct). However, this factor interacted with sex, such that the advantage was less for males. Since males are generally thought to have greater visual–spatial ability, this interaction could be taken as weak evidence for a dual-coding position in which an optional visual strategy can be employed. However, one could not say that the girls were *not* using imagery, since the left-hemisphere advantage could arise from the initial verbal comprehension process. Unfortunately, the image-ability of the problem was not manipulated in this study.

Overall, then, there is no good evidence that transitive inference requires a *visual* mode of representation. At best, the evidence of Shaver *et al.* and van Duyne and Sass might be taken to support a dual coding position in which imagery relates to an optional strat-egy. Introspective reports of mental imagery are subject to problems of interpretation (cf. Chapter 2) and there is no clear evidence of their functional significance in transitive reasoning, at least so far as the visual aspect is concerned. This section has, however, looked only at the format of representation. In line with our earlier dis-tinction we should now look for differences between the Imagery and Linguistic theories in information-processing structure. The next section concerns such a distinction.

Evidence for linear representation

The issue between Imagery and Linguistic theorists has been some-what redefined by authors of recent papers (e.g. Trabasso, 1977; Higgins, 1976; Potts and Scholz, 1975). The opposing viewpoints are now seen as follows:

(1) The information contained in the premises is combined into a single linear order at the time of comprehension. The form in which the information was originally presented is irrelevant to sub-sequent reasoning.

(2) The information in the premises is stored separately for each premise at the time of comprehension, and is not combined until the subject attempts to answer the question. Linguistic properties of the premise are retained in storage.

Whilst conditions (1) and (2) clearly correspond to the 'Imagery' and 'Linguistic' theories, the issue defined has nothing to do with the presence of mental pictures, or competition with visual percep-tion. The notion of linear orderings at the comprehension stage is thus defined in a manner which exorcises the ghost of 'mental imagery' and all its associated problems. This, in turn, renders the assessment of the relative merits of the two alternative positions amenable to ready empirical test. As we shall see, there is considerable evidence in favour of the first position. Some of the evidence comes from the rather indirect source of 'memory for inference' studies. For stimulating, argumentative reviews of recent work in this area, the reader is referred to Potts (1978) and Griggs (1978). The relevant experiments for the present purpose are those which present information about linear orderings, for example, A>B>C>D. The general paradigm is one in which subjects are presented with a prose passage which contains information about adjacent pairs – (A, B), (B,C), (C, D). An example of a passage used by Potts (1974) is the following:

> In art class, Sally showed her nature painting to the teacher. Her teacher felt that certain parts of the picture were drawn better than others. The teacher said her tree was better than the grass, her sky was better than her bird, and her bird was better than her tree. Upon hearing this, Sally decided to drop art and major in psychology.

In this piece A = sky, B = bird, C = tree, and D = grass.

Subjects were subsequently presented with test sentences to evaluate which were either true (A>B) or false (B>A) and either *adjacent* (A>B) or *remote* (A>C). The most interesting aspect of the results is response latencies are quicker to question about *remote* pairs than the adjacent pairs, even though the former were not presented. In other words, subjects have better recall for *inferred* relations than those actually presented (see also Potts, 1972; Scholz and Potts, 1974). Similar findings have been reported by Moyer (1973) in semantic memory experiments, where subjects are asked to assess statements on natural linear orderings such as animal size.

These results strongly suggest that a linear ordering is constructed during comprehension. The superiority of remote pairs is explained by Moyer in terms of an 'internal psychophysics'. Items further apart on the internal scale are more 'discriminable'. However, the Potts studies (e.g. Potts, 1974) show that this cannot explain all the data. There is also an interaction with truth value, which suggests some kind of 'end-anchoring' effect, in retrieval. Subjects respond more quickly 'true' to any pair starting with A, and 'false' to any pair starting with D. They are sure to be correct on such cases, because the items concerned are at the top and bottom ends of the scale.

These experiments suggest that subjects make transitive inferences during comprehension, even when not asked to do so. What evidence is there for a similar process on the more conventional reasoning tasks?

Some evidence comes from developmental studies of transitive inference. Research on children's reasoning appears to be polarised between two camps, the Piagetians on the one hand and those interested in information-processing approaches on the other. Transitive reasoning has long been used as a Piagetian test of the level of the child's conceptual thought. In a typical experiment the child is given information about the relative length of pairs of coloured sticks. He is then questioned about the relation of remote pairs. In Piaget's theory transitivity requires reversibility and hence concrete operations, and correspondingly is claimed by his followers to develop at about 8 years of age. Information-processing psychologists such as Bryant and Trabasso (1971), however, have claimed transitivity at ages as young as 4 years. Klahr and Wallace (1976) explain the discrepancies in terms of methodological differences in the criteria used to assess the presence of transitivity.

It is the information-processing approach which has provided the most relevant data for our purpose. The study of Trabasso, Riley and Wilson (1975) is particularly relevant, and will be discussed in some detail. The experiment was run on three age groups: 6-year-olds, 9-year-olds and adults (college students). Each subject was presented with adjacent pairs of six sticks of different lengths and different colours. During the Training phase each pair was presented behind a screen so that the subject could see the difference in colour but not in length. All *adjacent* pairs were presented in random order. The subject said which stick he thought was longer and was then given one of two types of feedback. Half the subjects were given verbal feedback and half a visual display of the sticks, fully visible, as well.

Subjects were trained to criterion and then a graph of errors during training was plotted over 'serial position'. If the largest stick is called 1 and the shortest 6, then the scale runs from the comparison of (1,2) through to (5,6). The errors showed a serial position effect, with most errors being made on comparison of middle items. Although the curve appeared more sharply peaked for younger children this is due to a greater absolute frequency of errors. When errors are computed as a percentage of total errors the curves coincide.

Since the pairs are presented in random order, this strongly supports the hypothesis that subjects are learning a scale rather than individual comparisons. Furthermore, the bowed nature of the curve suggests that they are 'end-anchoring' i.e. learning the end items first. The results of a subsequent test phase confirmed this. As in the memory-for-inference studies, subjects more quickly and accurately answered questions about remote comparisons (*not* presented in training) than adjacent comparisons.

The only developmental trend of interest concerned the type of feedback administered. Performance on the test trials improved significantly with age for verbal feedback groups but was uniformly high on visual feedback. This suggests that while young children have the capacity for constructing a linear representation, they may have difficulty in encoding verbal statements in this manner. This does, then, constitute suggestive evidence that the representation may be visual in nature. However, Adams (1978) has pointed out that the superiority of visual feedback could arise for other reasons, such as maintaining the child's attention during the long training phase. She administered visual and verbal feedback, but in one case the sticks were barely discriminable in length. Although subjects shown highly discriminable sticks learned the adjacent pairs quicker, they did no better on the subsequent transitive inference test (performance was generally high). In fact, other controls suggested that a genuinely integrated sequence was more likely to be constructed in the group given *low* discriminable visual feedback. With highly discriminable sticks there is some evidence that the children compare absolute memories of particular sticks when given a transitive test. However, this memory explanation cannot account for other groups tested by Adams, who provides excellent evidence of integration of transitive information in children as young as 5 years.

A corollary of the linear-order hypothesis is the assumption that linguistic information, for example lexical markedness, is lost after the comprehension stage. Potts and Scholz (1975) tested this hypothesis by giving subjects three-term series 'letter–name' problems, with a modified procedure. Subjects were given as long as they liked to read and understand the problems. They were timed from presentation of the question: 'Who is best?/worst?' only. Clark's predictions of congruence disappeared completely, although they were observed in a control group using standard latency measurement. (This effect is substantiated by the data of French, 1979, who overlooks the significance of this aspect of his results and fails to discuss them.) In failing to observe any interaction between the adjective used in premise and question, Potts and Scholz are led to question a general independent assumption of Huttenlocher's as well as Clark's theory (cf. Figure 3.2):

> The absence of such an interaction . . . leads one to question whether performance in the standard paradigm can be accurately described using a model which posits independent encoding and answering stages.

This is an interesting observation in the light of the discussion in Chapter 3 where it was suggested that the fit of sentence-verification models based on independent additive stages might be specific to the type of paradigm adopted.

Higgins (1976) has also looked at the question of whether the 'presupposition' information underlying the premises is retained as proposed in Clark's Linguistic theory. He claims that 'There is now general agreement that Clark's model is not adequate as an explanation of how the information contained in three term series premises is combined' but that it is an independent issue, 'whether presuppositional information contained in the premises of three term series problems can affect the process of combining information from the two premises.' He suggests that it is particularly difficult to see how the information could be combined in heterogeneous syllogisms, where the comparisons and hence the underlying presupposition differs between the two premises. For example, in the syllogism 'A is better than B, C is worse than B' the first premise presupposes 'good' and the second 'bad'.

Higgins claims that some adjective pairs have stronger presuppositions than others, and tests the hypothesis that such pairs will increase the difficulty of integrating heterogeneous premises. The results supported the hypothesis leading to the conclusion that, 'These results suggest that subjects do retain the presuppositional information contained in the premises.' This interpretation should be treated cautiously however. It is not clear how strong the linguistic basis is for claiming that some pairs have stronger presuppositions than others. The only basis cited is the linguistic analysis of Huttenlocher and Higgins (1971) which has been criticised in various respects by Clark (1971).

In summary, then, there is reason to believe that subjects do combine transitive information into a linear ordering during comprehension. There is suggestive evidence that the linguistic presuppositions may influence the ease of this construction, but no evidence that linguistic properties of the premises affect the subsequent answering of questions.

Conclusions

This summary of the transitive inference literature illustrates the difficulties associated with imagery explanations discussed in Chapter 2. We have seen that imagery theorists have been highly influenced by introspective reports of their subjects. This has led to two assumptions about the representation underlying transitive inference (i) that it uses a visual mode, (ii) that premise information is combined into a linear sequence during comprehension. As we have seen, experimental evidence gives clear support only to the second of these assumptions. So the subjects' introspections are in a sense helpful and in a sense misleading. What lesson should be learned from this? Perhaps that subjective reports should, at most, serve as heuristic sources of hypotheses about cognitive processes, which should then be subjected to rigorous experimental test. I certainly agree with Pylyshyn (1973) that the functional significance of what a subject experiences and reports cannot be assumed.

Anderson's (1978) distinction between representation and process is also relevant. The problem with Clark's Linguistic theory does not lie in its assumption of propositional representation. The theory fails in an assumption about the manner in which those representations are *processed* (i.e. after rather than before the question). The propositions versus imagery debate is probably rather vacuous. As Johnson-Laird (1979) points out, a propositional representation is essentially a *description* of an internal model. It is hence a theoretical device which is not incompatible with an analogue model, with or without modality related mechanisms.

A more important issue, discussed in Chapter 2, was that of whether singular or multiple cognitive mechanisms are involved in representing and processing sentences. In the review of sentence verification (Chapter 3) it was noted that the main models assumed that a common semantic code was used for comparing sentences and pictures. However, it was also pointed out that dual coding mechanisms could not be ruled out on the evidence available. In transitive inference the models of both Clark and Huttenlocher have assumed a single format of representation (propositional and visual respectively), with the sequential stages of comprehension, inference and response (Figure 3.2). However, the soundness of such models is questioned by Potts and Scholz (1975) and suggestions of unclear evidence for dual coding is found in the studies of Shaver *et al.* (1975) and Van Duyne and Sass (1979).

In Part I we have looked at simple reasoning tasks in which subjects are usually able to provide the correct answers, if given sufficient time. The psychological limitation of studying such tasks is recognised by Newell and Simon (1972): 'To the extent that behaviour is precisely what is called for it will give us information about the task environment' (p.55). The point is that the models proposed to account for sentence verification and transitive inference are essentially analyses of the information processing requirements of the task, rather than the information-processing characteristics of the subjects. It is hard to infer very much about reasoning mechanisms when the problems lie within the subjects' competence. What could we have learned about the mechanisms of memory if we did not lead it to the point where forgetting occurs?

Of course, the work reviewed in Chapters 3 and 4 is of psychological value. However, the focus on latencies, rather than errors, probably tells us more about comprehension processes than reasoning *per se*, important though these are in understanding inference. We carry forward to the study of more complex reasoning some important knowledge. For example, negatives are difficult to process and tend to be either converted to affirmatives or encoded as false affirmatives. We also know that latency data will conform to simple additive models where they are appropriate to the task, but the fit of such models is subject to variations in procedure. Thus subjects appear to devise purpose-built strategies to fit tasks. While this tells us that subjects are flexible information-processors, it limits the psychological value of the models. Sequential stages, for example, may be a feature of the task structure rather than a general characteristic of cognition. This flexibility of strategy generation may encompass alternative forms of representation, in line with dual coding, although there is insufficient evidence to decide this at present.

In order to advance our understanding of reasoning, we must then look at more difficult problems which do not lie so comfortably within the competence of the subjects. To quote Newell and Simon again, 'To the extent that behaviour departs from perfect rationality, we gain information about the psychology of the subject, about the nature of the internal mechanisms which are limiting his performance.' Parts II and III abound with evidence of non-rational behaviour, at least by the standards of formal logic. As we shall see, representation and process models retain much of the popularity they have enjoyed on the simpler reasoning tasks, with 'error' built in at either or both stages. We shall also examine some explanations of reasoning performance based on an entirely different approach.

Part II

Syllogistic reasoning

5 An introduction to syllogistic reasoning

Syllogistic logic was devised by Aristotle and was utilised by the earliest psychologists to study deductive reasoning with formal problems (Woodworth and Sells, 1935). It is also employed in a number of current studies, as we shall see in Chapter 6. The present chapter is concerned with explaining the nature of the logical system, the psychological paradigms based on it, and the general nature of the psychological issues involved.

The logic of syllogisms

The premises of classical syllogisms always express one of the four relations shown in Table 5.1. Since the statements all refer to relations between two sets, it is easiest to understand their meaning with reference to Venn diagrams. There are five possible relations between two sets as shown in Figure 5.1. In situation 1 (set equivalence) the membership of sets A and B is identical. For example, A might be the set of male persons, and B the set of persons having an XY chromosome pair. In situation 2 sets A and B overlap but there are some A that are not B, and some B that are not A. An example would be if A represented men and B represented cigarette smokers. In situation 3 (set inclusion) the set B is a proper subset of the set A. That is all B are contained within A but some A are not B. A example would be if A represents the set of animals and B the set of dogs. Situation 4 is the reverse of 3, A being a subset of B. Finally, in situation 5, A and B are mutually exclusive, i.e. have no common members. An example would be if A represented cats and B dogs.

TABLE 5.1   *The four basic relations in syllogistic logic*

Name	Code	Relation	Possible situations*
universal affirmative	A	All A are B	1,4
universal negative	E	No A are B	5
particular affirmative	I	Some A are B	1,2,3,4
particular negative	0	Some A are not B	2,3,5

* cf. Figure 5.1.

FIGURE 5.1   Venn diagrams of possible relations between two sets

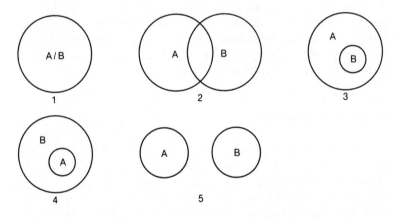

Now let us consider the four basic relations in Table 5.1. The universal affirmative (A), *All A are B*, holds if either A and B are equivalent (situation 1) or if A is a proper subset of B (situation 4). The universal negative (E), *No A are B*, is true only in situation 5 where the two sets are mutually exclusive. The particular affirmative (I) *Some A are B* is true of any situation *except* mutual exclusion i.e. situations 1, 2, 3 and 4. Finally the particular negative (O), *Some A are not B*, is true for situations 2, 3 and 5. If the reader is confused by the last two, it is probably due to use of the word 'some'. In logic this does not exclude 'all', but means 'at least some'. Hence, for example, *Some A are B* is always true in a situation where *All A are B* is true.

Before looking at syllogisms as such, we can illustrate the nature of deductive logic by asking a simple question of each of the four relations: does each relation imply its converse? The converse of a statement is one in which the terms (A and B) are interchanged. In other words does:

(1) *All A are B* imply *All B are A*?
(2) *No A are B* imply *No B are A*?
(3) *Some A are B* imply *Some B are A*?
(4) *Some A are not B* imply *Some B are not A*?

The reader may like to attempt to answer these questions before reading on.

To make progress we must first recall what is meant by logical implication. One statement implies another logically if whenever the former is true the latter is necessarily also true. In this case, a relation will imply its converse, if there is no possible situation we can construct such that the relation would be true and its converse false. Bearing this principle in mind we will now answer each of the above four questions.

The A statement *All A are B* is true in situations 1 and 4. In situation 1 its converse *All B are A* is also true. However, in the other situation, 4, the converse is *not* true. Hence, there does exist a situation such that the A relation is true and its converse false. Thus the answer to question (1) is 'No'. A thematic example such as 'All dogs are animals' which depicts situation 4, shows immediately the fallacy of conversion 'All animals are dogs'.

The E relation, *No A are B* is only true in one situation (5). However, in this situation its converse *No B are A* is also true, so the answer to question (2) is 'Yes'. The answer to (3) is also 'Yes'. In any situation but 5 at least one A is a B and hence, of course, at least one B is an A. Question (4) is the least easy to answer. In fact the answer is 'No'. *Some A are not B* is true in situations 2, 3 and 5. Its converse *Some B are not A* is true in situations 2, 4, and 5. Hence there exists one situation (3) where the statement could be true and its converse false. A thematic example in which one can readily perceive the fallacy of conversion is 'Some animals are not dogs'.

The reasoning becomes more complex when one is asked to decide what is implied by two premises in combination. This is required by the syllogism which consists of two premises and a conclusion. The syllogism is termed *valid* if the conclusion necessarily follows from (i.e. is implied by) the two premises. Consider the following syllogism:

> No B are C
> Some A are B
> Therefore, some A are not C

Now the question we have to decide is whether or not this syllogism is valid. We must ask whether there exists a situation such that *both* premises could be true and the conclusion false. If so the syllogism is fallacious; if not then the syllogism is valid. We could attempt to solve this by constructing all possible Venn diagrams where both premises are true. We know that the second premise *Some A are B* is true for situations 1, 2, 3, and 4 (Figure 5.1). To these we must add a third set C in such a way that it does not overlap with B (on account of the first premise). This third set C may or may not overlap A, but however we place it C cannot entirely contain A, because it cannot contain those elements that are linked to members of B. Thus, however we draw the diagrams the conclusion *Some A are not C* will be true. If the conclusion had read *Some C are not A* the syllogism would have been fallacious. The validity of the original syllogism may perhaps be more easily perceived if expressed in thematic terms, e.g.

> No singers are tone deaf
> Some men are singers
> Therefore, some men are not tone deaf

We will now consider the structure of syllogisms in classical Aristotelian logic. The conclusion consists of a subject (S) and predicate (P). One premise, the *major*, relates the middle term (M) to the predicate, while the other *minor* premise relates the middle term to the subject. In classical logic the major premise always precedes the minor premise, but the two terms of each may appear in either order. This produces the four classical *figures* of the syllogism (cf. Table 5.2, Figures I – IV).

The *mood* of a syllogism is defined independently of its figure. The mood refers to the type of relation specified in the major premise,

TABLE 5.2   *Eight possible figures for syllogisms*

Classical figures

I	II	III	IV
M – P	P – M	M – P	P – M
S – M	S – M,	M – S	M – S
Therefore, S – P	Therefore, S – P	Therefore, S – P	Therefore, S – P

Reversed figures

I'	II'	III'	IV'
S – M	S – M	M – S	M – S
M – P	P – M	M – P	P – M
Therefore, S – P	Therefore, S – P	Therefore, S – P	Therefore, S – P

minor premise and conclusion. If all these were universal the mood would be AAA. Four distinct classical syllogisms of this mood would be possible according to the figure. The logical structure of a syllogism is thus uniquely defined when both mood and figure are specified. The example discussed above is, for example, in mood EIO and Figure I. There are 64 possible moods of a syllogism and as a result a total of 256 possible classical syllogisms when figure is taken into account. Only 24 of these are, in fact, valid. If premise order is reversed, so that the minor premise is presented first (Figures I' to IV', Table 5.2) the logical validity of the syllogism is unaffected. From a psychological perspective, however, premise order may affect the ease of reasoning. Hence, a further 256 syllogisms produced by reversing premise order should be considered for possible psychological investigation.

Paradigms

There are several ways in which subjects may be asked to assess the validity of a syllogism:

(1) The whole syllogism may be presented, and the subject asked whether or not the conclusion necessarily follows from the premises.

(2) The two premises may be presented, followed by a list of alternative conclusions from which the subject must select. To accommodate invalid syllogisms, an alternative such as 'None of these'

is normally included. This alternative is described as a *non-propositional conclusion*.

(3) The premise pair may be presented, and the subject asked to produce what conclusion, if any, he believes to follow.

In practice method (1) is rarely adopted, and method (2) is the most common. Consequently, a number of researchers in the field inaccurately refer to premise pairs (without a conclusion) as a 'syllogism'. This may lead to ambiguity in the definition of figure. For example, the premises of Classical Figure I (Table 5.2) only belong to that figure because it is known that the conclusion is of the form S – P. If no conclusion were stated, then it might be in the form P – S. In this case the figure would actually be a Figure IV with reversed premise order (Figure IV'). This problem only really arises under method (3), however. In method (2), all the alternative conclusions will have the S – P order, thus making the figure clear.

Other experimental paradigms involving syllogistic premises will be considered in Chapter 6. These include attempts to measure subjects' representation of the premises by asking them to construct or evaluate Venn diagrams. We will also examine research in which several A premises are embedded in a prose passage. It is pertinent here to observe that an A relation is *transitive*. Hence, if *All A are B*, *All B are C* and *All C are D* it follows that *All A are D*, and so on.

What of the independent variables employed in syllogistic reasoning experiments? There are essentially two types of variables, relating to *form* and *content*. In the former category, attention has been focused on how the structural characteristics of the syllogism, i.e. mood and figure, affect the ease of reasoning. Most of this research has employed abstract materials, frequently using letters to represent class names as in Table 5.1. However, the effect of the problem *content* has also been investigated, by using as terms words which refer to real-life properties ('thematic content'). It is possible, for example, to see whether such thematic content facilitates correct inference, and also to look at the effect of *a priori* attitudes towards thematic content.

The issues

In studying research into syllogistic reasoning, we will consider one of the most important issues in the psychology of reasoning as a whole, that of logical versus non-logical explanation (see Chapter 1). The fundamental question is whether or not people behave rationally, i.e. whether they *reason*, when confronted with a logical task in the laboratory. The assertion that they do so will be referred to as the logical or *rationalist* approach, even if it is supposed that the logic employed differs in some respect from that of philosophers. The alternative *non-logical* approach supposes that subject behaviour is determined by response biases, or attention to aspects of the problem irrelevant to its logical structure. Between these extremes of course, it is possible to assume that behaviour is determined partly by logical and partly by non-logical processes.

The question of whether or not people behave rationally in reasoning experiments is by no means easy to answer (cf. Chapter 1). The basic problem is that the logicality of the observed response to a reasoning task does not necessarily indicate the logicality of the underlying process. The arguments in this respect have been most clearly laid out by Henle (1962) whose paper is considered in detail below.

Early research on syllogistic reasoning, dating from the paper of Woodworth and Sells (1935), was largely concerned with investigating non-logical biases. Such was the impact of Henle's (1962) paper, however, that subsequent research has been dominated by the rationalist school. Two recent collections of papers published in the USA are effectively devoted to her cause (Falmagne, 1975; Revlin and Mayer, 1978). In a foreword to the latter of these, Henle states categorically, 'I have never found errors which could unambiguously be attributed to faulty reasoning.' We cannot assess the evidence for this claim without first of all considering problems which arise concerning the interpretation of reasoning data.

Smedslund (1970) has pointed out that a circular relationship exists between logic and understanding. Suppose I set someone a reasoning task and observe their performance. If I assume that they understand the problem then I can determine the logicality of their reasoning by considering the accuracy of their conclusions. Conversely, if I assume that their reasoning is logical, I can determine the accuracy of their understanding of the problem. What I cannot do is to determine both simultaneously.

How does one escape this dilemma? In an earlier article (Evans, 1972a) I suggested a multi-paradigm approach. If an effect is due to difficulty of interpretation, then it should manifest itself on various reasoning tasks where a particular linguistic form is used. Conversely, if a particular reasoning operation is the cause of difficulty, then this should appear whenever the reasoning operation is required, irrespective of the linguistic structure. This approach has been adopted with a certain degree of success in the study of propositional reasoning (see Part III).

The rationalist approach seeks to exploit the ambiguity identified by Smedslund in a different way. Since the assumption is that the reasoning process is logical and since errors frequently occur, the general supposition is that subjects have misunderstood or misrepresented the problem. In other words, it is supposed that the reasoning is logical given their own personal interpretation of the premises.

Henle (1962) does, however, identify another source of error which she calls 'failure to accept the logical task'. This occurs, for example, when a subject evaluates the conclusion of a syllogism on its merits, without considering whether it follows from the premises. This is apparently most likely to occur when realistic materials are used towards which subjects have emotional attitudes (see the section on content in Chapter 6).

However, Henle claimed that subjects who do accept the task make errors through misinterpretation. Specifically, they may (i) restate either a premise or the conclusion in such a way that the intended meaning is changed, (ii) omit a premise, or (iii) add additional premises. She obtained evidence that subjects do this from an experiment in reasoning with thematic syllogisms, i.e. syllogisms phrased in terms of real-life situations. Henle presented no quantitative data, but cited selective verbal protocols, to illustrate these distortions. The use of such qualitative data is problematic. Wason and Evans (1975) have shown that protocols may reflect a rationalisation of a reasoning response rather than an introspection of a thought process (see Chapters 9 and 12). According to this view, the conclusion is arrived at by a process of which the subject is unaware and which may be non-logical. The subject is, however, highly logical in constructing an explanation consistent with his response. The Henle protocols could be rationalisations, with the distortions of interpretation inserted *post hoc* to produce apparently consistent reasoning.

However, most psychologists adopting the rationalist approach have used quantitative measures, normally the frequency of correct answers. Certain difficulties arise in assessing the evidence for rationality in such experiments. For example, how do we know whether or not the subject has 'accepted the logical task?' Do we suppose that those subjects whose behaviour cannot be fitted to a rational model have in fact refused the task? Such a position would clearly be circular and impossible to refute. In my view, one can only assess the rationalist hypothesis by assuming that subjects *do* accept the logical task. Even so the theory may be hard to test on a single paradigm. To return to the point of the Evans (1972a) article, we must also assume that any distortion of interpretation of a particular sentence will be consistent across paradigms.

Although the logical/non-logical issue will form the main focus of discussion, we will also consider the merits of specific theories and models, and attempt to extract any general empirical findings. In the next chapter experimental studies of syllogistic reasoning are considered in detail.

6 The experimental psychology of syllogisms

In this chapter the major experimental work on the psychology of syllogisms will be reviewed. This will be broken down into three major sections, the first two of which are concerned with effects of the form of syllogisms and the last with content variables.

The effect of mood

Much of the research into syllogistic reasoning has been concerned with the likelihood of error as a function of the mood of the syllogism. Bearing in mind that one can only normally determine the validity of a syllogism if one knows both its mood *and* figure, any predictions based on mood alone would appear to be of non-logical type. This is certainly true of the 'atmosphere effect' theory of Woodworth and Sells (1935) and Sells (1936). They proposed that the mood of the premises creates an atmosphere which induces the subject to choose a conclusion of similar type. When the conclusions are homogeneous, i.e. of same mood, the prediction is straightforward. AA premises should induce an A conclusion, EE premises an E conclusion, and so on.

In order to perceive the non-logical nature of the performance predicted by this theory, examine the four possible (classical) figures of the AAA syllogism (Table 6.1.). Only in Figure I is the syllogism valid, a fact which readers can verify for themselves by following the procedures described in Chapter 5. Atmosphere theory predicts, however, that subjects ignore the figure, and hence logical nature of the task, and would classify all four of these syllogisms as valid.

Note that in the case of Figure I the subject will be correct, but for the 'wrong' reason.

TABLE 6.1 *The four classical figures of an AAA syllogism*

I	II
All B are C	All C are B
All A are B	All A are B
Therefore, all A are C	Therefore, all A are C
III	IV
All B are C	All C are B
All B are A	All B are A
Therefore, all A are C	Therefore, all A are C

Where premises are heterogeneous, supplementary principles are necessary for this theory. The combined effect of the original and supplementary principles is most succinctly stated by Begg and Denny (1969). They distinguish the quantity of syllogism (universal/particular) from the quality (affirmative/negative). The predictions are stated as follows:

1 If the quantity of at least one premise is particular then the conclusion is particular, otherwise it is universal.

2 If the quality of at least one premise is negative then the conclusion is negative, otherwise it is affirmative.

Sells (1936) also suggested a 'caution' principle, by which it is supposed that universal conclusions are more incautious than particulars. This explains why particular conclusions are often endorsed when the premises are, in fact, universals. He conducted an experiment which he claimed to provide evidence for both the atmosphere and caution principles. Like most of the studies to be considered in this section, his experiment used 'abstract' materials, with letters rather than words. He presented subjects with a large number of syllogisms most of which were invalid. Unlike most subsequent researchers, he presented complete syllogisms and asked subjects to rate the truth of their conclusions.

Sells's methodology has been criticised by Chapman and Chapman (1959), who also obviously object to the irrational conception of man incorporated into the atmosphere theory. They claim that the support for this theory could be partially due to an artifact. For example, if subjects consider an A conclusion to follow from a given pair of premises, what happens if they are asked to evaluate a I conclusion, as in a syllogism of mood AAI? Sells would claim an endorsement of this syllogisms as evidence for the caution principle. However, as Chapman and Chapman point out, the I conclusion *Some A are B* is logically entailed by the A conclusion *All A are B*. Since subjects have only one conclusion to evaluate on each problem, they could simply be demonstrating internal consistency.

Chapman and Chapman (1959) overcame this problem by presenting subjects with a list of conclusions to choose from. The list included a statement in each of the four moods plus 'none of these' (the non-propositional conclusion). Since all 42 syllogisms they presented were invalid, the last alternative would have been correct throughout. In the event subjects frequently endorsed definite conclusions. The interest is in whether these 'preferred error tendencies' conform to atmosphere predictions.

Atmosphere theory *without* caution incorporated (as in Begg and Denny's statement) fitted well to all but three problems – IE, OE and EO. Despite this rather good performance of the theory, Chapman and Chapman considered it to be refuted by these exceptions, and so formulated an alternative. One suspects that the motivation was more to impute rationality to the subjects than simply to improve the fit to the data. In any event the Chapmans' theory does envisage a reasoning subject, albeit one who makes erroneous inferences from the standpoint of formal logic. Two types of erroneous reasoning are proposed, illicit conversion and probabilistic inference.

In Chapter 5 it was demonstrated that while the E and I imply their converse statements, A and O do not. The Chapmans suggest that subjects make the converse inference for these two statements as well. This principle would explain, without reference to the concept of atmosphere effect, why subjects endorse a number of invalid syllogisms. Consider again the AAA syllogism (Table 6.1). If the converse of the A statement is accepted then *All A are B* implies *All B are A*, etc. In this case *all* four figures of the syllogism would be valid. Thus 'atmosphere' could be an illusion created by a subject who is indeed *reasoning*, but with an erroneous rule.

Not all fallacies could be explained in these terms, so the Chapmans introduce the notion of probabilistic inference, in which the subject reasons that things that have common qualities or effects are likely to be the same kinds of things, but things that lack common qualities or effects are not likely to be the same. For example, consider a Figure III syllogism:

> Some B are C
> Some B are A
> Therefore, Some A are C

This fallacy is endorsed by the majority of Chapman and Chapman's subjects. It is, of course, predicted by atmosphere theory, but probabilistic inference permits an alternative explanation. Since some A and some C have B (by (valid) conversion of the premises) then some A must be the same as some C. The fallacy of the argument is demonstrated by a thematic example:

> Some doctors are men
> Some doctors are women
> Therefore, Some women are men

Much subsequent research has focused on the debate between these two theories, which is a form of the logical/non-logical argument. The illicit conversion hypothesis can be regarded, à la Henle, as an error of interpretation rather than a fallacious rule of inference. For example, a subject might interpret the statement *All A are B* as meaning '*A* is equivalent to *B*', thus envisaging only situation 1 of Figure 5.1 as a possible reading. The principle of probabilistic inference does not seem amenable to the same treatment, which may account for its being relatively ignored by subsequent authors.

Studies of syllogistic inference

Begg and Denny (1969) set out to distinguish the two theories empirically. They decided that the predictions of atmosphere theory (minus caution) converge with those of the Chapmans' theory for all premise pairs except IE, EO and OE. However, even here they pointed out that the probabilistic inference principle is ambiguous, and one of its predictions in each case corresponds to atmosphere theory. Begg and Denny presented all 64 premise pairs with a choice of four alternative conclusions in the different moods. They did not include a 'none of these' choice, but subjects were instructed to put a question mark in the margin if none appeared correct. Their data fitted extremely well to atmosphere theory as they stated it (see earlier), without need to add the caution principle. They also fitted well to Chapman and Chapman's theory, with the ambiguous cases this time coming out in the manner predicted by either theory.

Wason and Johnson-Laird (1972, Chapter 10) describe an experiment which they claimed to give evidence against the atmosphere theory. Their experiment differed from the usual procedure in that only premise pairs from which a valid conclusion could be drawn were presented. Furthermore, subjects were given no conclusions to evaluate or select, but asked to write down their own. It was found that significantly more errors occurred which were incompatible with atmosphere predictions than compatible. These data are less damaging for atmosphere theory than they appear, however. For one thing, the authors exclude all *correct* responses from the analysis, most of which *are* compatible with atmosphere. Just because an answer is logically correct, it does not mean that it is based on a logical process. Secondly, their statistical comparison is dubious in· that the number of available erroneous conclusions that are compatible with atmosphere is considerably less than those which are incompatible. Finally, most of the evidence for atmosphere theory in the literature is based on experiments which have used predominantly fallacious inferences. Even if the effect were restricted to the latter, it would still be of psychological interest.

The atmosphere/conversion argument has been investigated by use of a number of variations in the nature of the task. Before considering these, however, we will first of all examine some information processing models devised to account for data on the usual paradigm, i.e. when syllogisms of all types are presented in abstract form with a choice of conclusions.

Revlis (1975a) formulated two models incorporating the atmosphere and conversion principles: the feature selection model and the conversion model. He criticised the atmosphere theory on two main grounds. One was that the presentation of so many invalid syllogisms will induce an acceptance of fallacies, as subjects will have a bias against an excessive number of non-propositional conclusions. He argued that subjects are hardly likely to expect so many invalid problems. This point seems very reasonable, but in fact Dickstein (1976) found no effect of manipulating the relative frequency of valid and invalid syllogisms.

Revlis's (1975a) major criticism is that the atmosphere theory is too vague and lacking in psychological explanation: 'the hypothesis does not specify why reasoners should fail to grasp the nature of the relationship between subject and predicate terms, nor does it provide a statement of the overall probability of an error for a specific problem.' He consequently reformulates the theory as a representation and process model. This differs from those considered in Part I of this book in that it is devised to predict the frequency of errors rather than latencies. The feature selection model has four stages:

1   Premise representation
Each premise is represented on both the dimensions of quantity (+ ve universal, ;− ve particular) and quality (+ ve affirmative, − ve negative).
2   Composite representation
At this stage the subject compares the representations of the two premises on both quantity and quality. If they match (e.g. universal – universal or negative – negative) then the composite sign is that of the match. If they mismatch (e.g. universal – particular or negative – affirmative) then the composite sign is −ve. An extra operation is required for a mismatch.
3   Representation of the conclusion
Each conclusion is represented as in Stage 1.
4   Comparison process
The composite representation is compared with that of a given conclusion. If they are congruent the subject accepts the conclusion. If not he responds 'invalid' or examines another possible conclusion depending on the paradigm.

At first glance this model appears formally equivalent to the atmosphere theory as restated by Begg and Denny (1969). However, the model does have some extra implications, since it is assumed that each operation required is prone to error. This means that the atmosphere effect will be less strong for problems where an extra operation is required at the composite representation stage, i.e. when heterogeneous premises are involved.

The Revlis (1975a) conversion model, however, differs considerably from that of Chapman and Chapman (1959). The model again has stages of encoding, composite representation, conclusion encoding and comparison. It is supposed that subjects initially encode both premises (regardless of mood) in a *converted* form. This extraordinary assumption means that a subject given *All A are B* encodes *not* as '*A* is equivalent to *B*' as suggested by Chapman and Chapman, but as *All B are A*. At the composite representation stage the subject deduces a conclusion from his stored representations of the premises in a logical manner (if possible). The deduction is compared with each possible conclusion in turn. If a match is found the conclusion is accepted. If no conclusions can be accepted on the first run through, the subject makes a second pass, this time using the true rather than converted representations of the premises. If still no conclusion is possible, the subject guesses randomly between alternatives. In a variant of the conversion model guessing is biased by feature matching (see Revlis, 1975b).

Revlis reported an experiment to test these models. He presented 64 premise pairs, half of which entailed conclusions (valid), and half which did not (invalid). Subjects were given the usual choice of four conclusions, one in each mood, plus 'none of these'. Revlis's results are not very easy to assess with respect to the general atmosphere/conversion argument. This is because he presents the data entirely within the framework of his models' predictions, which do not necessarily conform to those of the theories from which they were derived. It appears that his feature selection model fitted quite well. The aspects which did not fit related to additional assumptions in Revlis's own model. So far as one can tell the data fitted traditional atmosphere predictions very well.

In general, the predictions of the conversion model were supported as well. For example, there were considerably more errors on valid problems whose conclusions are altered by conversion of premises, than on those which are not altered. This does not, however, prove that the converted form is considered first as specified in the model. If subjects simply assumed the conversions *in addition* to the true meaning this could lead them to several alternative conclusions – they are thus less likely to choose the 'correct' one. Which particular ones they choose could be influenced by the order in which alternatives are presented for assessment, which Revlis does not appear to have randomised.

The overall fit of the conversion model is considerably poorer than the feature selection model, especially on valid syllogisms. In view of this it is surprising that it is the conversion model, in a modified form, which Revlis has subsequently developed (Revlis, 1975b; Revlin* and Leirer, 1978). So far as I can see, the reason for this lies in his clear bias towards the rationalist position, as evidenced by the following quotations:

> the feature selection model fails to account for the observed rationality of the subjects (Revlis, 1975a). . . . The Conversion model was purposely developed as an alternative to the notion that reasoners' decisions are capricious and reflect idiosyncratic biases . . . the view taken here dates back . . . to Henle (1962) (Revlin and Leirer, 1978).

Notwithstanding Revlis's acts of faith, his data seem to do no harm at all to the atmosphere theory. We will, however, consider other aspects of his work later in the chapter.

We will now consider some experiments in which the usual paradigm has been modified in certain respects. Ceraso and Provitera (1971) presented some subjects with syllogisms which were modified to avoid misinterpretations (group M) and other subjects (group T) with traditional syllogisms. For example, the A statement *All A are B* can be taken as referring to a situation in which *A* is equivalent to *B*, or to a situation in which *A* is a subset of *B*. The modified syllogisms included problems disambiguated either way, e.g. 'whenever I have a red block it is triangular, and the triangular blocks are red' (equivalence) and, 'whenever I have a yellow block it is striped, but there are some striped blocks which are not yellow' (inclusion). If errors in the standard paradigm arise from illicit conversion, then they should only occur on the former of these modified presentations. In the actual syllogisms used by Ceraso and Provitero, the critical A premises were mixed with E and I forms, but O premises were not included.

The results of the T group exhibited the atmosphere effect, particularly when the conclusion was also logically valid. This result (also noted by Revlis, 1975a) is consistent with the idea of additive logical and non-logical tendencies, which has been suggested as an explanation of propositional reasoning data (see Evans, 1977a, and

* Revlis has recently changed his name to Revlin.

Part III of this book). The M group made considerably more correct responses. Comparison with the T group is difficult since the modifications change the correct answer in some cases. However, a substantial number of correct responses cannot be accounted for by atmosphere theory in this group, so the results give some support to the premise-misinterpretation hypothesis.

Another approach consists of training subjects to avoid either atmosphere or conversion errors. Simpson and Johnson (1966) were the first to use this method and found that anti-atmosphere training was much more effective than anti-conversion training in reducing errors. This result looks good for atmosphere theory, but unfortunately their study has several methodological weaknesses, which have been identified by Dickstein (1975). Dickstein also criticises these authors and others for considering only conversion as an alternative to atmosphere and not taking account of Chapman and Chapman's principle of probabilistic inference.

Dickstein's (1975) paper makes an important contribution to the study of syllogistic reasoning and deserves detailed consideration. He gave all possible 64 premise pairs to three groups of subjects. In addition to standard instructions, one group received additional instructions warning against atmosphere errors, and a second group received warning against conversions and probabilistic inferences (CPI); the remaining group was a control. On a gross comparison of total errors the CPI instructions proved significantly effective in improving logical performance, whereas the atmosphere instructions did not, a result which conflicts with those of Simpson and Johnson. However, this result was restricted to invalid premise pairs; the groups did not differ in the rate at which invalid conclusions were chosen for premise pairs which had valid conclusions.

Experiments which manipulate instructions as an independent variable are hard to interpret, because one does not know precisely what aspect of the instructions is having an effect. Were Dickstein's instructions totally equivalent in all respects other than the type of error described? Pollard (1979a) for one does not think so. The atmosphere instructions included the comment 'while these assumptions are sometimes correct they are by no means always the correct assumption to make', while at the corresponding point the CPI instructions say, 'these erroneous inferences are often responsible for errors on the syllogistic task'. The former comment appears less critical of the error described, but more subtly suggests that a relatively larger number of syllogisms might be expected to have a definite conclusion.

A more important aspect of the Dickstein (1975) paper concerns his use of a refined measuring technique. In the case of atmosphere theory, he suggests that the effects of atmosphere in the two dimensions of quantity and quality should be cumulative. That is to say if a pair of premises share both quantity and quality, the atmosphere conclusion should be more compelling than if they share only one or the other. The effect should be weakest if they share neither. Atmosphere theory predicts a conclusion in all four categories, of course, because of the rule that particulars and negatives dominate in heterogeneous premise pairs.

Dickstein did not, in fact, find any support for these predictions either in his own data or in re-analysis of previous studies, which he takes as evidence against the atmosphere theory. Strictly speaking this is *not* evidence against the theory of Woodworth and Sells or Begg and Denny, since these theorists did not propose cumulative effects. The finding diminished the atmosphere position only if one feels this to be a reasonable assumption.

Dickstein evaluated indirect evidence for the Chapmans' theory in an analogous manner. Here he predicted that where fallacies derive from conversion alone they should occur more frequently than on problems where probabilistic inference is also required. (Examples of both atmosphere and conversion categories are shown in Table 6.2.) Analysis of his own results and those of previous authors' data strongly confirmed the prediction for conversion categories. The comparison is problematical, however, in that the problems are not otherwise equivalent. For example, the problems which lead to error by conversion alone all contain at least one A premise, while none of those requiring probabilistic inference include a premise of that type. In the case of the atmosphere prediction the four premise types were equally distributed over the four categories compared. However, the Chapmans' theory, as extended by Dickstein, is clearly better supported than his extension of atmosphere theory.

To summarise the evidence so far, both atmosphere theory and the Chapmans' theory fit well to the data collected on the standard, traditional paradigms. Recent theorists, with their rationalist perspective, have tended to favour the Chapmans' theory, and modifications to the standard paradigm have tended to provide some

TABLE 6.2   *Example of Dickstein's categories of premise pairs (none permitting valid conclusions)*

Atmosphere categories

1   Premises share quantity and quality, e.g.
        All C are B
        All A are B

2   Premises share quantity, e.g.
        Some C are B
        Some A are not B

3   Premises share quality, e.g.
        Some C are not B
        No B are A

4   Premises share neither quantity nor quality
        All B are C
        Some A are not B

Conversion categories

1   Conversion sufficient for fallacy, e.g.
        All C are B
        All A are B

2   Probabilistic inference required, e.g.
        Some B are C
        Some A are B

---

evidence in its favour. What, however, of genuinely different paradigms? According to the strong testable version of the Henle hypothesis discussed in the previous chapter, the results should generalise to different tasks. It is not reasonable to expect the subjects' interpretation of sentences to be independent of the linguistic form and content of their expression. It is, however, reasonable to expect them to be independent of the processing requirements of the task.

Research with other paradigms

If subjects make illicit conversions of A and O propositions, this should be reflected in tasks which do not require them to combine the two premises of the classical syllogisms. Consider the A proposition, *All A are B*. According to the Henle hypothesis, conversion of this statement occurs by logical processing. This means that subjects must be interpreting the rule as '*A* is equivalent to *B*'. Referring back to Figure 5.1 of the previous chapter, this means that the subject would *only* envisage situation 1, and *not* also situation 4 (set inclusion). Any logical subject who perceived both situations as possible would have to refuse the converse inference, since he is aware of a situation (4) where it would not hold. Similarly a subject who converts an O proposition *Some A are not B*, can only be logical in the Henle sense if he restricts his interpretation. Specifically, he should overlook situation 3, in which the converse statement *Some B are not A* is clearly untrue. These restricted interpretations should occur frequently, according to the rationalists, who explain away apparent atmosphere errors in these terms. What, then, of experiments which ask subjects explicitly to assign Venn diagrams of the sort shown in Figure 5.1 to the various propositions?

An experiment reported by Wason and Johnson-Laird (1972, Chapter 11) did just this. In the case of the A proposition *all* subjects selected our situation 4 (set inclusion) as a possible situation. Furthermore, 75 per cent of the subjects included situation 3 as possibly described by the O proposition. No Henle-like subject should both do this *and* convert such propositions.

However, the Wason and Johnson-Laird experiment used thematic content, which in some circumstances improves logical performance (see Chapter 9). A fairer test is provided by the developmental study of Neimark and Chapman (1975) who used A's and B's as the terms of their premises. Subjects were shown the possible Venn diagrams, and asked to indicate whether or not each was correctly described by the statement. The A proposition was correctly interpreted as either equivalence *or* class inclusion by around 70 per cent of 7th grade children, rising to nearly 80 per cent for college students, who would be typical of populations sampled in the syllogism experiments. Performance was much poorer for O propositions, but this seems to be due to assuming that 'some' means 'not all', and a corresponding drop in performance on I propositions also occurred. Universal statements (affirmative or negative) were much better interpreted than particulars.

A more complex task administered in the same study required subjects to score the diagrams for compound propositions. For example, an I.O. compound might be *Some B are A and some A are not B*. Performance here was largely predictable from subjects' treatment of individual propositions. The study as a whole, then, provides very little evidence for the conversion hypothesis.

Nevertheless, Erikson (1974; 1978) has claimed that syllogistic reasoning data *can* be predicted from the measured interpretation of individual premises, by use of a probabilistic model. (The model will not be considered here, but for a critique see Dickstein, 1978b.) The experiment from which he derives his estimate of interpretation, however, obtains much more evidence of conversion than the studies considered above. This may be due to a difference in methodology. In the Erikson experiment subjects were asked to draw Venn diagrams rather than evaluate them. On A statements, about 40 per cent consistently constructed equivalence rather than set-inclusive interpretations. On the basis of parameter estimates from this study, Erikson (1978) was prepared to predict the data of a number of studies differing in subject populations, techniques of presentation, etc. It might be argued that he should equally be willing to estimate his parameters from these other studies; and, if he used the data of Neimark and Chapman, his model would presumably fit rather badly.

Why, though, should a construction technique produce more evidence of conversion? Perhaps subjects do not spontaneously think of the set-inclusion situation unless it is explicitly presented for their evaluation. This would explain the apparently frequent conversion errors on syllogistic reasoning tasks, when different interpretations are not drawn to the subjects' attention. In following such an argument we are, of course, departing from the assumption that interpretation is independent of task structure. Once we do this then the Henle hypothesis tends to become circular and untestable (cf. Chapter 5).

A recent developmental study by Bucci (1978) is relevant here. Her experiment 1 compared construction and evaluation task performance on the interpretation of universal affirmative (A) statements. The paradigm did not, however, involve Venn diagrams. On the construction task subjects were asked to make toy buildings following instructions such as:

'Make a building in which all the yellow bricks are square.' Their understanding was subsequently checked by probe questions.

In the evaluation task subjects were given sentences and instances to evaluate as true or false. A sample sentence is:

'On this card all the yellow blocks are square.'

On the construction task, logical performance of the children even at 11–12 years of age was poor. They tended to restrict their building entirely to the items mentioned (yellow bricks in our example) and deny that any other bricks were permitted. This interpretative failure cannot be explained as taking the instruction to be an equivalence, for this would permit blocks containing neither named attribute to be used. Bucci suggests that people encode the proposition *All A are B* as an unordered string 'All *A, B*' which she calls a structural-neutral interpretation. In her introduction she suggests that it is this failure in interpretation which underlies errors in adult syllogistic reasoning. Other aspects of her data do not bear this out, however. For one thing logical performance on the evaluation task was good, even 6- to 8-year olds being 84 per cent correct. Moreover, the adult subjects tested showed good logical performance on both construction and evaluation tasks, being correct on 80 per cent and 85 per cent of items respectively. In this case, the construction/evaluation task discrepancy appears only in the children. Taken as a whole, the Bucci experiment provides evidence against the strong form of the Henle hypothesis. If reasoning errors are due to misinterpretations, then the latter are themselves dependent on changes in task structure.

The final paradigm to be considered here is that of inferential memory. Research in this paradigm was discussed with reference to transitive inference (Chapter 4), but the same authors have concerned themselves with quantified statements of the universal affirmative form (see Griggs, 1978; Potts, 1978). The paradigm is essentially similar, in that prose passages are presented which give set inclusion relations between 'adjacent' pairs of classes. The following example is taken from Griggs (1976):

All the Fundulas are outcasts from other tribes in Central Ugala. These people are isolated from other tribes because it is the custom in this country to get rid of certain types of people. All the outcasts of Central Ugala are hill people. The hills provided a most accommodating place to live. All the hill people of Central Ugala are farmers. The upper highlands provide excellent soil for cultivation. All the farmers of this country are peace-loving people. This is reflected in their artwork. All together, there are about fifteen different tribes in this area.

Now, the statement *All A are B* expresses set inclusion, $A \subset B$. The passage above includes a number of such relations $A \subset B$, $B \subset C$, $C \subset D$, etc. Since set inclusion is itself a transitive relation, the 'remote' pairs such as $A \subset D$ are logically deducible. Subjects are presented with adjacent and remote pairs in both the correct and reverse order of items. For example,

Adjacent correct:	*All A are B*
Adjacent reverse:	*All C are B*
Remote correct:	*All A are C*
Remote reverse:	*All C are A*

Subjects are instructed to respond true to any statement that was either presented, or is logically deducible from information presented. It will be recalled from Chapter 4 that when passages are constructed with transitive relations such as 'better than', a clear pattern of results occurs (e.g. Potts, 1974). In that case the remote (inferred) relations are better recalled than the adjacent ones, leading to the supposition of stored linear representations.

The pattern of results with set relations is, however, quite different (see, for example, Griggs, 1976). With 'true' items performance gets worse rather than better as the relations tested become more remote. On 'false' pairs performance becomes progressively better as the relations become more remote. That is, subjects frequently endorse a near reverse relation, $B \subset A$, but more rarely a remote one such as $D \subset C$. Griggs (1976; 1978) interprets this distance $\times$ truth-value interaction as resulting from logical processing errors. Firstly, he supposes that subjects often fail to realise that the relation $A \subset B$ is a transitive one. This accounts for the failure to endorse 'true' remote pairs. The second error is our old friend, illicit conversion. This accounts for the high false positive rate on adjacent reverse pairs, e.g. a subject might decide on the basis of the above paragraph that the statement, 'All the hill people are outcasts of Central Ugala' must be true. This error reduces on remote pairs because the subject again fails to *make transitive* inferences. Such failure with an illicitly converted premise will lead to (correct)

performance – a case of two wrongs making a right! This explanation is over-simplified, however, since the change in error rate on
both true and false pairs is progressive over different levels of re-
moteness. Thus one has to assume that the transitive inference does
not fail entirely, but is probabilistic. Hence the more transitive
inferences required (the more remote the pairs) the less the chance
that the conclusion will be reached.

How does Griggs's hypothesis compare with the conversion theory of syllogistic reasoning? The assumption of conversion obviously
fits, but simple lack of transitivity does not. If subjects did not
regard the relation *All A are B* as transitive, for example, none of
the syllogisms shown in Table 6.1 would be regarded as valid, even
if conversions of individual premises were made. The notion of
probabilistic transitivity copes much better, since the chance of
making the inference could be quite high when only one transitive
step is required, as in the classical syllogism.

Potts (1976; 1978), however, has proposed an alternative explanation that does not involve conversion at all. He assumed that the
information is stored in an integrated structure. However, he suggested that subjects encode *All A are B* as '*A* is similar to *B*'. Let us
denote such a similarity relation as *A s B*. The point is that such a
relation is symmetric, that is *A s B* implies *B s A*, but *non*-transitive.
Potts then explains the decreasing tendency to make true judgments
on remote pairs (irrespective of the order of items) as a distance
effect, similar to that observed in various other paradigms. Potts
(1976) adduced strong evidence for this claim by showing that
subjects who do not make logical errors have identical latency
profiles to those observed with linear orderings (remote pairs faster).
This finding was not, however, replicated by Griggs and Osterman
(1980), although these authors also emphasise the importance of
looking at individual differences in processing strategies.

One difficulty in assessing the relevance of this work to the atmos-
phere/conversion argument is in the nature of the material used.
The syllogistic reasoning tasks considered so far have used abstract
materials. Although the inferential memory studies have used *artificial* set inclusions (not present in the subjects' semantic memory)
they are nevertheless phrased in concrete terms. However, Griggs
and Osterman have demonstrated the usual pattern of results with
abstract materials in one of their experiments.

The notion that subjects convert the A premises, but otherwise make logical deductions, clearly does not account for the data of these memory studies. Atmosphere theory fares no better, however. Since all test statements (A's throughout) are congruent with the presented statements, presumably they should all be endorsed. The false positive responses to reversed adjacent statements are consistent with either theory, but the truth value × distance interaction is quite beyond the scope of both.

Conclusions

The atmosphere/conversion controversy, plus or minus probabilistic inference, has encapsulated the non-logical v. logical debate. Although the evidence slightly favours the conversion theory when standard paradigms are modified, this theory fails to account adequately for subjects' treatment of syllogistic propositions on other paradigms.

   The implications for the logical/non-logical argument will be considered at the end of the chapter. The material reviewed in this section also points to another question of general interest. To what extent can performance on different paradigms be explained by a single theory? All the paradigms considered in this chapter have produced systematic and generally reliable effects; but explanations constructed for one paradigm do not seem easily to carry on to another. When evaluation or construction tasks are introduced to determine subjects' 'interpretation' of individual propositions, the information-processing requirements of these tasks evidently affect the behaviour. Each task seems to require its own paradigm – specific model of explanation. The point is reinforced by consideration of inferential memory paradigms.

   As discussed earlier, syllogisms differ from each other in two ways: they vary in mood and in figure. So far in this chapter we have considered the effects of the first of these variables; we turn now to an examination of effects of the second variable.

The effect of figure

The nature of syllogistic figures was explained in Chapter 5. In general, one needs to know both the mood and figure of a syllogism to determine its logical validity. The atmosphere theory of mood effects assumed that subjects ignored figure in making validity judgments; for this reason, the atmosphere theory is a non-logical account of syllogistic processing. The conversion theory offered in contrast a 'rational' explanation of atmosphere effects, since if all premises are considered convertible, the figure of the syllogism has no effect on the validity decision. Analogous issues arise in the study of the effects of the figure of syllogisms. If figure determines performance and mood is ignored, the effect appears non-logical. Rationalistic models can, however, be constructed to explain such effects.

The figural equivalent of atmosphere theory has been proposed by Frase (1968; see also Pezzoli and Frase, 1968) and is illustrated in Table 6.3. Frase supposed that subjects' evaluation of syllogisms will be influenced by mediated associations analogous to those observed in verbal learning research. If the item mentioned first in a premise is considered a 'stimulus' and the item mentioned second a 'response' then each figure corresponds to a different learning paradigm: Figure I to forward chaining, Figure II to stimulus equivalence, Figure III to response equivalence and Figure IV to backward chaining (see Table 6.3).

TABLE 6.3 *Analysis of syllogistic figures by mediated association theory (Frase, 1968)*

Figure			Analysis
I	M – P	forward	S – M – P
	S – M	chaining	
Therefore,	S – P		
II	P – M	stimulus	$\begin{array}{c} P \\ \diagdown \\ \diagup M \\ S \end{array}$
	S – M	equivalent	
Therefore,	S – P		
III	M – P	response	$\begin{array}{c} \diagup P \\ M \diagdown \\ S \end{array}$
	M – S	equivalent	
Therefore,	S – P		
IV	P – M	backward	P – M – S
	M – S	chaining	
Therefore,	S – P		

Frase predicted that the order of difficulty should correspond to the ease of learning the equivalent paradigm. This led to the prediction that errors should decrease from Figure I to II to III to IV.

Whilst the data of Frase (1968) and Pezzoli and Frase (1968) do come out in this direction, the effect is very weak. However, these experiments used only a few of the possible syllogisms, and did not attempt to control for effects of atmosphere or conversion. This control was introduced by Roberge (1971a) who also gave subjects a choice of conclusions for each premise pair. His results do not fit too well, except for finding fewer errors in Figure I than Figure IV (forward versus backward chaining). The best fit is found in the study of Erikson (1974) using *valid* syllogisms. Frase used only invalid syllogisms, and Roberge a mixture.

The study of figural effects has been developed considerably in recent papers by Dickstein (1978a) and Johnson-Laird and Steedman (1978), both of whom prefer an information-processing approach. Both claim that subjects tend to work in a direction determined by the order of items on the premises. There are analogies here to the principles such as direction of working, end-anchoring and 'natural order', proposed to explain reasoning with linear syllogisms (cf. Chapter 4). However, the papers differ in the detail of both their methodology and theory, and each will be considered in turn.

The Dickstein model

Dickstein (1978a) assumes that subjects deduce a conclusion from the premises that follows logically, but only in a direction (S – P or P – S) determined by the order of items in the premises. For Figure I problems, the order will be S – P, the same as that given in the choice of conclusions, and hence this problem involves 'forward processing'. For Figure IV subjects will initially deduce a conclusion in the order P – S and then convert it, *regardless of mood*, to the order S – P. This 'backward' processing can lead to errors for two reasons, (1) because no conclusion is deducible in the backward direction although a valid forward conclusion exists, or (2) because a conclusion correctly derived backwards is not legally convertible into the forward direction.

In general, the model predicts that Figure I will be the easiest and Figure IV the hardest. Figures II and III are intermediate because they may induce either a forward or backward processing. Unlike in Frase's theory, however, these predictions are subject to consideration of mood. This is because backward conclusions are legally convertible in some moods and thus do not lead to errors.

In constructing problems to test this theory, it is important to control for other sources of error such as conversion of *premises*. Dickstein's problems were carefully chosen with respect to such considerations. Consider for example an EI premise pair in Figure I:

No M are P

Some S are M

The O conclusion may be validly inferred – *Some S are not P*. As this conclusion can be reached by forward processing it should be relatively easy to deduce. Since conversion of E and I premises is legitimate, the same conclusion follows logically in any other figure, such as Figure IV:

No P are M

Some M are S

However, backward processing will not lead to any valid conclusion in the direction P – S. The subject will thus arrive at a non-propositional conclusion, with nothing to convert into the S – P form. Dickstein also included invalid premise pairs (e.g. IE) where backward processing would lead to erroneous endorsement of a propositional conclusion. In both cases he found that, as predicted, fewest errors occured in Figure I and most in Figure IV.

This finding does not, in itself, distinguish the theory from Frase's. To do that, Dickstein had to demonstrate that figural effects do *not* occur in problems where forward and backward processing should have the same result. This includes problems where both forward and backward processing fail to produce a propositional conclusion, and those where the two types of processing lead to the same propositional conclusion. As predicted from Dickstein's theory, in none of these problems was the effect of figure significant.

While these results provide strong evidence for Dickstein's theory, they also indicate that figural bias can only be a partial explanation of the data. In the case of valid EI syllogisms, the error rate was as high as 20 per cent in Figure I and as low as 36 per cent in Figure IV problems. Thus although the model is described as an algorithm, its predictions are confirmed only in terms of statistical tendencies.

The Johnson-Laird and Steedman model

The experiments described so far have all presented subjects either with a single conclusion or with a choice of conclusions to evaluate. The 'direction of working' idea can, however, be more directly assessed by simply presenting the premise pairs and asking the subject to state what conclusion (if any) follows. This technique was adopted by Johnson-Laird and Steedman (1978). The four premise pairs they use cannot consequently be defined uniquely in terms of classical figures (see Chapter 5).

Consider the following premise pair:

All B are C
Some A are B

There are two valid conclusions that might be drawn, 'Some A are C' and 'Some C are A'. Figural bias would predict that subjects would produce the former rather than the latter.

Table 6.4 shows the premise pairs used, along with the typical bias in responding which they observed, on both valid and invalid premise pairs. Note that the general preferred direction of conclusion for pairs (i) and (ii) conforms both to the direction of processing induced by the premises in Dickstein's terms and to a preference for forward over backward chaining in Frase's terms. In pairs (iii) and (iv), where no consistent direction of working is determined by the premises, there was, in general, no bias to prefer A – C to C – A conclusions. As in Dickstein's study, figural bias was by no means the only determinant of responding. As one would expect, the mood of the syllogism exerted considerable influence.

To account for these results, Johnson-Laird and Steedman presented a new theory of syllogistic reasoning (developed from Johnson-Laird, 1975). The theory has four stages:

1   Semantic interpretation of the premises.
2   An initial *heuristic* combination of the representations of the two premises.
3   The formulation of a conclusion corresponding to the combined representation.
4   A *logical* test of the initial representation that may lead to it being modified or abandoned.

TABLE 6.4 *Problems and general findings of Johnson–Laird and Steedman (1978)*

	Premise pair	Figure*	Conclusion preferred by subjects
(i)	A – B B – C	I' or IV	A – C
(ii)	B – A C – B	I or IV'	C – A
(iii)	A – B C – B	II or II'	Neither
(iv)	B – A B – C	III or III'	Neither

* cf Table 5.2

It will be recalled from Chapter 4 that the theories best fitting the solution of *linear* syllogisms were those that assumed that representations of the premises were combined prior to seeking the conclusion. The Johnson-Laird theory has a similar broad structure, with the addition of the fourth stage. This addition does, however, reduce the testability of the theory.

Space limitations preclude detailed discussion of the theory, but one example will be considered. Take the premise pair:

All A are B
Some B are C

In the following discussion, members of the sets A, B, C, will be designated as a,b,c. In representing the first (A) premise the subject realises that all a's are linked to b's, but also considers the possibility of b's that are *not* linked to a's. This is written as follows:

a   a
↓   ↓
b   b   (b)

The second (I) premise is represented:

b   b
↓
c (c)

The subject here links (some b's to c's) but considers possible examples of each that are not linked. At stage 2, the heuristic combination is formed as follows:

All A are B   a   a
             ↓   ↓
Some B are C   b   b   *(b)*
             ↓
                  c   *(c)*

This combination immediately suggests the conclusion *Some A are C* due to the left-hand vertical pathway. The inference is fallacious, however, since the b's that are c's need not be the same b's as the one attached to a's. (A similar error process is also suggested by Dickstein, 1978b.) However, the logical re-assessment at stage 4 *may* lead to correct re-assessment of the representation, and hence eliminate the fallacy.

The theory assumes that links between elements in the representation are drawn in a direction conforming to that of the class names in the premises. With premise pairs (i) and (ii) (Table 6.3) this will lead to formation of a chain of a, b, c, in a given direction, so leading to conclusions in line with the figural bias. For pairs (iii) and (iv) lines will be formed in opposite directions so no clear bias operates on the direction of the conclusion constructed. The theory attempts to explain the effects of mood as well as figure, however. Reasoning errors previously attributed to either atmosphere or conversion (e.g. the fallacious argument illustrated in the above example) are now attributed to heuristic errors in representation.

The authors claimed that a computer simulation derived from their model provides a good fit to the data. Proper evaluation of the theory, however, must await its application in other contexts, since it is both unparsimonious, i.e. rests on a large number of assumptions; and also seems to have been constructed on a somewhat *post hoc* basis.

Conclusions

Both Dickstein (1978a) and Johnson-Laird and Steedman (1978) criticise atmosphere theory for failing to predict the figural effect.

Such criticism is vacuous since the atmosphere theory was not intended to predict the effects of figure. There is no reason why an atmosphere bias could not combine with a figural bias in determining responding – a hypothesis which fits the data quite well. What is clear, however, is that there is no one simple single explanation of the effects of mood and figure. Atmosphere and figural biases, if conceived of as non-logical tendencies, cannot explain all the data. There is evidence of influence of logical validity that cannot be explained in those terms. For example, atmosphere conclusions are more readily endorsed if they are also valid (e.g. Revlis, 1975a; 1975b; Johnson-Laird and Steedman, 1978), and error rates on valid and invalid syllogism are significantly correlated across subjects (Dickstein, 1975).

The simple Henle-style conversion hypothesis which cannot even explain the effect of mood on all paradigms has little to offer to the explanation of figural bias. The only authors who have attempted complete explanations of the effects of mood *and* figure are Johnson-Laird and Steedman (1978) and Dickstein (1978a; 1978b). In both cases a large number of *post hoc* assumptions are needed. We will now turn from considerations of syntactic structure to those of semantic content.

The effect of content

Thus far the experimental studies considered have used only one type of lexical content, and in nearly every case this was of an abstract nature (an exception being Johnson-Laird and Steedman's study). In this section we will consider studies in which the primary manipulation of interest is in the nature of the content of the problems with which the subject is reasoning. The effect of this variable is of considerable psychological interest for several reasons. From the standpoint of Piagetian theory (cf. Chapter 11), adult subjects at the stage of formal operations should be able to analyse the logical structure of a problem in a content-free manner. However, in view of the far-from-perfect level of performance intelligent adults produce with abstract materials, it is interesting to see whether thematic materials will facilitate reasoning. In Piagetian terms, such facilitation would indicate at least partial failure to develop beyond concrete systems of thought.

In terms of the more general rationalist position which has been considered here, reasoning accuracy is dependent upon the accuracy of subjects' understanding of the premises. This might explain any facilitation by thematic content. On the other hand, the use of realistic materials might give evidence of irrationality, if subjects' beliefs and attitudes about the material override considerations of logical validity; here one might find that performance is *worse* with thematic content than with abstract content.

Facilitation by realism

One of the most widely quoted studies of the effect of thematic content is that of Wilkins (1928). She employed classical syllogisms, and used premise pairs with a short list of alternative conclusions from which the subjects were required to choose. Some problems entailed valid conclusions and some did not. The content was of four types:

(A) *Thematic*. Problems were phrased in everyday terms, but constructed such that the subject could not determine the truth of the conclusion from stored knowledge.
(B) *Abstract*. Letters were used in place of words.
(C) *Unfamiliar*. Obscure or nonsense words were used.
(D) *Belief bias*. Problems were constructed in a thematic form such that subjects' beliefs *conflicted* with logical validity. Hence, conclusions which followed logically were empirically false, and those which did not follow were empirically true.

Examples of the four types of problem are shown in Table 6.5 along with the mean percentage correct in each category. Wilkins quotes no statistical analysis, but since the sample size and standard deviations are given, it is possible to assess differences with t tests. It emerges that performance on category A problems is highly significantly superior to that on B and C, and marginally significantly superior to that on category D. No other significant effects emerge. Thus familiar content does appear to facilitate, but the benefit is appreciably reduced if subjects' beliefs are put into conflict with the logical structure.

TABLE 6.5 *Examples of premise pairs (minus list of conclusions) used by Wilkins (1928) in four categories*

		% correct* (n=81)
A	*Thematic*	
	All the people living on this farm are related to Joneses, these men live on the farm;	84
B	*Abstract*	
	All x's are y's	76
	All z's are x's	
C	*Unfamiliar*	
	All lysimachion is epilobium	
	All adenocaulon is lysimachion	75
D	*Belief bias*	
	All Anglosaxons are English	
	All British are Anglosaxons	80

* Averaged over the whole category.

Belief bias

Recent investigations of the effect of thematic content have concentrated on other paradigms (see especially Chapter 10). However, a considerable number of studies subsequent to that of Wilkins (1928) used syllogistic problems to investigate the belief bias effect.

In all these studies the believability of the syllogistic *conclusion* is manipulated. The validity judgment, which subjects are supposed to make, can be seen as a conditional truth judgment. Instructions frequently ask subjects to decide whether the conclusion is true, *assuming that the premises are true.* Belief bias occurs when a subject makes an absolute truth judgment on the conclusion, i.e. assesses it with respect to personal beliefs rather than with respect to the premises given. A study by Janis and Frick (1943) claimed stronger evidence for the effect than Wilkins. Performance was found to be worse on thematic problems in which beliefs conflicted with validity than it was on abstract problems. An analysis simply in terms of the correctness of performance is unsatisfactory, however, owing to the frequency, and the systematic nature, of the errors which occur with abstract problems. Morgan and Morton (1944) attempted to distinguish atmosphere from belief bias errors in comparison of thematic and abstract problems. An example of one of their problems is as follows:

Some ruthless men deserve a violent death; since one of the most ruthless men was Heydrich the Nazi Hangman:
1. Heydrich the Nazi Hangman, deserved a violent death.
2. Heydrich the Nazi Hangman, may have deserved a violent death.
3. Heydrich the Nazi Hangman, did not deserve a violent death.
4. Heydrich the Nazi Hangman, may not have deserved a violent death.
5. None of the given conclusions seem to follow.

According to Morgan and Morton no valid conclusion may be drawn since Heydrich might or might not be one of the ruthless men who deserve a violent death. Hence the correct choice is 5. Belief bias would, however, lead subjects to choose alternative 1. The authors claim that the atmosphere choice is 2 since the premises have a particular affirmative atmosphere. They are assuming here that 'may' applied to an individual is like 'some' applied to a category. This is highly dubious, and 2 seems actually to be a *valid* conclusion since the premises do establish this possibility. However, relative to an abstract control choices of 2 and 5 decreased, and choice of 1 increased which does seem to point to a belief bias effect, since 1 is certainly not justifed by the premises.

Whilst inaccurate wording marred several of Morgan and Morton's thematic problems, as in the above example, their results do support the belief-bias predictions, *provided* that we accept the authors' *a priori* assumptions about beliefs. They report no attempt actually to measure attitudes towards the materials concerned. Henle and Michael (1956) tested subjects on Morgan and Morton's problems with similar results. However, they *did* also test subjects attitudes to the conclusions and did *not* find the expected relation to reasoning performance. They also found other evidence against the belief-bias hypothesis. For example, when in one problem 'peoples of India' was substituted for 'peoples of Russia' it made no difference, though presumably emotional attitudes to the two countries would differ considerably. In another experiment of Henle and Michael's very little evidence of the effect of attitudes to Russia was found. Some evidence of effects of attitudes on this subject *was* claimed by Gorden (1953) but it is very weak. When one considers the strength of emotions aroused by the subject of Russia in the

USA at that time, one would have expected such material to provide a strong test of the belief-bias hypothesis.

Some studies which have claimed evidence for the effect have assessed beliefs by asking the same subjects subsequently to assess their attitudes to the conclusions (e.g. Feather, 1964; Janis and Frick, 1943; Lefford, 1946). This is unsatisfactory since performance on one task may influence performance on the other. Much research on 'cognitive dissonance' (see Zajonc, 1968) has shown that if people are induced to behave in a particular way, then verbally expressed attitudes tend to shift towards agreement with the behaviour. The response to the reasoning task could be regarded as a behavioural commitment to the attitude. This was controlled in a study by Kaufman and Goldstein (1967), who obtained ratings of attitudes and syllogistic reasoning scores from *separate* groups. They did indeed find an increased tendency to accept fallacious conclusions which were strongly believed, as opposed to neutral, fallacious conclusions. However, they also found an increase in the acceptance of conclusions that were strongly disbelieved!

Some experiments by Frase (1966; 1968) provide evidence that runs against the belief-bias hypothesis. He varied the degree of compatibility between the items in the conclusion. For example, 'All mothers are evil' was rated as highly incompatible. Presumably, incompatible statements appear to be untrue, and so should not be rated as likely conclusions. He found that incompatibility increased the number of logical 'errors'. Since the majority of the problems were fallacious, this suggests that subjects are more likely to *accept* (erroneously) a semantically incompatible conclusion. This appears to go against the alleged effects of belief bias, but since he does not report separate data for valid and fallacious problems it is hard to be sure.

A recent study by Revlin and Leirer (1978) has provided new evidence. Henle (1962) was happy to suppose that subjects sometimes 'fail to accept the logical task'. Revlin and Leirer, however, carry the rationalist position further. With reference to the theory of Revlis (1975a; 1975b), they state:

Since the Conversion Model assumes that reasoners' decisions follow rationally from the nature of the representation of the syllogism's premises, it cannot entertain illogical inference rules.

We must show, therefore, that the previous findings are artifacts of the confounding of Representation and Inference.

They claim that realistic conversions are 'blocked' by semantic content. For example, no one would convert 'All dogs are animals' into 'All animals are dogs' since the latter is obviously false. Not all thematic statements need be blocked, however: consider, for example, 'All people entitled to vote are over eighteen years of age'. Revlin and Leirer account for the effects of realistic content in reasoning solely by reference to this 'blocking effect'. They assert:

> The Conversion Model makes the strong claim that performance on concrete syllogisms is usually superior to that found on abstract syllogisms because only the former permit conversion to be blocked in the encoding of the premises.

It is highly doubtful whether the evidence for belief bias in the previous literature could be explained in this way. For example, Wilkins (1928) found that facilitation by realistic content was reduced when beliefs conflicted with the logic. This could only be explained in Revlin's terms if with valid problems the premises were more convertible than with invalid problems. Such systematic artifact could not be introduced accidentally by Wilkins and others. Unless experimenters were aware of the variable and deliberately confounded it, the effect would be randomly distributed. Furthermore, some belief-bias effects cannot be explained by conversion at all. The example quoted earlier from Morgan and Morton (1944) can only be explained as a 'rational' inference if the 'some' of the first premise was misinterpreted as 'all'.

Another objection to Revlin and Leirer's approach is the peculiarity of saying that realistic materials 'block' a process postulated to explain performance on an artificial reasoning task. It is almost as if they assume that reasoning in the laboratory is the important thing to understand, while effects in 'real life' are irritating complications, to be explained away. Revlin and Leirer's *experiment*, in which they control convertibility while manipulating belief bias, is nevertheless a useful contribution to the literature.

Paradoxically, their well-controlled experiment provides some of the best evidence for the belief-bias effect. They found subjects to be correct on 83 per cent of problems when beliefs accorded with logic, and on only 67 per cent when beliefs conflicted with logic. We saw in the previous section how Revlis (1975a) obtained evidence unfavourable for his conversion model and yet argued for this model. Revlin and Leirer (1978) again do their best to play down the evidence they have found against the rationalist position.

To summarise the evidence reviewed in this section, the evidence for facilitation by concrete materials relies heavily on the work of Wilkins (1928) so far as syllogistic reasoning is concerned. A number of studies have investigated the notion that beliefs and attitudes influence performance on such tasks, however. Many of these contain flaws of design or produce equivocal evidence. On balance, there appears to be some evidence that the effect exists, but only as a relatively weak influence.

General conclusions

The research into syllogistic reasoning reviewed in this chapter leads to several general conclusions. The most obvious aspect of these studies is the low level of logical performance. It is the high frequency of logical errors which sharply distinguish these studies from those discussed in Part I. In view of the higher-than-average intelligence level of the samples used (subjects usually were undergraduate students), this is in itself quite interesting. Most interesting, however, is the nature of the errors, which are far from random.

Reasoning errors are reliably and systematically related to the structure of the syllogisms used. *How* performance is related to the mood and figure of syllogisms is well established, and only disputed in matters of fine detail. *Why* these effects occur is much trickier to determine, however. Though reliable, the effects observed are complex in nature, and irritatingly specific to the paradigm used. No simple and general theoretical principles seem to have been discovered which can explain all the major findings. Nor is the effect of semantic content well understood. In the syllogistic literature, evidence for facilitation rests too heavily upon the work of Wilkins (1928), while studies of belief bias are equivocal in their findings, and frequently of doubtful design.

The evidence for the extreme rationalist position, as proposed by Henle (1962), is not very convincing. It is true that much of the evidence for atmosphere bias can be explained as arising from misinterpretations of the premises leading to illicit conversions. On the other hand, such explanations are not consistent with performance on some other paradigms involving the same sort of statement. Furthermore, whichever theory of figural bias one prefers, all imply some extra-logical influences on subjects' thinking. Finally, as Revlin and Leirer (1978) concede, the evidence of (weak) belief bias effects is incompatible with a purely rationalist account of reasoning performance.

However, there is some evidence indicating a logical component of performance, when the various non-logical inferences are taken into account. Whether or not such a component could reveal an underlying system of logical competence will be discussed in Chapter 11. Further discussion of the rationality issue will be deferred, since much of the work on propositional reasoning (Part III) provides relevant evidence.

In the review of elementary reasoning tasks (Part I), a concern was expressed about the paradigm–specific nature of the theoretical explanations. A similar problem is evident in the syllogistic reasoning literature. The general assumption of sequential stages of comprehension and reasoning is also evident to some extent in the syllogistic literature, particularly in recent papers. Problem representation is again an issue, but there is less concern with the question of format of representation than with its content. In some respects the syllogistic reasoning work lacks theoretical interest, in that little attempt has been made to investigate the nature of possible cognitive mechanisms or processes that may be involved. The propositional reasoning literature, while developing the interesting and important debate about rationalism, has proved rather richer in other theoretical aspects; it is hoped that this is demonstrated in Parts III and IV.

Part III

Propositional reasoning

7 An introduction to propositional reasoning

Much recent research into deductive reasoning has utilised problems derived from the propositional calculus of logic (see, for example, Lemmon, 1965), which forms the basis of 'standard logic' in modern philosophy. This chapter is organised in similar fashion to the introduction to syllogistic reasoning (Chapter 5), and will explain the logic, paradigms and issues associated with this work. Experimental studies will then be considered in the following three chapters.

Propositional logic

As noted in Chapter 2, a proposition is a statement with truth value. In standard logic only two values are permitted: true (T) and false (F). The possibility of a third truth value will be considered later. It is conventional to represent propositions as p, q, r, etc. For example, a conditional relationship between propositions may be represented as *If p then q*. Any logical inference derived from such a statement holds no matter what propositions are substituted for p and q. A fundamental operation is *negation*, which in two-valued standard logic always reverses truth value. If a proposition p is true, then its negation *not p* is false. Conversely, whenever p is false, *not p* is true.

In propositional logic, the validity of arguments can be determined by two different but formally equivalent means. In assessing the validity of syllogisms (cf. Chapter 5), we adopted a fundamental principle: a false conclusion can never be logically derived from assumptions which are all true. This principle forms the basis of a

115

method known as *truth table analysis*. In this method all possible combinations of the truth values of the propositions involved are considered systematically, to check whether the principle can be violated. The method will be illustrated with reference to a particular problem, where our task is to decide whether the argument is logically valid:

PREMISES: 1 John is not both clever and rich
                   2 If John is clever then he is rich
CONCLUSION: John is not clever.

This argument contains two basic propositions – 'John is clever', and 'John is rich'. In the truth table approach we consider all four possible combinations of truth values:

(a) John is clever and rich
(b) John is clever and not rich
(c) John is not clever and rich
(d) John is not clever and not rich

The possibilities (c) and (d) can be disregarded since in either case the conclusion of the argument would be true. Remember that our only problem is to ensure that a false conclusion could not be derived from conclusions which are all true. In the case of (a) and (b) the conclusion to the argument is false, so we must look at the truth value of the two assumptions. If (a) is the case then assumption (1) is obviously false, and if (b) is the case then assumption (2) is obviously false. Hence there is no possibility that a false conclusion can be derived from true assumptions, so we must conclude that the argument is valid.

The truth-table analysis is an infallible algorithm but provides little intuitive feeling of the correctness of the argument. An alternative method involves the use of *rules of inference*. The example quoted can be proved by a rule known as *reductio ad absurdum* (RAA). The rule works as follows:

(i)   Assume the negation of that which you wish to prove.
(ii)   Deduce a logical contradiction.
(iii) Infer that your starting assumption was false.

In the above example the conclusion is 'John is not clever'. Hence we start with the assumption of its opposite, i.e. 'John is clever'. If this were the case then from premise (1) it follows that John is not rich, and from premise (2) it follows that John is rich. We have derived a contradiction, so the assumption 'John is clever' must be false, hence the valid conclusion to the argument is 'John is not clever'.

In actual fact, the deductions from each premise involved additional rules of inference of a sort that will be considered later. Let us consider further the nature of a proposition. Since the premises of the argument given have truth value, they must be propositions themselves, compounded as they are of more elementary ones. If we have a compound proposition such as *If p then q* then we must have some means of determining its truth value, from that of its component propositions, *p* and *q*. Before considering this specific problem further, it will be useful to distinguish propositions from *relations*. Relations are devices for compounding propositions to form new ones. Some of the most important relations are shown in Table 7.1.

TABLE 7.1   *Examples of relations in propositional logic*

Relation	Logical form	Linguistic form
Negation	$\bar{p}$	Not p
Conjunction	$p \wedge q$	p and q
Inclusive disjunction	$p \vee q$	Either p or q
Exclusive disjunction	$p \ / \ q$	Either p or q but not both
Material implication	$p \supset q$	If p then q*
Material equivalence	$p \longleftrightarrow q$	If and only if p then q

* Other linguistic expressions of implication are possible, such as 'Not both p and q' or 'Either not p or q', but the conditional form shown is of primary psychological interest.

Table 7.1 shows the logical notation for expressing different re- tions, and also a suggested linguistic form. The nature of the gical relation has a precise definition in formal logic. Linguistic ᴐrms do not have such precise definition and are simply suggested ᴐy philosophers as examples of usages which correspond roughly to their defined logical relations. The extent to which these and other linguistic forms (sentences) are treated as logical relations is, in fact, the major point of interest in the psychological research, as we shall see later. First, we will consider briefly the relations shown in Table 7.1.

Research into people's ability to understand and use *negation* as a logical relation has been reviewed in detail earlier in this book (Chapter 3). Even with this relatively simple relation we saw that

(1) People experience difficulty in using the relation correctly, and

(2) Various extra-logical factors (e.g. context) affect performance.

These findings are good indications of the sorts of result we can expect in the study of people's use of other logical relations, as will become apparent in due course.

A conjunctive rule $p \wedge q$ ('p and q') is defined as being true only when both components p and q are true. If either or both are false, then the compound is false. Generally speaking adults have no difficulty understanding the logic of conjunctions.

Disjunctions, on the other hand, cause people a lot of problems (cf. Chapter 9). An inclusive disjunction, $p \vee q$, is true if either or both of its components are true. If both p and q are false then the compound is false. The exclusive disjunction $p \mid q$ is true when p is true and q is false and vice versa. If p and q are both true or both false then the compound is false. Philosophers usually regard the linguistic disjunction, *Either p or q* as conveying inclusive disjunction unless qualified by the additional words *but not both*. It cannot be assumed that this is a correct reading of actual linguistic usage, however. According to semantic context the form *Either p or q* may be read inclusively or exclusively. For example, the following would be read exclusively; 'A candidate for election to parliament must either poll more than 15 per cent of the votes cast or lose his deposit.' Anyone standing under this rule would be understandably enraged if he polled 30 per cent and still lost his deposit! On the other hand the following is clearly intended to be inclusive; 'Students on the M.Sc. programme must either hold a good honours degree or an equivalent professional qualification.' Obviously, no one would be excluded on the grounds that they qualified on both counts. The fact that people's interpretation of the relation underlying a linguistic form is not independent of the meaning of the context clearly complicates life for the psychologist.

Similar problems arise with the relations of material implication,

$p \supset q$ and material equivalence, $p \longleftrightarrow q$. In the former relation, p *implies* q so that one may never observe p to be true without also observing q to be true. If p is *equivalent* to q, however, the converse also holds, i.e. one may never observe q without p. p and q are equivalent in that they always occur together. Logicians often use the conditional sentence, *If p then q*, to express implication, with the modification *If and only if p then q* when it is extended to equivalence. In actual linguistic usage, however, people again tend to use the shorter form and let semantic factors determine the meaning which is read. For example, 'If it is a dog then it is an animal' obviously does not entail the converse. On the other hand use of a conditional as a threat or promise normally assumes equivalence (see Chapter 8). You may say to a child 'If you finish your homework then you may go to the pictures.' This carries the pragmatic (rather than the logical) inference that if he doesn't finish it then he will not be allowed to go. If the two propositions are not regarded as equivalent the statement would be pointless.

The reasoning problems with which we are concerned in this book are set in terms of sentences and words, rather than abstract relations and propositions. The linguistic forms that have received most attention are disjunctives and conditionals. It is necessary now to look in more detail at the logic of the relations that these forms may be taken to convey. One way to do this involves looking more precisely at the truth-table analysis of these forms. Table 7.2 presents two possible truth tables for a disjunctive sentence and three possible truth tables for a conditional sentence.

The truth-table cases are formally defined in terms of the truth values of the constituent propositions. For example the TF case is that which occurs when the first proposition (p) is true, and the second (q) is false. In the case of the form *Either p or q* it has been pointed out that this might be read as either inclusive or exclusive disjunction. The *logical* relations corresponding to these readings are defined by the truth tables given. The difference is that TT is 'true' for an inclusive and 'false' for an exclusive relation. Two of the truth tables shown for a conditional rule correspond to the logical relations of implication and equivalence. The former is falsified only by an observation of TF, and the latter also by FT.

The third 'defective' truth table goes beyond the limits of standard logic with its two truth values. A possible third truth value is 'indeterminate' or 'irrelevant', symbolised here as '?'. Wason (1966)

TABLE 7.2   *Possible truth tables for disjunctive and conditional sentences*

(a) Disjunction

Sentence	Truth-table case		Truth value of sentence	
	pq		Inclusive	Exclusive
Either p or q	TT	(pq)	T	F
	TF	(pq̄)	T	T
	FT	(p̄q)	T	T
	FF	(p̄q̄)	F	T

(b) Conditional

Sentence	Truth-table case		Truth value of sentence		
	pq		Implication	Equivalence	Defective
If p then q	TT	(pq)	T	T	T
	TF	(pq̄)	F	F	F
	FT	(p̄q)	T	F	?
	FF	(p̄q̄)	T	T	?

has proposed that people may well have a defective truth table for the conditional such that it is considered irrelevant to cases where the first part of the rule is false. For example, the sentence, 'If it is a table then it has four legs' is clearly true of a four-legged table (TT) but false if applied to a three-legged table (TF). According to the logic of material implication, the sentence must be true of anything which is *not* a table. Wason suggests that people see such instances as irrelevant to the rule, rather than as verifying examples of it. The rule simply *does not apply* to things which are not tables.

It was stated earlier that arguments may be made by use of *rules of inference*. Such rules have been associated with disjunctives and conditionals, and may be derived from the truth-table analysis. The rules are simply statements of whether or not basic syllogistic inferences are valid. The classical Aristotelian syllogisms discussed in the previous part of this book concerned class relations, and may be more precisely defined as *categorical syllogisms*. Similar problems involving conditional sentences are sometimes known as conditional or hypothetical syllogisms. However, to avoid confusion they will be designated *conditional inferences* in this book. In each case, the major premise is the conditional sentence containing two propositions, and the minor premise an assertion or denial of one of its component propositions. In the conditional, the first component (p) is known as the antecedent, and the second component (q) as the consequent.

TABLE 7.3 *Conditional Inferences*

Modus ponens		If p then q
(MP)		p
	Therefore,	q
Denial of the antecedent		If p then q
(DA)		Not p
	Therefore,	Not q
Affirmation of the consequent		If p then q
(AC)		q
	Therefore,	p
Modus tollens		If p then q
(MT)		Not q
	Therefore,	Not p

In the first inference modus ponens (MP) the minor premise asserts the antecedent and the conclusion asserts the consequent. This inference is valid *regardless* of which truth table shown in Table 7.2 applies. All the truth tables agree that we may not have a true antecedent with a false consequent (TF). So if the antecedent is true, then the consequent must be true as well. For similar reasons modus tollens (MT) is indisputably valid. In this syllogism the minor premise denies the consequent and the conclusion denies the antecedent. Since TF cannot occur, a false consequent can only be accompanied by a false antecedent.

To use the example given above, if we know that something is a table we can infer that it has four legs (MP), and if we know that something does not have four legs we can infer that it is not a table (MT). In actual fact, of course, one can have three-legged tables, but the inferences follow on the assumption that the given rule 'If it is a table then it has four legs' is true. The necessity of both inferences follows from its implication that one cannot have a table with any other number of legs than four, so they are still valid if the truth table is defective.

The other inferences DA and AC are valid only if material equivalence is assumed. This truth table also forbids FT, so a false antecedent must be accompanied by a false consequent, and a true consequent must be accompanied by a true antecedent. Under either implication or defective truth tables, DA and AC are fallacious syllogisms and cannot be adopted as linguistic rules of inference.

These inferences would seem absurd from the rule given above, since one would have to posit that *only* tables can have four legs. However, they would seem reasonable for a rule such as 'If a person is male then that person has an XY chromosome.' Semantics determine an equivalence reading, such that both DA (given not male, infer no XY chromosome) and AC (given XY chromosome, infer male) seem reasonable.

Similar disjunctive inferences can be constructed. For example, either component may be denied in the minor premise and the other asserted in conclusion, e.g.

> Either p or q
> Not p
Therefore, q

An inference of this form is valid under both inclusive and exclusive readings, since it is not permitted that both components can be false. A second type is when one component is asserted in the major premise and the other denied in conclusion, e.g.:

> Either p or q
> q
Therefore, Not p

This inference is valid only if exclusive disjunction is assumed, since only this relation excludes the possibility of both components being true at the same time.

With reference to the thematic examples given earlier, we can see that, for the semantically exclusive disjunctive, the alternatives of polling over 15 per cent of the vote, and losing one's deposit are incompatible. The truth of either proposition implies the falsity of the other, and vice versa. In the semantically inclusive example, it is clear that candidates for MSc must have at least one of the two qualifications specified. So if one qualification is not met they must have the other, but the converse obviously does not follow.

So far we have only considered compound propositions involving one relation. There are, however, no limits to the combinations of relations that may be used. The only combination that will arise in the work to be reviewed is that of negation with other relations. For example, there are four conditional rules that can be constructed by permuting the presence of a negated proposition in either component: (1) *If p then q*, (2) *If p then not q*, (3) *If not p then q*, and (4) *If not p then not q*. Similarly four disjunctive rules can be formed by permuting negatives. We shall see in the following chapters that the manipulation of the presence of negative components has led to interesting empirical findings, and stimulated important theoretical arguments.

Paradigms

Most experimental studies have focused on people's ability to reason with conditionals and disjunctives.

The most common method used is to present people with a conditional or disjunctive inference to evaluate. Procedures vary in that sometimes the whole argument is presented, and subjects asked to decide whether the conclusion necessarily follows. Alternatively, the subjects may be given the premises plus a list of possible conclusions to choose from, or simply asked to state what, if anything, follows from the premises.

Experimenters have also been interested in investigating the *psychological* truth tables that people 'possess' for conditional and disjunctive rules, although this presupposes a certain theoretical assumption. In addition to inferring such truth tables from inference tasks, there have been various 'direct' attempts to assess these. Subjects could be asked to *construct* instances which conform to, or contradict the rules. Alternatively, and more commonly, people are asked to *evaluate* the effect of presented instances on the truth value of the rule. This is essentially similar to the sentence-picture verification task (cf. Chapter 3), although the instances evaluated are not necessarily pictures. For example, subjects may be given the 'rule':

'If the letter is not A then the number is 3'

They may then be presented with a letter-number pair, A3, and asked if it conforms to, contradicts, or is irrelevant to the rule. The task differs only in complexity from the verification tasks reviewed in Chapter 3. Those involved single assertions and denials, whereas the above combines them with a conditional relation. The above example also has a third truth value (irrelevant) permitted.

The primary measurement used in these tasks has been the frequency of alternative answers given. However, some of the work, (see e.g. Evans, 1977a; Evans and Newstead, 1977; 1980) has employed response latency as a secondary measure. When latencies are measured on reasoning tasks it is not normally possible to eliminate those based on errors as is customary with simple cognitive tasks. This is because the definition of an 'error' is debatable, and also because the degree of variable responding is too large to make data dropping practicable. It is best to look upon the responses as reflecting *decisions* with two measurable characteristics: latency and outcome.

Two other tasks are considered in this part of the book, both of which were devised by Wason. While these tasks require understanding of propositional logic for their solution, they also involve additional devices such as hypothesis formation and active seeking of information. One of these tasks, the THOG problem, is designed to investigate people's understanding of the logic of exclusive disjunction and is discussed in Chapter 10. The other, known as the 'selection task' or 'four-card problem' has generated much recent research, and probably occasioned more interesting psychological work than any other single paradigm reviewed in this book. For this reason, it is accorded a chapter of its own (Chapter 9).

Issues

The issue of primary interest in the review of work on classical syllogisms (Part II) was the debate for and against rationalism. The Henle view that all reasoning errors were attributable to errors of interpretation rather than logic was examined in some detail. It was concluded that the hypothesis did not fare very well unless one assumes that the interpretation of a given sentence can vary across paradigms. It was also observed that rival explanations in terms of non-logical biases and intrusions of personal beliefs received equally good empirical support.

The same issue arises in the study of propositional reasoning, in which some authors have tried to apply Henle-type explanations. However, the issues broaden here in several respects. For example, a different aspect of the notion of rationalism is explored with respect to work on the selection task (Chapter 9). This is the idea that behaviour is determined by *conscious* strategies which are available to introspection. Evidence will be presented which causes difficulties for this view, and stimulates alternative theoretical proposals.

The discussion of propositional reasoning performance will also be influenced by the two-factor theory of reasoning (cf. Evans, 1972a; 1977a, 1977b) which was mentioned in Chapter 5, but must now be explained in more detail. The theory postulates that the variability observed in response to reasoning tasks is composed of two orthogonal statistical components, each of which reflects the influence of a distinct type of factor. With suitable controls – often involving the manipulation of negatives – it is possible to distinguish a *logical* and *non-logical* component of performance. The 'logical' component reflects the degree to which subjects' responses are related to the logical structure of the task – such responses need *not* be 'logical' in the sense of logically correct. The non-logical component reflects the extent to which subjects respond to logically irrelevant features of the problems.

The theoretical assumptions about the nature of the two factors underlying these components have evolved somewhat over successive papers, and a synthesis will be given here. The logical component is thought to arise from the subject's attempt to solve the task as instructed. The fact that some inferences are more readily perceived than others is attributed to linguistic influences – what Evans (1972a) calls *interpretational* factors – or to the amount and difficulty of the cognitive processing they require. The non-logical component is thought to reflect response biases, attention to logically irrelevant features or application of inappropriate heuristics.

Since the two components are statistically orthogonal, this implies that the underlying processes are *parallel* in nature. In other words a conflict model is assumed in which logical and non-logical influences compete for control of the subjects' responses. This means that the relative *weighting* given to the two factors must be taken into account in explaining the data. A formal model incorporating these properties has been developed by Evans (1977b) and will be explained in Chapter 9.

One way in which the two-factor theory is testable is in its assumption that linguistic factors affect only the logical component of performance, whereas non-logical biases arise from specific operational requirements of the task (see Evans, 1972a). An example of the latter is an apparent preference for endorsing arguments that have negative rather than affirmative conclusions (see Chapter 8). This sort of 'response bias' should be independent of the linguistic or logical structure of the task. Conversely, variations in the logical component attributed to linguistic influences should be manifest on tasks of different structure which involve the same linguistic forms. The formalisation of the theory in the form of a mathematical model (Evans, 1977b) also increases its predictive power, and we shall see in Chapter 10 how application of the model revealed an error in the application of the theory which might not otherwise have been detected. Finally and most recently Evans (1980a) has linked the two factor theory to the Wason and Evans (1975) 'dual-process theory' in which behavioural responses and verbalisations were attributed to distinct systems of thought. The consequent 'revised dual process' theory is explained and assessed in Chapter 12 (Part IV).

The two-factor theory leads to an interest in linguistic and interpretational factors, as do other theoretical approaches. It differs radically from representation and process models, however, in assuming *parallel* influences on behaviour rather than sequential stages. Also, while the logical component reflects the influence of interpretational factors as assumed by the Henle hypothesis, it does not attribute *all* reasoning errors to such influences. Indeed, many errors are supposed to arise from non-logical biases. Since the Henle approach would be preferred on the grounds of parsimony, it is necessary to demonstrate its inadequacy to account for the data and explain the need to postulate a two-factor explanation. The relative merits of these two positions will be considered throughout the discussion of experimental results in Part III.

In addition to the influence of task and linguistic *structure* on reasoning performance, the effect of problem *content* will be a matter of major concern. Logically, a problem's solution is unaffected by the meaning of the actual propositions substituted for p and q. Psychologically, however, content variables may have a profound influence as we saw in Chapter 6. This influence could arise from the presence of contextual cues which alter the interpretation of the problem sentences. Such effects can be handled by Henle's theory or the logical/interpretational component of the Evans two factor theory. The latter theory, however, permits of an alternative effect discussed by Evans (1977b); it may affect the *weighting* given to logical versus non-logical processes. The general implications of the effects of content and other variables will be taken up in Part IV.

8 Conditional reasoning

Studies of conditional reasoning have generally focused on sentences of the linguistic form *If p then q*, although a few studies have also utilised the form *p only if q*, and these will be discussed later in this chapter. Some of the work investigating conditional reasoning has had little or no theoretical content. In some cases the aim seems to be simply to discover whether or not people have the competence to perform certain logical inferences, and how such competence develops with age. The problem with this approach is that it assumes that the ability to perform, for example, a modus tollens inference is situation independent. If a subject can solve a *specific* experimental problem with this logical structure, then it is supposed that he 'possesses' it as part of his *general* logical competence. As we shall see, this assumption is hard to justify. The findings will, however, be discussed with reference to the theoretical positions adopted by Henle and by Evans (cf. Chapter 7).

Studies of conditional reasoning ability

Conditional inferences

A number of studies have assessed people's tendency to make the four inferences associated with conditional rules – MP, DA, AC, and MT (cf. Table 7.3). Frequently, abstract content is used. For example, the following defines an MT inference, when the subject is asked to reason about letter-number pairs:

GIVEN
(1) If the letter is A then the number is 6
(2) The number is not 6
CONCLUSION
The letter is not A

A subject might be presented with the above argument and asked to assess its validity. He may be asked to decide whether or not the conclusion *necessarily* follows from the premises, or else to rate the truth of the conclusion assuming the truth of the premises.

If subjects' observed responses reflect only their interpretation of the sentence, then two different reasoning patterns might be expected, according to whether *If p then q* is interpreted as implication or equivalence (see last chapter). In the former case, subjects should endorse MP and MT but not DA and AC. In the latter, they should endorse all four inferences. If group data reflect a mixture of subjects employing both interpretations then we should expect the frequency of MP and MT to equal 100 per cent, and the frequency of DA and AC to equal each other at some level intermediate between 0 and 100 per cent.

Most early experiments looked only at *affirmative* conditionals, *If p then q* (see Wason and Johnson-Laird, 1972). We will consider first some data for rules of this sort. Table 8.1 shows the results of three studies of adult reasoning. The data show a fairly consistent pattern. MP is very frequently endorsed. MT, though endorsed more often than not, is consistently and sometimes considerably, less often endorsed than MP. This causes problems for the Henle hypothesis, in which it is assumed that reasoning errors arise *solely* due to misinterpretation. It is not clear how the conditional could be interpreted such that MT would not be necessary. The other prediction, that DA and AC frequencies will be equal, fits pretty well within each study or experimental condition.

TABLE 8.1 *Percentage of adult subjects endorsing conditional inferences in several studies, for an affirmative rule, If p then q*

Study	MP	DA	AC	MT
Taplin (1971)	92	52	57	63
Taplin and Staudenmayer (1973)	99	82	84	87
Evans (1977a)	100	69	75	75

A number of studies have looked at children's ability to solve conditional syllogisms. Here, the interest has focused on Piaget's theory of formal operations. For example, Hill (1961) (cited by Suppes, 1965) claimed that children of age 6–8 were able to perform remarkably well on conditional reasoning problems, which ought to require formal operational thought. O'Brien and Shapiro (1968) confirmed this finding, although they did not, unfortunately, report data on the different kinds of conditional inference. Roberge (1970) and Kordoff and Roberge (1975) do report evidence for developmental improvement in conditional reasoning ability, but the general pattern of difficulty across inference types is similar to that of adults: that is, MP is correctly endorsed more often than MT at all ages, while the 'fallacious' DA and AC also tend to be endorsed (very often in young children).

The MP/MT difference is not hard to explain if a simple Henle position is abandoned. Given *If p then q*, the inference *p* therefore *q* is so evident that one would hardly wish to call it reasoning. It is hard to see how one could understand the meaning of the conditional without making MP. MT, however, does require some reasoning. With reference to the MT problem presented earlier, the subject might argue something like: 'A's always have a 6 with them, so any letter which does *not* have a 6 with it cannot be an A'. There are two other factors which might account for the extra difficulty of MT. Once concerns the *directionality* of the conditional: it is arguable that inferences from antecedent to consequent are easier to make than those in reverse. The second factor is negativity: MT involves a negated second premise and a negated conclusion. The directionality of conditionals will be considered in a later section; the problem of negativity will be considered now.

If negative components are introduced into the rules, then the additional premises and conclusions corresponding to the four conditional inferences are as shown in Table 8.2. It will be noticed that each inference is now associated with both affirmative and negative premises and conclusions, according to the rule.

A number of studies have shown that the pattern of response to the four conditional inferences is significantly affected by the introduction of negative components in the rules (Roberge, 1971b; 1974; 1978; Evans, 1972b; 1977a). The Roberge papers do not present the data in a way which enables one to see the patterns for each rule and inference separately, so Table 8.3 presents data for the Evans

TABLE 8.2 *Conditional inferences for rules involving negative components*

Rule	MP given	conclude	DA given	conclude	AC given	conclude	MT given	conclude
(1) *If p then q*	p	q	p̄	q̄	q	p	q̄	p̄
e.g. If the letter is A then the number is 7	A	7	not A	not 7	7	A	not 7	not A
(2) *If p then not q*	p	q̄	p̄	q	q̄	p	q	p̄
e.g. If the letter is C then the number is not 5	C	not 5	not C	5	not 5	C	5	not C
(3) *If not p then q*	p̄	q	p	q̄	q	p̄	q̄	p
e.g. If the letter is not R then the number is 1	not R	1	R	not 1	1	not R	not 1	R
(4) *If not p then not q*	p̄	q̄	p	q	q̄	p̄	q	p
e.g. If the letter is not W then the number is not 4	not W	not 4	W	4	not 4	not W	4	W

p̄ = 'not p'
q̄ = 'not q'

(1977a) study. Also included are the data of Pollard and Evans (1980, Experiment 1), who used a different paradigm which appears to be psychologically equivalent. They presented subjects with one conditional rule and asked them whether another conditional rule was entailed by it. For example, given that the (affirmative) conditional is true:

If p then q

subjects might be asked if any of the following must also be true:

If not p then not q (inverse)
If q then p (converse)
If not q then not p (contrapositive)

Their data are presented on the assumption that endorsing the inverse, converse and contrapositive are psychologically equivalent to endorsing DA, AC and MT. Reference to Table 8.2 should indicate the logical similarity of the two tasks. Empirically the two tasks do seem to produce similar results, with a rank correlation of 0.886 between the Evans, and Pollard and Evans data across conditions.

The Roberge, Evans, and Pollard and Evans studies all show certain systematic effects of negatives. For example, the MT infer-

TABLE 8.3   *Percentage of subjects endorsing conditional inferences for rules which contain negative components*

	MP	DA	AC	MT
If p then q				
Evans (1977a)	100	69	75	75
Pollard and Evans (1980)*	–	54	66	59
If p then not q				
Evans (1977a)	100	12	31	56
Pollard and Evans (1980)*	–	30	37	72
If not p then q				
Evans (1977a)	100	50	81	12
Pollard and Evans (1980)*	–	47	72	34
If not p then not q				
Evans (1977a)	100	19	81	25
Pollard and Evans (1980)*	–	37	64	44
Overall				
Evans (1977a)	100	38	67	42
Pollard and Evans (1980a)*	–	35	60	53

* Experiment 1.

ence is reliably less often made when the antecedent is negative, as in the following example:

GIVEN
  (1) If the letter is not D then the number is 7
  (2) The number is not 7
CONCLUSION
  The letter is D

The conclusion is valid, but most subjects rate it as 'indeterminate'. One possible explanation of this would be that an extra step of inference is required to deal with a double negative. MT leads the subject in the above example to infer that the letter cannot be not a D; he must then realise that this implies that the letter must be a D. If the difficulty is due to an inability to deny a negative, then the DA inference should also be less frequent when the consequent is negative, as in

GIVEN
  (1) If the letter is B then the number is not 4
  (2) The letter is not B
CONCLUSION
  The number is 4

DA is indeed made significantly less often when the consequent is negated in both the Evans, and Pollard and Evans studies (cf. Table 8.3). However, the AC inference is also significantly more often endorsed in both studies on the rules with negative antecedents. Why should subjects find it easier to affirm a component which is negative? We shall return to this problem shortly.

It would be extremely difficult to explain the results of these studies by arguing that the negatives alter subjects' interpretation of the rules. For example, if AC occurs more often on the rules with negative antecedents because such rules are interpreted as equivalences, then a corresponding increase in DA inference should occur on these rules. It does not. Similarly, the reduced DA on rules with negative consequents should be accompanied by a corresponding decrease in AC, if these rules are more often interpreted as implication. In fact, in the Evans (1977a) study, AC significantly *increased* on these rules.

The results are best described within the framework of the Evans two-factor theory (see Chapter 7). It is assumed that the negatives do *not* affect the interpretation of rules, and hence the logical component, but affect certain non-logical response biases. In this case, Evans (1977a) proposed that subjects are more inclined to accept a conclusion which is negative rather than affirmative. The effects of negation on all three inferences (DA, AC, MT) accord with this bias. The lack of effect of negatives on MP is explained as indicating a weighting totally in favour of the logical component on these inferences (which people almost always evaluate correctly). To put it another way, MP is totally within the subject's logical competence and thus resistant to response biases.

Pollard and Evans (1980) have suggested that this 'negative conclusion bias' might be due to a cautious attitude on the part of the subjects. A negative conclusion is less likely to be false. For example, the conclusion 'The letter is A' is only true if one particular letter is actually present, whereas the conclusion 'The letter is not A' can only be falsified in one way. If in doubt, a negative might seem to be a safer bet. (This argument is elaborated in Chapter 11.)

When the inference rate is averaged across the four rules, then the influence of response bias is controlled for any given inference, since two affirmative and two negative conclusions are involved in the four problems pooled in each case (see Table 8.2). Unfortunately these averaged rates cannot be taken to indicate the relative strength of different inferences in the 'logical component'. For example, the average rate of MP is approximately double that of MT (Table 8.3). This does not, however, necessarily mean that there is a stronger tendency to make MP on the basis of subjects' understanding of the rule. This is because the *weighting* given to the logical component is not the same on the two inferences. As already noted, part of the variability on MT is accounted for by response-bias effects, whereas they have negligible effect on MP. The actual nature of the logical component can only be discovered by fitting a formal model. To date, this has been attempted only for data collected on the Wason selection task (see Chapter 9).

Pollard and Evans (1980) have, however, utilised an alternative technique to investigate whether there is a logical basis to any conditional inferences other than the MP inference. They analysed individual differences, to test the hypothesis that some subjects have more logical ability than others. If this were so, then the ability to make (say) an MT inference on one rule should be correlated with the ability to make it on another. When individual differences for base rate of offering conclusions was controlled, they found no evidence of such a correlation. In a second experiment, they looked at subjects' tendency to reject the opposite of an inference. For example, if an MT (contrapositive) problem is the following:

GIVEN   If the letter is B then the number is 2
CONCLUDE If the number is not 2 then the letter is not B
                     then its opposite, MT(O) is
GIVEN   If the letter is B then the number is 2
CONCLUDE If the number is not 2 then the letter is B

In this experiment subjects could say that the conclusion was either *necessarily true, necessarily false or neither*. The authors argue that, if the ability to say 'true' to the former is due to a logical appreciation of MT, then it should correlate with a tendency to say 'false' to the latter. They found only a weak association for MT and DA inferences, and they attributed the individual differences they found to differences in susceptibility to negative conclusion bias, rather than to differences in logical ability.

The degree of independence of people's response to different problems of related logical structure in this study is really quite remarkable, and appears to defy any rationalistic explanation. The above is one of very few studies that have looked at individual differences in reasoning, and this approach should surely be adopted more often.

Inferred truth tables

It is unfortunate, in view of the previous section, that most authors studying conditional reasoning have looked only at affirmative rules. Furthermore, many have tended to infer underlying interpretations or truth tables from subjects' observed responses to conditional syllogisms (e.g. Taplin, 1971; Taplin and Staudenmayer, 1973; Staudenmayer, 1975; Staudenmayer and Bourne, 1978; Rips and Marcus, 1977; Marcus and Rips, 1979). In this approach, subjects are classified as having a truth table for either implication (or conditional) or equivalence (or biconditional). The former involves subjects who make MP and MT but not DA and AC, while the latter classification is for subjects who make all four inferences.

The authors adopting this approach frequently present their data *only* in this classified form, without giving the actual frequencies of particular inferences. However, this classification system rests critically on the rationalist assumption that people reason logically given their personal interpretation of the rules. It will be evident that the theoretical position adopted in the previous section is quite incompatible with this. There it was proposed that the actual frequency of responding to conditional inference problems was considerably distorted by the non-logical negative conclusion bias.

If this assumption is correct, then one would expect that the attempt to infer truth tables from inference tasks would be rather unsuccessful. In particular, one would expect the data of many subjects *not* to conform consistently to a particular truth table. Let us look at the evidence. Taplin (1971) found that only 45 per cent of his subjects reasoned in a consistently truth-functional manner, the great majority of these being classified as 'equivalence'. Taplin and Staudenmayer (1973) found much higher consistency (about 80 per cent) with the majority again conforming to 'equivalence'. In a second experiment, however, less than 50 per cent were truth-functional, and the majority of these classified as *'implication'*. This last experiment differed from the others in that subjects were not asked simply to rate the conclusion as true or false, but given an intermediate 'sometimes true (or false)' option. Many subjects switched their response on DA and AC problems from true to sometimes true.

Apart from the unimpressive proportion of 'truth-functional' subjects in these three experiments, the discrepancy in the latter results casts doubt on the inferred truth-table approach. Subjects' interpretation of the rules should surely not depend on the method of testing their inferences. Actually, some form of indeterminate choice, as in Taplin and Staudenmayer's second experiment, is logically necessary. Consider the following AC syllogism:

GIVEN
    (1) If the letter is H then the number is 7
    (2) The number is 7
CONCLUDE
    The letter is H

A subject asked to rate the truth of this conclusion, given the truth of the premises, can only be logically correct if he makes an indeterminate response. The conclusion might or might not be true, so a true/false forced choice forces the subject to make one of two erroneous inferences.

Staudenmayer (1975) included a 'sometimes' category. He conceded the existence of non-logical factors in conditional reasoning tasks, but nevertheless maintained the classification of responses into underlying truth tables. In these experiments subjects were given different semantic contexts, the effects of which will be discussed in a later section. Our concern here is the consistency with which such classifications are made. The proportion of consistent subjects was 78 per cent with abstract material and only 55 per cent with concrete material. However, consistent subjects were not necessarily truth-functional, and their classifications of truth tables did *not* require absolute consistency, so the data are hard to assess.

Staudenmayer and Bourne (1978), requiring only 75 per cent consistency, failed to classify an alarming 33 per cent of their subjects in one experiment. A recent study by Marcus and Rips (1979) produces even worse figures. Over a variety of semantic contexts, responses to conditional inferences were logically contradictory for an average of 53 per cent of subjects tested.

In assessing these figures two points must be borne in mind. Firstly the fact that some subjects *do* consistently conform to a truth table may not be because they are 'using' it. Non-logical factors would conceivably produce the same response pattern. Secondly, some subjects may appear consistent *by chance*. If all subjects behave in a probabilistic manner, certain highly probable combinations will appear consistently for some subjects but not for others. In other words, one cannot be sure from any one experiment that some subjects have qualitatively distinct interpretations from others.

The question of consistency across tasks will be reconsidered later. We now turn to so-called 'direct' attempts to measure truth tables for conditional rules.

'Direct' measures of psychological truth tables

In the previous section truth tables were referred to as representing either implication or equivalence. However, it was pointed out in the previous chapter that the truth tables may be 'defective', i.e. contain 'irrelevant' or indeterminate truth values (see Table 7.2). Even if truth tables could be inferred from syllogistic performance, this could not lead to the detection of defective values. For example, MP and MT both follow from the fact that a true antecedent-false consequent (TF) combination is forbidden, regardless of how FT and FF are represented.

One of the earliest attempts to achieve direct measurement of an underlying truth table was by Johnson-Laird and Tagart (1969). They expressed the implication relation $p \supset q$ in four linguistic forms:

(1) If p then q
(2) Not p if not q
(3) Not p or q
(4) Never p without q

The actual sentences used referred to combinations of letters and numbers on cards. Subjects were given a pack of cards which included combinations corresponding to all four logical possibilities – TT, TF, FT, and FF. They were asked, for each rule, to sort them into three piles, corresponding to the classifications 'true', 'false' and 'irrelevant'.

Now, the defective truth table for implication proposed by Wason (1966) classifies TT as true, TF as false, and FT and FF as irrelevant. This can be abbreviated as TF?? This was indeed the modal response pattern for the conditional rule (form (1)). Of the others, only rule (4) produced a similar pattern. Subjects' responses to rules (2) and (3) were highly variable. Thus, while supporting Wason's hypothesis for the affirmative conditional *If p then q*, Johnson-Laird and Tagart's experiment also shows that subjects' understanding of implication is highly dependent upon its linguistic expression.

In the review of work on conditional inferences, it was claimed that a substantial amount of responding was attributable to non-logical factors, which could only be identified by the manipulation of negative components. The same manipulation occasions similar conclusions when truth-table tasks are used (Evans, 1972c; 1975; Evans and Newstead, 1977). The first study along these lines was that of Evans (1972c), which attempted to replicate Johnson-Laird and Tagart's findings with a different technique, the hope being to generalise their results to rules with negative components. In this experiment subjects were given an array of coloured shapes, along with a rule presented on a card, e.g.

IF THE SHAPE ON THE LEFT IS A RED CIRCLE, THEN THE SHAPE ON THE RIGHT IS NOT A GREEN SQUARE.

For each rule, subjects were given both a verification and a falsification task. In the verification task, subjects were asked to place two figures from the array side by side to make the rule true. They were asked to indicate *all* possible ways of doing this, but allowed to generalise, e.g. 'A red circle on the left, together with anything except a green square on the right makes it true'. In the falsification task, subjects were asked to demonstrate all possible falsifying combinations. Because each procedure was exhaustive, any logical case not constructed on either could be *inferred* to be 'irrelevant', without explicitly pointing the subject to such a classification.

TABLE 8.4 *The combinations of affirmed (matching) and negated (mismatching) values corresponding to each logical case on each rule, in the truth table task.*

	Logical Case			
Rule	TT	TF	FT	FF
(1) *If p then q*	pq	pq̄	p̄q	p̄q̄
e.g. If the letter is A then the number is 7	A7	A3	G7	H2
(2) *If p then not q*	pq̄	pq	p̄q̄	p̄q
e.g. If the letter is C then the number is not 5	C8	C5	L9	D5
(3) *If not p then q*	p̄q	p̄q̄	pq	pq̄
e.g. If the letter is not R then the number is 1	Q1	L5	R1	R9
(4) *If not p then not q*	p̄q̄	p̄q	pq̄	pq
e.g. If the letter is not W then the number is not 4	A6	J4	W5	W4

p̄ = not p   q̄ = not q

In order to understand the analysis one must first consider the combinations of values producing the different logical cases, as negatives vary in the rules (Table 8.4). A *pq* combination occurs when a solution matches both values named in the rule. This corresponds to TT for the affirmative rule *If p then q*. However, this matching combination corresponds to a different logical case on each of the other rules. In the above example the rule is of the form *If p then not q*. Hence the double match (red circle – green square) makes the antecedent true but the consequent false (the TF case). It can be seen from Table 8.4 that in each rule the four logical cases are produced on each rule by each of the four combinations – pq, pq̄, p̄q, p̄q̄. However, the mapping of 'matching' values on to logical cases is different for each.

TABLE 8.5   *(i) Evans' (1972c) results pooled over the four rules and classified by (a) logical case and (b) by matching case. Results are percentage frequencies (n = 24)*

		Classification	
	True	False	Irrelevant
(a) *Logical Case*			
TT	99	0	1
TF	3	80	17
FT	14	34	52
FF	33	23	44
(b) *Matching Case*			
pq	34	52	14
pq̄	41	33	26
p̄q	40	27	33
p̄q̄	34	25	41

TABLE 8.5   *(ii) The frequency of construction of each logical case on rules where they constitute a double match, pq, (data from same experiement).*

Logical Case	Rule		% Frequency	
		True	False	Irrelevant
TT	If p then q	100	0	0
TF	If p then not q	0	96	4
FT	If not p then q	8	75	17
FF	If not p then not q	29	38	33

The results of the Evans (1972c) study are shown in Table 8.5, pooled over the four rules. When we look at the data by truth-table case (Table 8.5 (i)(a)), we see that the prediction of the defective truth table is upheld. The modal response is 'true' for TT, 'false' for TF and 'irrelevant' (i.e. non-constructed) for FT and FF. However, when FT and FF *are* constructed, the former is often seen to falsify and the latter to verify.

Table 8.5 (i)(b) shows the data arranged by 'matching case'. Since each matching case appears equally often as each logical case, when pooled over the four rules, any effect of this factor is seen as 'non-logical'. If one looks at the 'irrelevant' column, then a clear trend can be seen for these (non-constructed) choices to increase as the number of *mis*matches increases. In other words subjects are more likely to construct an instance if its items match those named in the rule. Evans (1972c) termed this effect 'matching bias'. The discovery of this apparent non-logical response bias parallels the finding of negative conclusion bias on the conditional inference tasks, and lends support to the Evans two-factor theory of reasoning (cf. Chapter 7).

The nature of the 'logical component' is somewhat easier to determine than on the inference tasks, because there are three responses, of which only one – 'irrelevant' – is affected by the non-logical matching. Thus the construction of TT as 'true' and TF as 'false' does indeed seem to reflect subjects' understanding of the rule. The FT and FF cases are more difficult to interpret. It could be that the high 'irrelevant' rate is due to the possession of a defective truth table in the logical component. Alternatively, there could be less *weighting* given to the logical component on these cases, with the 'irrelevants' arising from matching bias. Evans and Newstead (1977) have, for example, shown that matching bias is much stronger on the FT and FF cases. If we assume that the matching effect is really a suppression of responding on mismatching cases, then we can resolve the problem. Is there still a higher irrelevant rate on false antecedent cases if we look only at rules where such cases match? Let us look at the frequency of selecting each logical case in the Evans (1972c) data, on the rules when a double match is involved (Table 8.5 (ii)).

Although there is more 'irrelevant' responding to FT and FF, it is relatively low in cases that match. Thus the evidence for the defective truth table may be a partial artifact of greater susceptibility to response bias on these cases. So far as FT is concerned, the logical component appears to determine primarily a 'false' classification. Responding to FF is roughly random across available responses. This analysis again rests upon the assumption that the interpretation of the conditional is not affected by the presence of negative components. Otherwise the high rate of classification of FT as false in the rule *If not p then q* might be taken to indicate that this particular rule is interpreted as equivalence. However, the effects of matching on 'irrelevant' classifications cannot, in general, be explained as an illusion created by interpretational effects of negatives. For example, TF should be rated as 'false' under any interpretation of the conditional, but significant increases in 'irrelevants' occur on this case, as the number of mismatches increases.

The matching bias effect is not restricted to construction tasks such as that of Evans (1972c). It has also been demonstrated on evaluation tasks, where all truth table cases are presented in turn with each rule. The subject is normally asked to decide whether the instance conforms to the rule, contradicts the rule or is irrelevant to it. When these responses are classified as 'true', 'false' and 'irrelevant', a remarkably similar set of data is obtained (e.g. Evans, 1975, Evans and Newstead, 1977). Thus, not only are subjects less likely to construct a mismatching case, but they are also less likely to consider it relevant (true or false) if it is presented to them for evaluation. Our analysis of the logical component is also substantiated by the data of these later studies.

A more extreme form of matching bias has been observed in young children (Paris, 1973), who tend to classify all matching cases as 'true', and all other cases as 'false', irrespective of the linguistic form of the rules presented. It is possible, as Wason (1969a) suggests, that in complex reasoning tasks adult subjects may, to some extent, regress to childhood patterns of thought, and this could be what is happening to adult subjects exhibiting matching behaviour.

What other explanation can be offered for this matching (response) bias? The obvious answer lies in an appeal to the difficulty of negativity (cf. Chapter 3). The subject finds it hard to think in terms of a 'not 7', and so is more likely to attend to the values named in the rule (Evans, 1975; see also Johnson-Laird and Wason, 1970). A problem with this explanation, however, is the interaction of matching case with logical case. We have noted already that TT constructions were unaffected in the Evans (1972c) study, and that Evans and Newstead (1977) also showed that the effects of matching bias were largely restricted to the FT and FF cases, using an evaluation task procedure. Further problems arise in interpreting the effect, from inconsistent results of reasoning studies using disjunctive rules (Chapter 10). Further discussion of the matching bias effect will hence be deferred for the time being.

Conclusions

It has been shown that it is not easy to infer the nature of the logical component of performance on these tasks. The problem is that the strength of response bias effects is not independent of the logical cases under consideration. Thus we must distinguish the nature of a response tendency related to the logical structure, from the extent to which that tendency competes with non-logical tendencies. We can, however, say with some confidence that subjects make the inference MP, and see TT as verifying and TF as falsifying in truth-table tasks. These 'logical' tendencies are a direct consequence of understanding a conditional rule. They amount to a recognition by the subject that *If p then q* means that any observation of *p* must be accompanied by an observation of *q*.

One other possible interpretational effect suggested in these analyses is a tendency for some subjects to interpret the rule *If p then q* as an equivalence. This would explain the evidence of a tendency to regard FT as falsifying on the truth-table task (Table 8.5) and also the relatively high overall AC rate on inference tasks (e.g. Table 8.3). This still leaves the problem of why the MT and DA rates are relatively low. On average, MP is made about twice as often as MT, and AC about twice as often as DA, over all rules (Table 8.3.). It was pointed out earlier that MT requires more reasoning to achieve than MP and is more susceptible to competing response biases. The AC/DA difference could be explained in a similar way. If the subjects treat the rule as an equivalence then they are reasoning not only with original rule *If p then q* but also its converse *If q then p*. In effect AC and DA are the MP and MT inferences for this converse rule, and presumably have the same relative strength as in the original.

There are some interesting parallels here to the work on syllogistic reasoning discussed in Chapter 6, where it was shown that there is quite a lot of evidence to suggest that people treat universal statements (*All A are B*) as equivalences. Another parallel is the preference for forward processing of syllogisms. One further possible explanation of the MP/MT difference is a preference for reasoning forwards. The AC/DA difference is likewise a preference for forward processing with the *converse* rule *If q then p*. The evidence for directionality effects is discussed in the next section.

The discussion of possible connections between the 'logical' components of the inference and truth-table tasks shows how hard it is to explain more than a small proportion of the data in terms of logical reasoning processes. It is not surprising that if 'interpretations' are imputed on the assumption of wholly logical reasoning (à la Henle), the consequence is very large discrepancies between tasks. Marcus and Rips (1979) used an evaluation task in which subjects were allowed only two responses; 'consistent' and 'inconsistent': the former category including both 'true' and 'irrelevant' responses. Even when they looked only at the 82 per cent subjects who could be classified as making either implication and equivalence interpretations, they found many 'errors' of reasoning on an inference task relative to the 'interpretation' derived from the truth-table task. Marcus and Rips responded to these findings by constructing a model of reasoning to account for error on the inference task. They assume that reasoning on the truth-table task is more or less error free. This assumption is impossible to justify in the light of the matching bias effects discussed here, a problem of which the authors were apparently unaware, since they failed to cite any work employing negative rules.

This review of work on conditional reasoning has revealed the presence of non-logical response biases in both conditional inference and truth-table tasks. There is, however, some evidence of a common logical component of performance underlying the two types of task. The remainder of this chapter is devoted to consideration of linguistic factors which may influence the logical or interpretational component of conditional reasoning.

Linguistic factors in conditional reasoning

In this section the term *interpretational* rather than logical component will be preferred. It will be assumed that any effects of syntactic or semantic linguistic factors are orthogonal to the non-logical effects demonstrated by the manipulation of negative components (conclusion bias, matching bias). This means that even if only affirmative rules are used, any shift in, say, the rate of MT inference, occasioned by manipulation of linguistic content, will be assumed to be mediated by the interpretational component.

Syntactic factors: directionality and 'only if' rules

Several allusions were made in the previous part of the chapter to the fact that the superiority of MP over MT could be due to a 'directionality' effect. The supposition is that the linguistic form *If p then q* must invite antecedent to consequent inferences far more strongly than in the reverse direction. (High AC rates were attributed to equivalence interpretations rather than to backward reasoning.) Several authors have independently postulated that such directionality might be reversed by an alternative linguistic expression of implication, *p only if q* (Rips and Marcus, 1977; Evans, 1977a; Braine, 1978).

It is essential here to appreciate that *p only if q* has the same truth table as *If p then q*, and *not* the same one as *If q then p*. Evans (1977a) illustrates the point with the following examples:

E1 If he is a policeman then he is over 5'9" in height.
E2 He is a policeman only if he is over 5'9" in height.

Some reflection on these examples will indicate that they are indeed logically equivalent. In either case the rules can only be falsified if a policeman is found who is *not* over 5'9" in height (the TF case). Neither would be falsified by finding someone who is not a policeman to be over 5'9". Thus, in each case, the first proposition (he is a policeman) implies the second proposition (he is over 5'9" in height).

The two sentences do not appear to be *linguistically* equivalent, however, and it is important to ask why two alternative linguistic forms should have precisely the same logical form. Evans (1977a) points out that there are two distinct logical properties of implication, and suggests that the 'If . . . then. . .' (IT) linguistic form is used to emphasise the one, and the '. . . only if. . .' (OI) linguistic form to empasise the other. The first property is that *the antecedent is sufficient for the consequent*, i.e. knowing that someone is a policeman is sufficient to infer that they are over 5'9". This property is that *the consequent is necessary for the antecedent*. In other words, one cannot be a policeman *unless* one is over 5'9". This second property is expressed by MT.

Evans (1977a) proposed the intuitive hypothesis that the IT form is used in natural language to express sufficiency of the antecedent, and the OI form to express necessity of the consequent. It was predicted, therefore, that more MP inferences would occur in IT and more MT inferences in OI. This was tested in an experiment in which the presence of negative components was also manipulated.

TABLE 8.6   *Percentage frequency of reasoning responses to IT and OI rules, pooled over rules in which the presence and absence of negated components is manipulated.*

(a) *Inference Task* (Evans, 1977a)

	If . . . then (n=16)	. . . only if . . . (n=16)
MP	100	76
DA	38	38
AC	67	84
MT	42	59

(b) *Truth table evaluation* (Evans, 1975)

	If . . . then (n=24)			. . . only if . . .(n=16)		
	True	False	Irrelevant	True	False	Irrelevant
TT	89	5	6	82	12	16
TF	9	81	9	11	58	30
FT	19	29	52	13	57	30
FF	30	11	57	44	16	40

Note: deviations of some totals from 100 per cent are due to rounding errors.

The results of this study are shown in Table 8.6 (a), averaged over rules containing negatives. The two predictions were significantly confirmed: there was more MP in the IT group than in the OI group ($p < 0.002$, 1-tailed) and more MT in the OI group than in the IT group ($p < 0.05$, 1-tailed). There was also significantly more AC in the OI group than in the IT group ($p < 0.05$, 2-tailed). This last result might suggest that equivalence interpretations are more common on OI. There is, however, no corresponding increase in DA rate.

The interpretation of the Evans (1977a) data is complicated by the absence of significant conclusion-bias effects on the OI rules. However, the trends were in the expected direction, and OI rules are clearly not generally exempt from response bias effects, since they have been shown to suffer from strong matching effects on truth table tasks (Evans, 1975; Evans and Newstead, 1977; Manktelow, 1979). The frequency of logical classifications on such tasks (averaged over negatives) shows marked differences, however (cf. Table 8.6 (b)). Corresponding to the reduced MP response (antecedent to consequent directionality) we see that there is a sharp increase in 'irrelevant' responses to cases where the antecedent condition is fulfilled (TT and TF), and a drop in such responses to cases where it is not (FT and FF). The direction of classification, true or false, is consistent between IT and OI rules on each logical case.

Rips and Marcus (1977) encompass the directionality idea in a *suppositional* theory of conditional reasoning. They propose that people evaluate a conditional in the form *If p then q* by supposing the truth of the antecedent, and assessing it against the current data base:

> By the current data base, we mean the set of propositions presently held to be true, that is, our present beliefs. The seed proposition corresponds to the hypothesis we wish to entertain. In the special case of the conditional sentence, this seed will be the proposition expressed in the antecedent clause.

They postulate that conditionals are evaluated by first of all taking the antecedent as the 'seed proposition'. 'The conditional should then be confirmed in case the consequent is an element of, or inferrable from, this supposition, and otherwise disconfirmed.' This theory predicts both the defective truth table – one does not evaluate the rule at all if the antecedent is not supposed – and the superiority of MP over MT inference. One normally proceeds by assuming the truth of the antecedent, not by assuming the falsity of the consequent. Presumably MT can only be made according to a suppositional view if it is achieved by a *reductio ad absurdum* argument, as Wason and Johnson-Laird (1972) suggested.

For example, consider the following MT problem:

      (1) If the letter is A then the number is 7
      (2) The number is 3
Therefore,   The letter is not A

In an RAA argument one starts by assuming the *opposite* of the intended conclusion. In this case one must start with the assumption that the letter is A. If Rips and Marcus are right, this is the natural supposition induced by the first premise. The consequence of this assumption is the deduction that the number is 7 from the first premise. This, however, leads to a contradiction, since we are told in the second premise that the number is, in fact, 3. Hence, the original supposition is false and the conclusion demonstrated.

Surprisingly, Rips and Marcus (also Marcus and Rips, 1979) do not make this point, and attribute MT difficulty to problems of negativity – an argument discounted in the early part of this chapter. Braine (1978) gets closer to the right line in claiming that MT involves more computation than MP, but unfortunately commits the logical error of claiming that it does not follow from a defective truth table. It was shown earlier that forbidding the occurence of TF is sufficient to justify both MP and MT inferences.

Rips and Marcus (1977) test this theory, in one experiment, by comparison of IT and OI rules. They suggest that while the antecedent will be interpreted before the consequent in *If p then q* the reverse may be true for *p only if q*. They test this hypothesis in a most ingenious manner. Subjects are given a diamond split into a number of cells, with a pair of letters in each. They are given rules to follow, such as:

E3 If there is a B in a square, then there is an X.
E4 There is a B in a square only if there is an X.

The two are logically equivalent, with E3 in the IT form, and E4 in the OI form. Subjects are then asked to indicate which cells are consistent with the given rule, numbering them in the order that they check them. The experimenters can then see whether, for example, the subject searches by the cells headed with the letter mentioned in the antecedent. As predicted, this does occur with IT rules. Contrary to their expectations, OI rules are not consistently evaluated by searching for consequent values, nor, for that matter, by antecedent values. Rips and Marcus suggest that 'subjects have difficulty in interpreting *only if*, treating it as a 'simple conjunctive'. This suggestion does not accord with other data, however (cf. Table 8.6). What their results do show is that a preference for testing IT rules by inspecting the antecedent does not generalise to the OI rules, a finding which supports the antecedent to consequent directionality of the former.

Evans (1977a) suggested that directionality effects in IT and OI rules might be related to temporal or causal factors. Subjects were asked to construct thematic examples of the two forms of rule at the end of the experiment, and included the following examples:

E5 If it rains on Tuesday, then I shall go swimming.
E6 The match will take place only if the weather improves.

Both E5 and E6 are clearly logical implications. E5 would only be false if it rained on Tuesday and I did not go swimming, and E6 would only be false if the match took place and the weather did not improve. Note, however, that in the IT sentence (E5) the antecedent event precedes the consequent event in time. If one attempts to convert the rules into the alternative form they become semantically anomalous. Thus, E5, in an OI form is:

It will rain on Tuesday only if I go swimming.

and E6 in an IT form reads:

If the match takes place then the weather will improve.

It was suggested that the natural linguistic function of IT and OI rules might be to express implication according to the time order of the antecedent and consequent events. This was tested experimentally by Evans and Newstead (1977) using a truth-table task. Subjects were presented with a rule followed by successive presentations of two letters (a three-field tachistoscope was used). Examples of IT rules used were as follows:

E7 If the first letter is B then the second letter is R
E8 If the second letter is Z then the first letter is T

Equivalent examples in OI form are:

E9   The first letter is B only if the second letter is R
E10 The second letter is Z only if the first letter is T

The truth-table cases were produced by the succession of letters. Thus a B followed by a P would be a TF case for rules E7 and E9. An X followed by a Z, on the other hand, would be the TF case for rules E8 and E10, since the second letter is a Z, but the first (X) is not a T.

It was hypothesised that E7 would be more linguistically 'natural' with 'forwards' time order as compared with the backwards order of E8. For OI rules, however, it is the backwards order that should be more natural, so E10 should be easier than E9. This hypothesis was confirmed by Evans and Newstead in the analysis of response latencies. Their problems also manipulated the presence of negatives, but the negatives factor did not interact with the temporal order effects.

Direction of time order interacted significantly with rule form in both comprehension and verification time analyses. The mean *total* times (CT + VT) were as follows:

IT forwards	12.8 seconds
IT backwards	14.7 seconds
OI forwards	16.8 seconds
OI backwards	15.6 seconds

Evans and Newstead consider an alternative explanation of this result. It is possible that subjects may, illicitly, convert the rule *p only if q* into *If q then p*. (Note that this is not the same as treating it as an equivalence. In that event the converse is assumed in addition to, rather than instead of, the stated rule.) If subjects do, in fact, make such a conversion, then what has been classified as a forwards time order for the OI rule, would in fact be backwards for the converted IT rule that it has become to the subject (and vice versa). Following a detailed analysis of the response-frequency data, however, Evans and Newstead conclude that most subjects retain the original implication of the OI rule, rather than convert it. Consequently, the hypothesis proposed by Evans (1977a) is generally well supported by the Evans and Newstead (1977) study.

The superiority of subjects' ability to reason forwards rather than backwards with the IT rule is further substantiated by work on the Wason selection task (see Chapter 9). The work reviewed in this section suggests that this results from the natural linguistic function of the normal conditional form, and that it is normally applied to situations where 'forward' thinking is appropriate. In the next section we look at the way in which other types of content and contextual factors influence subjects' understanding and use of conditional sentences.

Semantic factors: content and context effects in conditional reasoning

The effect of content on logical reasoning was discussed with respect to classical syllogisms in Chapter 6. One hypothesis considered was that concrete materials might facilitate 'correct' reasoning relative to abstract materials, provided that prior beliefs about the conclusions do not bias judgments. This hypothesis has been investigated extensively with regard to conditional sentences, but nearly all of this work has employed the Wason selection task, and will consequently be discussed in the next chapter.

There has, however, been some discussion of the manner in which the semantic context of a conditional will influence the inferences which people may draw from it. An important idea here is that *pragmatic* inferences may arise from context, even though they are not implied logically. Social psychologists have become interested in the degree to which pragmatic inferences may arise in communications, and the implications that this has for codes of advertising practice, rules of courtroom procedure, etc. (See Harris and Monaco, 1978.) A similar idea has been proposed with specific reference to conditional reasoning. Geiss and Zwicky (1971) suggested that use of a conditional sentence in certain contexts *invites* the DA or AC inference, even though it is not phrased as a biconditional (indicating equivalence). This is particularly true of promises or threats, and other situations where strong causal or temporal connections exist between antecedent and consequent, e.g:

If you mow the lawn, I'll give you five dollars.

clearly 'invites' the DA inference:

If you don't mow the lawn, I won't give you five dollars.

This hypothesis has been tested empirically by Fillenbaum (1975; 1976), who argues that DA should not be seen as a 'fallacy' but rather as a pragmatically reasonable inference in some contexts. Indeed, he is rather disparaging about the sort of studies described earlier in this chapter, which employ abstract propositions with arbitrary connections. His approach emphasises the fact that real-life inference always takes place in a semantic context in which presuppositions and additional knowledge will inevitably influence the process of reasoning.

In one experiment (Fillenbaum, 1975) subjects were given a conditional sentence and asked whether its converse was a 'reasonable, natural inference' to make from it. This appears similar to the methodology of Pollard and Evans (1980) described earlier in this chapter. In the case of their study, the inverse inference appeared psychologically equivalent to DA.

TABLE 8.7   *Percentage frequency of acceptance of inverse (DA) inferences in Fillenbaum's (1975) study*

Rule	Promises	Threats	Contingent universals
(1) If p then q	85	83	67
(2) If p then not q	84	90	60
(3) If not p then q	83	86	54
(4) If not p then not q	83	81	67

Fillenbaum's materials included promises, threats and contingent universals (e.g. 'If the mushroom is red it is edible'). The data for these categories are shown in Table 8.7. It is immediately apparent that the DA rate for threats and promises is very high, and is in fact, significantly higher than on contingent universals. Certainly the DA inference with abstract conditional rules (Table 8.3, second column) is much lower. Another comparison between Fillenbaum's data and that observed with abstract rules is possible, since he included rules with negative components. His data show no evidence of a bias to accept negative conclusions, which should increase acceptance of the inference on rules (1) and (3) relative to (2) and (4).

The most plausible explanation of these differences is that the use of thematics increases DA due to the 'invited inference' effect postulated by Geiss and Zwicky. The lack of conclusion bias can be attributed either to the general increase overriding the bias, or else to a switch to more 'rational' reasoning in the absence of artificial content. Some cautionary comments must be made, however. For one thing, the abstract reasoning experiments were presented as logical reasoning tasks, while Fillenbaum's subjects were clearly asked to make pragmatic inferences. Another problem arises from a lack of attention to the exact nature of his sentences. He gives very few examples of the sentences used, so it is not possible to assess possible confounding by belief bias effects, etc.

Fillenbaum also investigated inferences with conditionals of a temporal/causal nature (e.g. 'If he goes to Paris he will visit the Louvre'). He found similarly high rates of DA inference with such sentences, which are again interpreted as pragmatic inference.

An alternative approach, more consistent with the Henle hypothesis, is to suppose that the context induces a biconditional or equivalence interpretation of the rule, from which DA (and AC) follow logically. Staudenmayer (1975) classified people's inferential patterns as indicating an 'underlying' interpretation as either conditional (COND) or biconditional (BIC) – a technique of analysis criticised earlier in the chapter. He found that abstract rules phrased as *p causes q* led to more BIC classifications than those in the conditional form *If p then q*. He also manipulated people's linguistic presuppositions about causality by the use of thematic content. Consider the following:

E11 If I turn the switch then the light will go on.
E12 If the switch is turned then the light will go on.

Staudenmayer argues that in E11 the antecedent will be seen as sufficient but not *necessary* for the consequent – since someone else might turn the switch. On the other hand presuppositions might lead us to expect that the antecedent is both sufficient and necessary in the case of E12. His results appeared to confirm the hypothesis; sentences of type E12 were associated with considerably more BIC interpretations for subjects who were statistically consistent. Unfortunately, the presentation of data in terms of these dubious classifications, rather than raw frequencies of inference, makes a clear assessment of his findings difficult.

Legrenzi (1970) argued that subjects were likely to interpret a conditional as equivalence if its antecedent and consequent referred to situations which were strictly binary: that is, situations in which there are only two possible events, which are mutually exclusive. He showed subjects apparatus in which a ball could roll down either a left or right channel after which either a red or a green light lit. Subjects were then asked to evaluate the truth table of a rule such as:

E13 If the ball rolls to the left then the green lamp is lit.

Each truth-table case was evaluated as consistent, inconsistent or irrelevant. Twenty-two out of thirty subjects evaluated as follows:

left – green	(TT)	Consistent
left – red	(TF)	Inconsistent
right – green	(FT)	Inconsistent
right – red	(FF)	Consistent

This is the truth table of material equivalence. Although Legrenzi does not report abstract controls, we know from previous research that with an affirmative rule the 'defective' truth table is dominant (FT and FF classed as irrelevant). It is reasonable to assume that the semantic context is responsible for the discrepancy.

Rips and Marcus (1977) pointed out that it might be either the binary nature of the situation *or* causality *per se* that was responsible for Legrenzi's results. They repeated Legrenzi's experiment with extensions to separate these explanations. Thus their conditionals referred to either two (binary) or three (non-binary) possible alternatives, and were placed in either causal or non-causal contexts. They attempted to classify subjects' responses as MC (material conditional) or MB (material biconditional). However, they found another response pattern for the non-binary problems. Some subjects imposed a one-to-one matching between the three antecedent and three consequent values. This cannot be distinguished from MB on binary problems, so Rips and Marcus invent a joint category – 'MB-matching'. Such classifications were significantly more frequent for causal than non-causal contexts, but were not affected by the binary/non-binary manipulation. Thus it appears that it is the *causality* which is responsible for Legrenzi's effect – a conclusion consistent with Fillenbaum's and Staudenmayer's findings. However, a subsequent experiment suggested that it was the perceived *correlation* between antecedent and consequent values, rather than causation *per se* that determined the MB matching response.

When Rips and Marcus (see also Marcus and Rips, 1979) turned their attention to conditional inferences rather than truth-table tasks, the situation became more complicated. Although the causal context was associated with more MB classifications, most subjects are unclassifiable on this task. The problem of attempting to classify syllogistic responses into 'inferred truth tables' was discussed in an earlier section.

Overall, the studies reviewed in this section support the idea that people's behaviour is dependent on the content of the conditional sentences. Attempts to classify behaviour in truth tables à la Henle are not promising, however. If the notion of converted or pragmatic inference is adopted instead, then this can be incorporated into an *interpretational component* of performance. Non-truth functional behaviour will be observed, of course, since other sources of error in the reasoning process, such as response biases, will also influence behaviour.

Conclusions

Originally, Evans (1972a) classified the two main sources of variance on reasoning tasks as *interpretational* and *operational*; in subsequent work the latter has become more specifically defined as non-logical response bias. Marcus and Rips (1977) asserted a similar view:

> [This discrepancy] helps put at rest the long standing debate as to whether errors in logical tasks are due to misinterpretations of the premises or errors in the reasoning process itself. To the extent that this argument can be settled experimentally, our data implicate both sources.

The fact that Marcus and Rips formulated an error-prone process model to explain their non-logical effects, whereas Evans postulated response-bias effects, is a matter of theoretical taste: in both cases, there is a rejection of Henle's attribution of errors *only* to misinterpretation. In my view the elimination of the simplistic rationalist approach is essential if progress is to be made in this field, and it is hoped that the uncommitted reader will perceive its inability to explain the data of the various studies reviewed.

The picture of conditional reasoning that has emerged in this chapter is complex, but not hopelessly so. Studies of conditional reasoning with abstract materials indicate some degree of logical competence, but a considerable amount of systematic error. While the description of these non-logical patterns as response biases is preferred here, it is recognised that others may wish to offer explanations in terms of misguided reasoning strategies. The more general theoretical issues involved will be explored in Part IV. Whilst the interpretational component of performance is only a partial determinant of responding, it is clearly of considerable interest. The review of linguistic factors (syntactic and also semantic) has revealed evidence of a number of influences on the reasoning process which can be interpreted within a psycholinguistic framework.

9 The Wason selection task

In the previous chapter, the focus was on conditional reasoning as measured by inference and truth-table evaluations. In the present chapter, people's reasoning with a conditional sentence *If p then q* is also investigated, but with a *meta-inference* task. Subjects are not simply required to draw or assess immediate inferences. Rather, they are invited to entertain alternative hypotheses with respect to the truth or falsity of a rule, and asked to test these hypotheses. The problem requires some understanding of the logic of conditionals for its solution, but is not *simply* a deductive reasoning problem. It may be regarded as an analogue of scientific hypothesis testing, in which the subject must appreciate the need to seek conditions which could *falsify* his hypothesis (cf. Popper, 1959).

The problem was first described by Wason (1966). So much work has been done on the problem since, however, that it is possible to describe a standard paradigm, an example of which is the following:

The subject is told that a set of cards has been constructed each of which has a letter on one side and a number on the other. In some experiments subjects are given packs of such cards to examine. They are then shown four cards lying on a table (see Figure 9.1).

The subject is then told that the following rule applies to these four cards and may be true or false:

If there is an *R* on one side of the card,
then there is a *2* on the other side of the card.

The subject is then asked to indicate those cards and *only* those cards that he would need to turn over in order to decide whether

FIGURE 9.1   A set of four cards that might be used in a selection task

the rule is true or false. Any reader who has not met this problem before may wish to attempt a solution before reading on.

The simple structure of this task is deceptive – most intelligent adults fail to solve it. Correct selection of cards requires the appreciation of several factors. Firstly, one must understand that in order for the rule to be true it must be obeyed by every card. Thus if any one card was turned over and found consistent with the rule this would not, in itself, prove the rule true. Conversely, only one card need to be found which does *not* obey the rule in order for the rule to be falsified. Once this *falsification principle* is grasped, the problem reduces to one of searching for any cards which could falsify the rule if turned over.

The next step, then, is to decide under what conditions the rule would be false. In effect the subject must consult a truth table for the rule. If subjects regard the rule as expressing implication, then they would classify only the TF case as falsifying the rule. In our example this would mean a card with an R on one side, that does *not* have a 2 on the other. This falsifying case could be discovered by turning over the R or the 8 (not a 2). With an equivalence truth table, the FT case would also falsify – a 2 without an R would contradict the rule. In this case the 2 and the J (not an R) would also need to be selected.

It should be noted that the existence of defective truth tables does not affect the correct solution. In defective implication FT and FF are seen as irrelevant, and in defective equivalence FF is seen as irrelevant. These truth tables contain the same falsifying cases as the corresponding two-valued tables, however, so choices according to the falsification principle are unaltered.

In general terms, for a rule of the form *If p then q* the correct choices would be *p* and *q̄* (not *q*) for an implication reading and all four cards for an equivalence reading. Reaching one of these correct solutions, as we have seen, involves several principles. In summary:

(i)   The subject must appreciate the falsification principle.
(ii) He must have a truth table to determine possible falsifying situations.
(iii) He must decide whether each of the four cards could reveal such a situation.

In practice very few subjects offer either of these solutions. Some typical data are shown in Table 9.1. It can be seen that most subjects (79 per cent) choose either p and q or p alone. Assuming the logic of implication, there are two characteristic errors; (i) failure to select $\bar{q}$ (most subjects), (ii) redundant selection of q (about half the subjects). Under equivalence, selection of q is appropriate, but then the omission of $\bar{p}$ and $\bar{q}$ is erroneous. Regardless of interpretation, the omission of the $\bar{q}$ card is a logical error.

TABLE 9.1   *Percentage frequencies of selections on the Wason selection task pooled across four experiments (from Johnson-Laird and Wason, 1970)*

Cards	% frequency
p,q	46
p	33
p,q,q̄	7
p,q̄	4
others	10

Wason (1966) proposed that subjects possess a truth table for defective implication. This would not lead to error, however, if the falsification principle were adopted. He explains the observed selections by supposing that subjects operate a *verification principle* instead. That is, they search for cards which could verify the rule when turned over, rather than those which could falsify it. With the defective truth table, the only verifying combination is p and q so these are the cards that subjects should tend to select. This explanation is in accord with Wason's (1960) assertion that he had demonstrated a verification bias on an inductive reasoning problem. The question of why subjects choose as they do on the selection task has occasioned considerable debate in the subsequent literature, as we shall see later. First, though, we shall examine some early experiments devised to give subjects insight into their erroneous performance on the task.

The 'therapy' experiments

In line with his theoretical account of subjects' errors, Wason (1968) devised procedures to emphasise the falsifying potential of the $\bar{q}$ card. In one experiment, subjects were invited to 'project falsity', that is to say what if anything on the back of each card could make the rule false. The curious finding was that while the majority of subjects did project a falsifying value (p) on to the back of the $\bar{q}$ card, this had little effect on their subsequent tendency to choose it on the selection task. In a second experiment, subjects were asked to identify falsifying combinations, and all picked out the $p\bar{q}$ card as the only case. Again, this 'therapy' was of no benefit on a subsequent selection task, as compared with control group performance.

A number of other experiments have been run in which an attempt is made to facilitate selections by making subjects aware of the falsifying case, and the fact the $\bar{q}$ selection can produce it (Wason, 1969a; Wason and Johnson-Laird, 1970; Wason and Shapiro, 1971, Experiment 1; Wason and Golding, 1974). Some general features arise from these studies:

(1)   Generally, subjects have no difficulty in recognising the falsifying case of the rule, and will see, if led, that turning $\bar{q}$ will lead to this.

(2)   The administration of such procedure improves performance of some subjects but it is quite ineffective for subsequent selection task performance for a number of others, who still decline to select the $\bar{q}$ card.

(3)   Subjects' introspective comments, if taken, often reveal inconsistent and self-contradictory thought processes.

The fact that subjects can identify the falsifying case is not too surprising, in view of the results of research into psychological truth tables (cf. Chapter 8). The fact that doing so produces only limited facilitation of selection-task performance is most interesting, however. Let us return to the analysis of the three points of understanding required for solution. Clearly the availability of the falsifying case from truth table (step (ii)) is not the problem. Since the subject is directed to think of the consequences of selecting the $\bar{q}$ card, presumably step (iii) is not the problem. Is it, then, the first requirement, the possession of a falsification principle? In other words, it may be that subjects, though aware that $\bar{q}$ could falsify, do not see this as a good reason for selecting it. However, instructions specifically asking for selections to prove the rule false or untrue do *not* produce a high rate of correct selections (cf. Wason, 1968; Wason and Golding, 1974).

One procedure which does seem quite effective in facilitating selection of $\bar{q}$ is reducing choices to selection of consequent cards (q and $\bar{q}$) only (Johnson-Laird and Wason, 1970; Lunzer, Harrison and Davey, 1972; Roth, 1979). It could be that this is due indirectly to the antecedent-consequent directionality of the conditional (see Chapter 8). Perhaps subjects on the full task consider antecedent choices first. Those subjects who select only p on the standard task may think other choices are unnecessary, since turning p will decide the issue – a q on the back will prove the rule true, and a $\bar{q}$ will prove it false. This would, of course, reveal an inductive fallacy – rules cannot be proved true unless all examplars are examined. The snag with this explanation is that subjects frequently choose q in the standard task, so they obviously do consider consequent choices. Roth suggests that the absence of the p card weakens the tendency to base responses on matching (see next section).

Returning to the problem of the relatively ineffective therapies, there is clearly something mysterious about this. Many subjects are, in effect, saying that the $\bar{q}$ card could falsify the rule, but that they do not need to turn it over in order to find out whether the rule is true or false. Not surprisingly, introspective reports reveal self-contradictions in such cases. For example, Wason and Johnson-Laird (1970) asked subjects to make an initial selection and then to evaluate the consequences seeing the p and $\bar{q}$ cards turned over (the latter revealing the falsifying p on the back). They were then asked to revise selections. Although the therapy was effective for a number of subjects, the interest focused on the substantial minority who failed to select $\bar{q}$ in their second selection. The authors quote various verbal comments made by subjects. Some subjects seemed aware of the conflict and tried to rationalise it; others saw no conflict and kept their selection and evaluation processes quite separate. Wason and Johnson-Laird suggest that the selection process tends to dominate these subjects, who become fixated on their original choices. They also comment on the apparent independence of selection and evaluation processes which 'may either interact or pass one another by', and 'conflict in some individuals but not in others'.

Elsewhere, Wason has claimed that protocols give evidence of irreversible thought processes (e.g. Wason and Golding, 1974) and has suggested that subjects may regress, under experimental stress, to primitive childish thought patterns (Wason, 1969a). Further discussion of the problem of self-contradiction and puzzling protocols will be deferred to a later section. Meanwhile, we will focus on the question of why people tend to select p and q in the first place.

The effect of negative components

Understanding the origin of selections really depends upon finding conditions under which selection performance improves, or at least substantially alters. The therapeutic attempts classified above are essentially rationalistic in nature. They are based on the notion that subjects have not properly considered the logical possibilities, or understood the importance of falsification. A rather different approach consists of manipulation of aspects of the task presentation, including the linguistic properties of the rule. In early experiments, as Johnson-Laird and Wason (1970) note, the selection pattern appeared remarkably robust, and indifferent to a number of presentation factors. These included expressing the rule in quantified form: 'Every card that has a p on one side has a q on the other', using strictly binary situations for $p/\bar{p}$ and $q/\bar{q}$, and presenting antecedent and consequent values on the same side of partially masked cards.

In the early 1970s, however, two factors were discovered to have significant effect on selection frequencies – without the necessity for 'therapy'. One of these factors was the introduction of realistic rather than abstract content into the rules (Wason and Shapiro, 1971). A number of studies have explored this factor and will be discussed in detail later in the chapter. For the time being we will focus on the question of why people behave as they do in the abstract task. Apart from reduced presentation, referred to earlier, the only factor of major significance has been the presence and absence of negatives in the rules.

In studies of conditional reasoning using other paradigms, this manipulation has considerably influenced observed reasoning frequencies, and yielded evidence of non-logical response biases (cf. Chapter 8). On truth-table tasks, there was evidence of a 'matching bias', i.e. a tendency to focus unduly on values named in the rule. Since all early experiments on the selection task used only affirmative rules, and since the predominant choices are *p* and *q*, it could well be a factor here as well. Evans and Lynch (1973) carried out an experiment to distinguish a *verification bias* explanation of selection choices (Wason, 1966) with a *matching bias* explanation (cf. Evans, 1972c). They characterised the logical status of the four cards on the standard selection task as follows:

p	true antecedent	(TA)
p̄	false antecedent	(FA)
q	true consequent	(TC)
q̄	false consequent	(FC)

The interesting question is whether subjects' choice of TA and TC are due to their logical status as potential verifiers, or to their matching status as cards named in the rule. If the selection task is administered with the presence of negatives varied, then the two explanations can be distinguished. Evans and Lynch performed this experiment, and their findings are shown in Table 9.2.

TABLE 9.2 *Percentage of cards selections in the Evans and Lynch (1973) experiment (n=24)*

		Card Selected		
Rule	TA	FA	TC	FC
(1) If p then q	(p) 88	(p̄) 8	(q) 50	(q̄) 33
(2) If p then not q	(p) 92	(p̄) 4	(q̄) 8	(q) 58
(3) If not p then q	(p̄) 58	(p) 29	(q) 58	(q̄) 42
(4) If not p then not q	(p̄) 54	(p) 46	(q̄) 29	(q) 75
ε	73	22	36	52

It has been argued throughout Part III that response biases *combine* with interpretational tendencies in producing the observed data. Consequently, evidence for matching bias must be assessed by comparing the frequency of selection of matching and mismatching cases while *holding the logical case constant*. For each logical case – TA, FA, TC, FC – Evans and Lynch predicted that the card would be selected more often on the two rules where it matched (p or q) than on the two which it mismatched ($\bar{p}$ or $\bar{q}$). Thus for TA and FA the comparison is between rules with affirmative and negative antecedents, and for TC and FC between rules with affirmative and negative consequents. Inspection of Table 9.2 reveals that all trends were as predicted, and indeed all were highly significant.

If the frequency of selection of logical cases is considered when averaged across all four rules, then each has benefited or suffered equally from matching bias. Is there, then, evidence of a verification bias, i.e. a preference for TC over FC? (This comparison is reasonable, since the extent of the matching effect is similar in each case.) Inspection of Table 9.1 reveals the *opposite* to be the case, and the extra FC selection is in fact significant. This last finding should not, however, be taken too seriously. Manktelow and Evans (1979) repeated the Evans and Lynch study in two experiments. While the matching bias effects were replicated, the TC/FC difference was not. Across the four rules, the selection frequencies for 48 subjects on a comparable abstract task were as follows: TA, 86 per cent; FA, 19 per cent; TC, 53 per cent; FC, 52 per cent. Taken together, the three experiments suggest the following conclusions:

(1)   Matching bias significantly influences the selection of cards, irrespective of their logical status.
(2)   There is also evidence of a 'logical' or interpretational bias to prefer TA to FA, but no reliable evidence of a preference between TC and FC.

These results appear to refute the verification theory of Wason. However, they only do so if the negatives are assumed not to affect the *interpretation* of the rules. Could one argue, in Henle fashion, that the negatives effect interpretational changes which alter the actual logical status of the cards? It is not easy to see how this could create the matching effect. Introducing a negative consequent 'improves' logical performance in that TC is less often and FC more often selected. However, the introduction of a negative antecedent worsens performance since selections of TA reduce and FA increase in frequency. No general interpretational shift (e.g. from implication to equivalence) could account for such changes.

The matching interpretation does seem compelling, but there are problems. Firstly, why do intelligent adults make such a primitive matching response in the first place? Van Duyne (1973; 1974) criticised the use of the concept of matching bias on the grounds that the origin of the bias was not explained, although that makes it none the less real. In reply, Evans (1975) suggested that subjects' attention was directed to named values. Whether a rule reads 'If A then not 3' or 'If not A then 3', it seems to be making statements *about* the A and the 3. This explanation ties in with linguistic considerations, since negatives are used to deny affirmative presuppositions and hence draw attention to them (cf. Chapter 3). More importantly, Van Duyne claimed that the matching bias effect did not generalise to disjunctive rules. This claim is examined in Chapter 10, where further consideration of the explanation of matching bias will be made. For the time being, the term 'matching bias' will be used to denote an experimental observation that any explanation of selection-task performance must take into account. Unfortunately, most published theories have avoided the explanation of the phenomenon by focusing entirely on the selection patterns for affirmative rules.

Insight models

Prior to the demonstration of the matching effect, Johnson-Laird and Wason (1970) had presented an *insight* model to account for the results of early selection task experiments. They were concerned with explaining not only the initial selection patterns, but also the modifications arising from 'therapies', including a tendency for some subjects to choose p, q and $\bar{q}$ (TA, TC, FC).

Johnson-Laird and Wason (1970) present two models postulating varying degrees of insights. We will consider only the second (revised) model here. They postulate three states:

No insight The subject selects cards which could verify the rule.

Partial insight The subject does appreciate the need to select potential falsifiers, but also chooses cards that could only verify. *Complete insight* The subject sees that *only* cards which could falsify need be selected.

The authors also postulate that 'the subject without insight will focus on cards mentioned in the rule'. This sounds like matching bias, but with two important differences: (i) they make no suggestion that this would generalise to rules with negative components, and (ii) they suggest that q is chosen as well as p only if the subject assumes that the rule implies its converse (equivalence). Under partial or complete insight, *all* cards are considered.

Johnson-Laird and Wason claim that subjects with no insight will choose p or p and q. Under partial insight they initially consider all cards. However, '$\bar{p}$ will be considered irrelevant because it could neither verify nor falsify.' All other cards *will* be chosen – p, q and $\bar{q}$ because they could either verify or falsify or both. Under complete insight q is eliminated because it could not falsify, and the subject chooses p and $\bar{q}$. There appears to be an inconsistency here (cf. Bree, 1973). If roughly half the subjects choose q under no insight because they think the rule is an equivalence, they should have $\bar{p}q$ as well as $p\bar{q}$ in their truth table as a falsifying case. Consequently, under either partial or complete insight, such subjects should choose *all four cards*. In fact, while therapies often produce $p,\bar{q}$ or $p,q,\bar{q}$ combinations, they rarely produce $p,\bar{p},q,\bar{q}$ selections.

Can the Johnson-Laird and Wason revised model account for the matching-bias effect observed by Evans and Lynch, when negative components are introduced? This depends on how we interpret their descriptions of behaviour under no insight – the state in which most untrained subjects are presumed to be. If subjects focus on the TA and TC, regardless of the presence of negatives, then the model makes the same predictions for negative rules as for affirmatives. In this case it could not account for the Evans and Lynch results.

Suppose, though, that we assume that subjects focus on p and q irrespective of their logical status. Would this lead to the prediction of matching bias? So far as the antecedent is concerned, the answer is definitely no. Given the rule *If not p then q*, the subject would *consider* p as well as q but he would not *select* it, since its logical status, FA, is 'irrelevant' in the defective truth table. Thus the increase in FA selections on rules where they match could not be explained. The drop in TA selections when they do not match (on rules with negative antecedents) should be much *more* marked than it actually is (cf. Table 9.2) on *If not p then q*; the TA case ($\bar{p}$) should not be considered, and hence selected, by any subject in a state of no insight.

The predictions of the effect of negative consequents are ambiguous. Consider the rule *If p then not q*. Is the significant increase in FC (q) selection, compared with the affirmative rule, predicted by the model? Certainly a no insight subject will now consider the FC case, since it is named in the rule. According to the *text* of their paper he will not, however, select it since it could only falsify and not verify the rule. According to the *flow-chart* published by Johnson-Laird and Wason however, he would select it. The discrepancy between flow-chart and text is not apparent when only affirmative rules are considered, since matching and verifying are then always confounded. Finally, the drastic drop in TC selections on rules with negative consequents *is* predicted by the model (text and flow-chart) since these unnamed values would not be considered. Overall, though, it appears that the Johnson-Laird and Wason model cannot be interpreted in such a way as to give a satisfactory explanation of the Evans and Lynch data.

Thus the Johnson-Laird and Wason model is not only slightly inconsistent in its explanation of affirmative rule performance, but also cannot account for selections on negative rules. Nevertheless, some evidence for the model has been claimed by Goodwin and Wason (1972). There is an inherent circularity in the model which they attempt to overcome. How does one know that a subject has, say, partial insight, other than by observing his response to be $p,q,\bar{q}$? Goodwin and Wason tried to overcome this by asking subjects to give written reasons for selecting or rejecting each card. They reasoned that this would show whether or not subjects were choosing in order to verify or falsify. The experiment employed only the affirmative form of rule.

Goodwin and Wason claim that their results

corroborate empirically the existence of the three levels of insight postulated by the information-processing model devised to explain performance on tasks of this type (Johnson-Laird and Wason, 1970). There is a close relation between the degrees of insight indicated by the protocols and the corresponding selection of cards.

This conclusion is based largely upon the inspection of subjects' protocols. The actual rule used was 'Every card which has a triangle on one half has red on the other half' and the stimuli were: triangle (p), square ($\bar{\text{p}}$), red (q) and blue ($\bar{q}$). A subject choosing p and q gave the following justifications:

p 'Triangle: only interested if it has red on.'
$\bar{p}$ 'It is irrelevant if the square has red or blue on it.'
q 'Red: want to know if it has triangle on it.'
$\bar{q}$ 'It is irrelevant if blue has triangle on it.'

This subject should, of course, be in a state of no insight. The authors claim that this protocol shows 'a strong set for verification which leads to the selection of only those stimuli mentioned in the rule'. In actual fact the subject makes no reference to proving the rule true – an alternative interpretation is that he is only interested in seeking the matching values.

The examples of partial insight and complete insight protocols cited are more convincing, however. For example, a subject choosing p, q and $\bar{q}$ gave the following justifications:

p,q 'The experiment mentions triangle and red, therefore we must look at both cards which show one of these features to see if its other half has the second feature required if the statement is true.'
$\bar{p}$ 'The experiment does not mention a square, so the card with a square on it need not be looked at.'
$\bar{q}$ 'We must look at the blue card in case it has a triangle on the other half, in which case the statement would be untrue.'

These comments seem to contain all the ingredients of partial insight. The first reveals a verification tendency; the second an 'irrelevant' attribution to the false antecedent, and the third a falsification tendency.

Subjects choosing p and $\bar{q}$, according to the model, have complete insight and should choose only in order to falsify. The following protocol appears to confirm this:

p 'I chose the triangle because if it has blue on the other half, it will disprove the claim.'

$\bar{p}$ 'I ignored the square because it has nothing to do with the claim.'

q 'I ignored the red card because it may have a triangle or a square on the other half.'

$\bar{q}$ 'I chose the blue card because if it has a triangle on the other half, it will disprove the claim.'

One point to bear in mind is that the Goodwin and Wason protocols do not constitute strictly independent evidence of the model. Johnson-Laird and Wason had been influenced by the therapy experiments in devising the model, a feature of which was the collection of verbal protocols. Hence remarks such as those cited could have influenced construction of the model. A second problem is that one needs to be sure that the verbal justifications are what they purport to be: an account of the actual *a priori* causes of selection. This issue will be discussed in detail in the next section.

Other insight models have been proposed to explain selection task performance. One of these, Bree and Coppens (1976), has been criticised by Moshman (1978), who identifies inaccuracies in the derivation of predictions and the presentation of data, as Bree and Coppens (1978) largely concede. The other main effort, by Smalley (1974), takes most comprehensive account of early selection-task studies. He suggested three main sources of variation between subjects:

(1) Interpretation of sentence.
(2) Interpretation of cards.
(3) Application of decision rules.

At stage (1) subjects may either interpret the rule as implication or equivalence (with 'defective' truth tables). At stage (2) the subject may or may not appreciate the reversibility of the cards. At stage (3) they may choose only to verify (no insight), to verify and falsify (partial insight) or only to falsify (complete insight). With reference to stage (2) of the model, Wason (personal communication) maintains that irreversibility is not a property of the cards as such, but is conferred on them by selection. The point is that evaluation of such cards in a truth-table task does not reveal such asymmetries.

Smalley's model makes more specific predictions than that of Johnson-Laird and Wason. For example, in his model partial insight only leads to selections of p, q and $\bar{q}$ if the subject has an implication interpretation, and perceives cards as reversible. The problem with Smalley's model, of course, lies in its testability – one needs to specify three parameters in order to predict the behaviour of each subject. In providing evidence for his model, Smalley, like Goodwin and Wason, relied heavily on subjects' verbal protocols including stated justifications for choices.

Interpretation of protocols

None of the insight models has been applied to selection tasks using negative rules. The demonstration of 'matching bias' by Evans and Lynch (1973) appears to embarrass these models. On the other hand, subjects' verbal justifications appear to give some support to the authors' claims of underlying insights or strategies.

Wason and Evans (1975) devised an experiment to resolve this paradox. Each subject was required to solve a selection task with an affirmative rule – *If p then q* – and a negative rule *If p then not q*. If subjects 'match' on both rules, i.e. select p and q, they should choose 'verifying' cases on the affirmative rule – TA and TC – but 'falsifying' cases on the negative rule – TA and FC. On each rule, subjects were asked to justify the decision to select or reject each card, in the manner of the Goodwin and Wason (1972) study.

The quantitative data were in line with the matching bias effect. None of the 24 subjects gave the correct selection (TA – FC) on the affirmative rule, and 12 of them chose p and q (TA – TC). On the negative rule 15 out of 24 gave the correct selection which is also the matching combination of p and q. Protocols were then rated for evidence of falsification, on the basis of statements such as 'If there is a 6 on the other side then the statement is false'. Falsification protocols were observed more often on the negative problem, particularly for those subjects who received it prior to the affirmative problem.

In essence, subjects tended to give logically appropriate justifications of the cards they had selected. Particularly interesting were the protocols of subjects who did the negative problem first, and matched on both rules. Wason and Evans report three such protocols which are reproduced in Table 9.3. To ease comprehension the lexical content – letter and number referred to – has been standardised.

Looking first at the justifications of the negative task, we see that S3 and S6 would have to be classified as demonstrating complete insight by the Goodwin and Wason technique. Not only do they choose the TA and FC cards, but they justify selections with reference to the possibility of falsification. By contrast, their protocols on the subsequent affirmative rule would be classified as showing no insight. Subjects choose TA and TC, in the case of S6, at least, suggesting a verification motive for choice.

These are essentially two interpretations of these results. One is to suppose that the negative component induces a genuine insight for some reason. But if this were so, why does it disappear on presentation of the affirmative rule? Also, we know from the Evans and Lynch (1973) study that the effect of introducing a negative *antecedent* is to make choices *less* logical (fewer TA's, more FA's). The alternative explanation, preferred by Wason and Evans, is to suppose that selections are highly influenced by matching, and that the verbal justifications are *rationalisations*. According to this view, the subject asked to justify his selection is *solving a new problem*. The problem is this: given (1) the instructions, (2) the selections, what is a good reason for having chosen as he did? Since the instructions asked subjects to 'establish whether the rule is true or false', he evaluates his selections in these terms. These verbalisations demonstrate an ability to recognise TT as verifying and TF as falsifying a conditional rule, a competence observed in truth-table tasks (Chapter 8).

An interesting feature of the protocols cited is that 'matching bias' not only influences the original selections, but appears to affect the process of justification as well. This is clearly illustrated by S6, who justifies the selection of B (TA) on each rule by considering the effect upon the rule, if the matching 3 is on the other side of the card. This leads him to a verifying justification of TA on the affirmative rule, and a falsifying justification of TA on the negative rule. This observation gives support to Evans's (1975) explanation of the

TABLE 9.3 *Three protocols from the study of Wason and Evans (1975)*

Cards and responses			Negative task	Affirmative task
			If there is a B. . . then there will not be a 3 *Reasons*	If there is a B. . . then there will be a 3 *Reasons*
S3				
	B	yes	'If the rule was false, there would be a 3 on the other side. If true there would not be a 3. B and 3 should be taken as part of the same assumption.'	'The rule says that B is related to 3. It does not say anything about there being a logical sequence of letters to numbers, so no assumptions about letters and numbers other than B and 3 can be made.'
	3	yes	'If the rule was false, there would be a B on the other side.'	'As above'
	U	no	'The rule only states that there is no relation between 3 and B. It does not state whether there is a relation between other numbers and letters'	'Logical extension of argument above.'
	6	no	'As above.'	'As above.'
S2				
	B	yes	'To see that it is not a 3.'	'To ensure that the reverse is 3.'
	3	yes	'To ensure that it is not a B.'	'To ensure that the reverse is B.'
	U	no	'It need not prove anything.'	'The result might be inconclusive.'
	6	no	'It need not prove anything.'	'The result might be inconclusive.'
S6				
	B	yes	'If there is a 3 on the other side, then the statement is false.'	'If there is a 3 on the other side, then the statement is true.'
	3	yes	'If there is a B on the other side, then the statement is false.'	'If there is a B on the other side, then the statement is true: othewise it is false.'
	U	no	'Whatever number is on the other side will not show if statement is true or false.'	'Any numbers may be on the other side.'
	6	no	'Any letter may be on the other side, therefore no way of knowing if statement is true.'	'If numbers are fairly random, then there may be any letter on the other side, thereby giving no indication unless the letter is B.'

origin of the matching effect. Subjects do indeed seem to think that the rule is making a statement about the named values, regardless of the presence of negatives. They evidently find it easier to consider an affirmative possibility, such as '3', than a negative, such as 'not 3'.

Evans and Wason (1976) report further evidence for the rationalisation hypothesis. Subjects were given the selection task, together with its 'solution'. They were assigned randomly to four groups according to how the solution was defined. They were told that either p; p and q; p, q and $\bar{q}$; or p and $\bar{q}$ was the correct answer. Subjects were then asked to justify the selection or rejection of each card, as specified in the 'solution' provided.

Very few subjects disputed the correctness of the alleged solution, although in many cases it would obviously differ from the selection they would have made if asked to solve it in the normal way. An inspection .of justification offered for q and $\bar{q}$ revealed that the majority not only gave a justification agreeing with the set solution (selection or rejection) but gave a high confidence rating of the correctness of this selection. This study shows that subjects can construct justifications for arbitrarily selected solutions, but does not prove that they are rationalising when justifying their own solutions in other experiments. The demand characteristics of the Evans and Wason experiment obviously exert a strong 'compliance' effect. It is worth reflecting, though, that if subjects do not have introspective access to the thought processes underlying selections, then a similar compliance effect may be operative when they are asked to justify their own responses. They may devise suitable 'reasons' simply because the experimenter has asked them to do so.

Wason and Evans went on to propose a dual process theory of reasoning, in which selections and justifications were attributed to distinct thought processes. The dual process theory has implications concerning the nature of thought, which go well beyond the explanation of selection task data. Since these implications will be explained fully in the final chapter of this book, it is unnecessary to divert attention to the dual process theory at this point. For purposes of the present chapter it is sufficient to note that this work casts serious doubt on the status of evidence for 'insight' or 'strategy' models, which is based upon subjects' verbal justifications.

Evans's stochastic model

The criticism of insight models is, of course, in keeping with the general opposition to rationalist approaches throughout this book. The stochastic reasoning model (Evans, 1977b) can be seen as a further attempt to offer an alternative to the rationalist account of reasoning. Readers may find its assumptions absurdly counter-intuitive. In this case, they might ask themselves whether this objection arises from introspection considerations. If so, consider the view that psychologists cannot reject purported explanations of behaviour simply on the grounds that people do not feel that they do things in such a manner. The work reported in the last section suggests that introspective reports may not be what they seem, a point which is elaborated in Chapter 12.

The Evans (1977b) paper starts with the question of where individual differences in reasoning performance arise. The predominant assumption has been that if two subjects make a different response to the same problem then they are in different states of insight, or are employing different strategies. An alternative possibility is that behaviour is intrinsically probabilistic, or stochastic. If a group of subjects all have a probability of 0.6 of making a given response, about 60 per cent of them would be observed to make it in a given experiment.

The object of the Evans (1977b) paper was to devise a stochastic model to account for reasoning performance in general, and the Wason selection task in particular. Insight models of the selection task place emphasis on the *combinations* of cards selected, e.g. p,q indicates no insight; $p,q,\bar{q}$ partial insight, and $p,\bar{q}$ complete insight. Evans (1977b), however, was interested in predicting the response probability of each card individually, and the first step was to check whether or not card selections were *statistically independent*. For example, if we know that a subject has selected q, are we able to predict that he is more or less likely to select $\bar{q}$? The analysis was restricted to q and $\bar{q}$ selection for two reasons:

(1)   Frequency of p is too high, and $\bar{p}$ too low, to permit useful statistical analysis.
(2)   It is the presence and absence of q and $\bar{q}$ selections that distinguishes different states in the insight and strategy models.

The Evans (1977b) paper presents a re-analysis of 17 selection-task experiments. In none of these was there a significant association between q and $\bar{q}$ selections. This statistical independence undermines the psychological significance of combinations of card selections emphasised by the insight models. Indeed, it suggests that data should be reported in terms of the raw frequencies of selecting each card – which many authors have omitted to do. The finding of independence also has an interesting implication for the selection patterns found after 'therapy', as will be explained.

Untrained subjects normally choose either p or p,q. The stochastic interpretation of this is as follows:

(1) Subjects have a high probability for selecting p.
(2) They have low probabilities for selecting $\bar{p}$ and $\bar{q}$.
(3) They have an intermediate selection probability for q.

Now supposing therapies are introduced with the specific aim of increasing $\bar{q}$ selections. This was attempted by Wason (1969a) using a progressive series of therapies with a selection task after each stage. Across the five tests, the selection probability of $\bar{q}$ rose from 0.06 to 0.88 – as measured by the proportion of subjects choosing it. However, the Evans (1977b) analysis showed that its selection remained independent of q selections on all five tests. Suppose, then, that the procedure has succeeded in raising the selection probability of $\bar{q}$ without affecting the probability of selecting any other card. What effect would this have on the observed combinations of cards? The answer is quite simple. The modal choices would switch from p and p,q to $p,\bar{q}$ and $p,q,\bar{q}$, which is exactly what happens when therapies are successful. Thus 'complete insight' and 'partial insight responses could simply be the statistical consequence of revising one of four independent card selection frequencies.

Pollard (1979a) analysed statistical associations between all four cards in several experiments. He replicated the independence of q and $\bar{q}$ selection, but found evidence of a correlation between $\bar{p}$ and $\bar{q}$ selections. He interprets this as arising from individual differences in susceptibility to matching bias. Some subjects tend strongly to ignore both mismatching cards. These findings parallel those of Pollard and Evans's (1980) inference task study (cf. Chapter 8) in which little correlation was found between performance on inferences of similar logical type, but some on the apparent basis of susceptibility to response biases.

If behaviour is stochastic at the level of individual subjects, then we might also expect independence in successive responses from the same subjects. This is not a *necessary* consequence of the stochastic assumption, however, since it is possible that the subject's response on the first presentation of the selection, while randomly generated, may affect his performance on a second test. Nevertheless Evans (1977a) does report an analysis of some new data provided by Bree, which provides some evidence of trial to trial independence.

The stochastic model of Evans (1977b) is based on the two-factor theory of Evans (1972a, 1977a). The idea is that interpretational (logical) tendencies combine with response-bias (non-logical) tendencies in providing the observed data. The model formalises the notion of *weighted* combination discussed previously. There are three parameters, all of which fall in the range 0 to 1:

I   Tendency to respond on the basis of the interpretational component.
R   Tendency to respond on the basis of response bias.
α   Weighting factor.

The model is represented schematically in Figure 9.2. It is written in a general form, but for consideration of the selection task the 'response' would be selection of a card. The model supposes that subjects *either* respond on the basis of interpretation (with probability α) or on the basis of response bias (with probability $1 - α$). The other parameters can be seen as conditional probabilities. I is the chance of selecting a card *given* that responding is based on interpretation; R is the probability *given* that a response bias is being used. By elementary probability theory the probability of a particular response (card selection) r is given by

$$P(r) = α.I + (1 - α) . R$$

In the paper, the model was tested against the data of Evans and Lynch (1973). In order to test the model it was necessary to assume that all subjects had the same parameter values, and to use the observed proportion of subjects making a given response as an

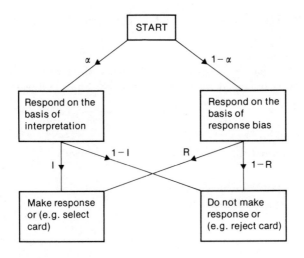

$$Pr(r) = \alpha.\ I + (1-\alpha).\ R.$$

FIGURE 9.2   Schematic representation of the Evans (1977b) stochastic reasoning model

estimate of the prior probability for each subject. It was also necessary to make several *a priori* assumptions about parameter values. These were as follows:

α values
Two values: α_a for antecedent choices
α_c for consequent choices

This was based upon the observation of Evans and Lynch (1973) that more weighting is apparently given to logic, and less to matching, on the antecedent selections. Thus we would expect $\alpha_a > \alpha_c$.

I values
$$I_{TA} = 1$$
$$I_{FA} = 0$$
$$I_{TC} = 0$$
$$I_{FC} = 1$$

Where I_{TA} = 'interpretational parameter for TA selections', etc.

This was based on Evans and Lynch's observation that when matching is balanced by pooling across the rules, subjects tended to be logically correct on this task.

R values
It was assumed that only two values were needed:

R_m for responses which match.
$R_{\bar{m}}$ for responses which mismatch.

On these assumptions it was possible to devise simplified expressions of the probability of selecting each card in the Evans and Lynch experiment. For example, consider selection of FA on the rule *If not p then q*. It is an antecedent choice, so the weighting parameter is α_a. FA matches on this rule, so the response bias parameter is R_m. Finally, I_{FA} is assumed 0, so the expression is:

$$P \ (FA/\textit{If not p then q}) = \alpha_a.0 + (1 - \alpha_a). \ R_m$$
$$= (1 - \alpha_a). \ R_m$$

Fitted in this way, two independent measures were found for each expression. They were consistently very close. It was also possible to predict equalities between pairs of differences or ratios of two observed probabilities (proportions) which again were impressively close. So it appeared that the model fitted well.

However, Pollard (1979a; 1979b) has shown that the *a priori* parameter assumptions used are incorrect. In attempting to fit the model to his own data, he found that estimates of α_c were frequently *negative*, whereas this parameter must lie in the range 0 to 1. This means that in his experiments, TC selections were more frequent than FC selections. This could not occur if the assumed values of I parameters were generalisable. On closer inspection, however, Pollard found that the assumed I values were not even consistent with the Evans and Lynch data. By manipulation of the equations of Evans (1977b), Pollard estimated the value of the following expressions:

$(1 - \alpha_a) \ (Rm - R\bar{m})$
$(1 - \alpha_c) \ (Rm - R\bar{m})$

The estimated values from the Evans and Lynch data were *identical*, an observation which indicates that $\alpha_a = \alpha_c$. However, on the Evans (1977b) parameter assumptions they had been estimated to have quite different values ($\alpha_a = 0.511$, $\alpha_c = 0.156$). This contradiction again arises from the *a priori* values which had been assumed for the I parameters, and these are clearly wrong.

Pollard does, however, find the model to fit well when these parameter assumptions are discarded. The psychological value of the model is, in fact, demonstrated by his criticism of the original parameter assumptions. In order to fit the data he is forced to reformulate the *psychological* analysis of the influence of interpretational tendencies. In simple English, the original parameter values were based on the following psychological theory: It was assumed that subjects have complete logical competence to solve the task contained in the interpretational component. However, while they could apply this competence more often than not on the antecedent choices, they could apply it much less often on consequent choices. The remainder of responding was biased by matching.

Pollard's critique alters the theory as follows: subjects give equal weighting to interpretational and response bias tendencies on all cards. However, the competence revealed by the I parameters is *not* uniform across cards, but more marked for antecedent cards. Thus the value of I_{TA} is high and I_{FA} low in accordance with logic, but the values of I_{TC} and I_{FC} are intermediate and little different from one another. Thus the superior logical performance on antecedent selections is attributed to superior logical tendencies and *not* to additional weighting of such tendencies. This distinction is of considerable importance to Pollard (1979a), who argues from a variety of sources of evidence that people have little or no logical competence regarding their treatment of the consequent of conditional rules.

Thus Pollard's critique does not amount to a refutation of the Evans (1977b) attempt to formulate a stochastic model of the two-factor reasoning theory. Rather it is a correction in its means of application. We will now proceed to consideration of the effects of thematic content on selection-task performance.

Facilitation by realism

All the selection-task experiments discussed so far have employed so-called 'abstract' materials. The rules refer to relationships between the presence and absence of arbitrarily chosen symbols (letters, numbers, coloured shapes, etc.) on either side of a card. Now, it can be argued that the high logical error rate, and the primitive matching bias, give a distorted impression of people's competence to understand logical relationships in real life. It will be recalled that Wilkins (1928) produced evidence that realistic content can facilitate performance on tasks employing classical syllogisms (see Chapter 6). A number of experiments have been performed to find out whether a similar facilitation of selection-task performance could be effected by the introduction of thematic content. The results of several of these are summarised in Table 9.4.

TABLE 9.4   *The results of some experiments manipulating thematic and abstract content.*[1] *(% correct ($p,\bar{q}$))*

	Abstract	Thematic
Wason and Shapiro (1971)	6	63
Johnson-Laird *et al.* (1972)	15	81
Van Duyne (1974)	33	54
Bracewell and Hidi (1974)[2]	8	75
Gilhooly and Falconer (1974)[2]	6	22
Manktelow and Evans (1979)[3]	7	7

Notes:
[1] Only affirmative rules of the form *If p then q* or *Every p has a q* are included.
[2] Only the conditions which repeat those of Wason and Shapiro are shown here.
[3] Data pooled over five experiments. The frequency of $p,\bar{q}$ is taken from the raw data; this measure was not reported in the paper.

Two experiments published in the early 1970s yield evidence of such faciliation. In the first (Wason and Shapiro, 1971, Experiment II) subjects were asked to investigate a claim made by the experimenter, such as:

'Every time I go to Manchester I travel by car.'

The four cards were used to represent journeys, with the means of transport written on one side, and the destination on the other. With the above rule, the subject might be shown the cards shown in Figure 9.3.

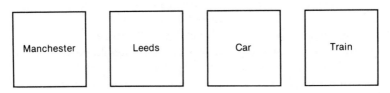

FIGURE 9.3   Four cards used in the thematic selection tack of Wason and Shapiro (1971)

Subjects were then asked which cards would need to be turned over in order to decide whether the experimenter's claim was true or false. The correct answer is 'Manchester' and 'train'. The abstract control condition employed rules such as 'Every card which has a D on one side has a 7 on the other'. 10 of the 16 subjects tested in the thematic group gave the correct $(p, \bar{q})$ answer, as compared with only 2 of the 16 in the abstract group.

This result is especially interesting when one considers that, in a sense, the abstract material is more *concrete* than the thematic. The abstract rule refers to the actual cards themselves, whereas the thematic rule refers to hypothetical situations, of which the cards are symbolic representations. In the second early experiment (Johnson-Laird, Legrenzi and Legrenzi, 1972), both the abstract and the thematic rules referred to the actual materials that the subject had to consider. In the thematic condition, subjects were asked to imagine that they were post office workers sorting letters. An example of the thematic rule was:

'If a letter is sealed then it has a 50 lire stamp on it'

Subjects are then shown not four cards, but four *envelopes*. Two had the front exposed, one bearing a 50 lire stamp (q) and one a 40 lire stamp ($\bar{q}$). The other two had their reverse sides facing, one sealed (p) and the other unsealed ($\bar{p}$). The abstract control employed the usual letter-number relations on cards. All subjects performed both tasks in counterbalanced order. Two aspects of the results are striking: (i) there was a massive facilitation effect, with 22/24 subjects showing superior logical performance in the thematic condition and (ii) those subjects who performed the abstract task after the thematic task gave the usual poor performance. Any 'insight' engendered by realism evidently does not transfer.

If the facilitation effect observed in these studies is genuine and reliable, then it clearly affects one's attitudes to the large number of studies employing only abstract content. One might regard the latter as having low ecological validity for assessing real life reasoning. More positively, one might ask why the reasoning abilities of intelligent adults are so dependent on content, and point to the discrepancy between these results and Piaget's theory of formal operations (see Wason, 1977, and Chapter 12 of this book). The reliability of the effect seemed to be established by a number of subsequent studies (Lunzer, Harrison and Davey, 1972; Bracewell and Hidi, 1974; Gilhooly and Falconer, 1974; Van Duyne, 1974). However, a recent study by Manktelow and Evans (1979) has failed to find any facilitation in five separate experiments. It is consequently necessary to look closely at the detail of the individual studies.

The study reporting the highest rate of solution with thematic content is that of Johnson-Laird *et al.* described above. This experiment can be criticised on the grounds that it is *too* realistic. The British university students tested at that time would certainly have experienced a similar rule in their own real-life experience. They would thus bring to the experiment the knowledge that one may not seal a letter with a *lower valued* stamp on it. They would also know that if a letter has a high-valued stamp it does not matter whether or not it is sealed, and that if it is unsealed it does not matter which of the two values of stamp is used. The point is that the subject can solve this problem without *reasoning* at all; he can transfer directly his learned response to an analogous real-life situation. It would be interesting to repeat the experiment with a higher-valued stamp (e.g. 60 lire) representing the $\bar{q}$ conclusion. The lesson here is that a reasoning task is not a reasoning task unless it is hypothetical to a degree; thematic materials must not be used which make the correct answer directly available from memory.

The towns and transport material of Wason and Shapiro (1971) have been employed by other workers. It was argued that the facilitation might result from thematic *terms* or else from a realistic *relation* between the terms. Two studies which investigated this produced conflicting results. Gilhooly and Falconer (1974) found the terms rather than the relation to be important, whereas Bracewell and Hidi (1974) made the reverse observation. However, both found significant facilitation in the situation similar to Wason and Shapiro – thematic terms *and* realistic relations – although in the Gilhooly and Falconer study the level of performance in this condition was still relatively low. The interpretation of Bracewell and Hidi's result is complicated by an interaction with the order of reference to antecedent and consequent in the sentence they used.

Manktelow and Evans (1979) have claimed that the evidence for facilitation has been overstated, and point to the fact that some studies (e.g. Van Duyne, 1974; Lunzer *et al.*, 1972) have only found the effect when other procedural changes are introduced such as instructions emphasising falsification, or the use of 'reduced' arrays of cards. However, it is the Manktelow and Evans study that is out of line with the rest of the literature, and it is necessary to look closely at *their* procedures. In four of the experiments 'food and drink' content was used so as to permit the introduction of negative components (in the first two experiments only). Examples are:

If I eat macaroni, then I do not drink champagne.
If I do not eat pork, then I drink red wine.
If I do not eat chips, then I do not drink brown ale.
If I eat haddock, then I drink gin.

Subjects were told that each card referred to 'what I ate and drank at a particular meal'.

In the first experiment, a group test, no difference was observed between performance on such sentences and abstract controls. Both groups showed the usual low logical performance and comparison between rules yielded evidence of matching bias with thematic as well as abstract content. This non-effect was replicated in three further experiments using individual presentation, including two experiments employing affirmative rules only. The final experiment repeated Wason and Shapiro's experiment with their materials and also produced no facilitation.

Pollard (1981) argues that the food and drink materials are not really realistic. He points to Wason and Johnson-Laird's (1972) emphasis on the importance of a believable story, and claims that the food and drinks materials lack plausibility.

On balance, the research to date suggests that the use of materials with realistic reference may have some facilitating effect on performance. The effect is not so strong or reliable as the early papers suggest, and there is clearly a need for further research to determine exactly how task content is affecting the manner in which subjects think about the problem.

Truth status effects

Much of the research into the effect of realistic materials on syllogistic reasoning (Chapter 6) was concerned with belief bias. These studies use thematic materials towards which the subject is likely to have attitudes. In particular, the evidence suggests that subjects may evaluate the truth of the syllogism's conclusion on the basis of *a priori* beliefs, rather than assessing the logical validity of the argument as instructed. People are more likely to assess an argument as 'valid' if they believe its conclusion to be true.

Van Duyne (1976) developed a theory of belief-bias effects in the thematic selection task. He proposed that subjects are motivated by 'cognitive self-reinforcement'. Essentially, his argument is that subjects will seek verifying evidence for a rule they believe to be true, and are more likely to seek falsifying evidence if they think the rule could be false. In order to test this hypothesis he asked subjects to make up conditional sentences which they thought either (1) necessarily true or (2) contingently true (sometimes true, sometimes false). Subjects wrote down five examples of each from which the experimenter selected one in each category for the selection task. Although Van Duyne's task is logically equivalent to Wason's, it is unusual in having not cards. Suppose the subject gives the following sentence as necessarily true:

If it is a camera then it has a lens.

The experimenter would ask the subject to suppose that he could know only one fact concerning either the first or second part of the sentence. He would be asked to consider:

(i) an object that was a camera (TA)
(ii) an object that was not a camera (FA)
(iii) an object that had a lens (TC)
(iv) an object that did not have a lens (FC)

In each case, he would be asked 'Would it be necessary in this case to look for additional information in order to find out whether the statement is true or false?' Subjects were also asked to give reasons.

Van Duyne claimed that there were significantly more correct answers in the contingency condition than in the necessity condition, in line with his prediction. However, he only scored a correct selection, e.g. FC, as 'correct' if the subject *gave the right reason for selecting it*. Pollard and Evans (1981) re-analysed his data in terms of the raw selection frequencies and found no differences at all between the conditions. Thus Van Duyne's procedure has affected not the selection of cards, but the verbal justifications that people offer for them. On closer inspection, his results arise almost entirely from people giving falsifying rather than verifying explanations for the choice of TA.

Van Duyne's results are best explained in terms of the dual process theory (cf. Wason and Evans, 1975 and Chapter 12 of this book). It is quite reasonable to suppose that a procedure might affect the verbal justification process, rather than the selection process. It is also not surprising that subjects rarely envisage a falsifying consequence of selecting TA when they believe the rule always to be true. It would be more interesting if the truth status of the rule affected the actual selections themselves. Pollard and Evans (1981) decided to give this a stronger test by repeating Van Duyne's experiment with some additional conditions. Subjects were asked to construct sentences that were:

(1) Always true.
(2) Sometimes true.
(3) Sometimes false.
or (4) Always false.

The crucial variable proved to be truth status (true v. false) rather than contingency (sometimes v. always). The card selection frequencies, pooled over the contingency variable, are shown in

Table 9.5. Although antecedent selections are unaffected, consequent choices show considerable logical improvement for sentences constructed to be *false*. The increase in FC selections was highly significant, although the drop in TC selections fell just short of significance.

TABLE 9.5   *Percentage frequency of card selections in the Pollard and Evans (1980) experiment.*

Card	TA	FA	TC	FC
TRUE SENTENCES	94	46	92	61
FALSE SENTENCES	92	42	79	87

Van Duyne's cognitive self-reinforcement might be used to explain this effect, but Pollard and Evans put forward an alternative associational explanation. If the subject believes *If p then q* to be true, then he will have learned a positive association between p and q, as in 'If it is a cat then it has whiskers'. When he believes a sentence to be false, he knows that if p is the case then q will *not* be, so p and q are negatively associated, as in 'If it is a cat then it can talk'. Thus, Pollard and Evans suggest that selections are mediated by strong TA-TC but weak TA-FC associations on true sentences. On false sentences the TA-TC association is weaker and the TA-FC association stronger.   The associational theory has the advantage of offering an explanation of the matching bias normally observed in the abstract task. When there is no semantic context to bring associations from real-life experience to bear, it may be that the strongest associational bias arises from the joint mention of two particular cards in the rule. Thus a p-q association might form regardless of the presence of negatives and the logical status of these selections.

Pollard (1979a) carried out several experiments which attempt to manipulate the nature of the associations formed in the abstract selection task, by prior training. Subjects were given a kind of probability learning task in which the likelihood of letter-number combinations was varied. For example, a subject might learn from repeated exposure to a pack of cards that an A usually or always has a 2 on the back. If he is subsequently given the rule 'If there is an A on one side of the card then there is a 2 on the other', and told that the four cards have been selected from the pack that he was trained on, this can be regarded as a 'true' rule. In this way it is possible to give people rules which are always or usually true or false, on the basis of their experimental experience. This permits a strong test of the associational theory, since the true rules are produced by training a TA-TC association, and the false ones by training a TA-FC association.

When affirmative-only rules were trained and tested the results were rather unclear, possibly due to competing matching associations which are thought to be strong on abstract rules. However, in one experiment Pollard also used rules with negative components. When matching was balanced by pooling across rules the associational predictions were confirmed. Subjects tested on false sentences selected significantly more FC and significantly less TC cards than those tested on true sentences. There was also a tendency to select less TA and more FA in the 'false' condition, although only the former was significant. These trends on antecedent selection, which Pollard claimed to be consistent with the associational theory, seem to preclude a rationalist explanation of the consequent effect. One cannot simply explain the latter as increased logical performance under falsity – the antecedent selections are becoming *less* logical.

Clearly on the selection task, as on syllogisms, the truth status of the sentences used affects people's performance. Very little work has so far been conducted, but already a theoretical divide has appeared between the relatively rationalist theory of Van Duyne, and the non-rational learning theory approach of Pollard. The associational theory will be examined further in Chapters 10 and 11.

Conclusions

It is arguable that research based on the Wason selection task has been more productive of psychologically interesting findings and theories than work with any other reasoning paradigm. The experiments have shown an extraordinary capability for illogical reasoning in intelligent adults. Subjects have been shown to maintain blatant self-contradictions and to treat simple stimulus cards as though their logical significance depended upon which way up they happen to be lying. Evidence has also been produced to suggest that the processes by which subjects select cards are quite separate from those which underlie verbal evaluations and justifications.

The selection task has stimulated construction of rival models postulating states of insight on the one hand and stochastic processes on the other. More generally, it has provided scope for theories based on rationalistic and non-rationalistic principles. The task has been the focus of recent attempts to look at the role of content in reasoning, with regard to both thematic facilitation and truth-status effects. It has proved remarkably well suited to the manipulation of experimental variables to test a whole range of theoretical ideas about thinking and reasoning.

The secret of the success of the selection task has been in what Wason (1969b) terms its structural simplicity and psychological complexity. The psychological complexity of the processes it evokes is extraordinary, but its structural simplicity facilitates the design of experiments to investigate their nature, and aids the clear construction of theoretical explanations. The broader ramifications of theoretical ideas inspired by people's behaviour on the selection task are considerable. These will contribute strongly to the discussion of general theoretical perspectives in the psychology of reasoning, which forms the last part of this book.

10 Disjunctive reasoning

Disjunctives have received far less attention than conditionals in experimental studies of reasoning. The studies that have been carried out nevertheless provide some interesting data of relevance to the theoretical issues which have arisen in the work on conditional inference. One aspect relates to the interpretational component of reasoning. All disjunctives can be expressed as logically equivalent conditionals. Exclusive disjunctives translate as equivalences, and inclusive disjunctives as implications. Thus, *Either p or q but not both* has the same truth table as *If and only if not p then q*, whereas *Either p or q or both* has the same truth table as *If not p then q*, assuming a two-valued logic (see Table 10.1).

It was argued in Chapter 8 that where two linguistic forms exist to denote the same logical relationship, they probably relate to different contexts in natural language usage. Evidence was presented to support this hypothesis in the case of 'If . . . then. . .' and '. . . only if. . .' sentences. What, then, might the distinct linguistic usage of conditionals and disjunctives be? One way of approaching this question is to examine some examples of 'natural' disjunctives and conditionals, and then construct them in their alternative form. This is done in Table 10.1. Two natural examples of an affirmative disjunctive are given with equivalent conditional formulations, and vice versa.

In the first two cases disjunctives of the form *Either p or q* are replaced by conditionals of the form *If not p then q*. It appears that the negative conditional is a perfectly reasonable alternative that could be used in natural language. Also, the addition of 'and only if' does not seem necessary to clarify meaning. The semantic cues that distinguish exclusive from inclusive readings of the disjunctive

TABLE 10.1   *Formal equivalence of disjunctives and conditionals*

Either p or q (or both) ⟷ *If not p then q*

Eg.   Either D or 7 or both
       If not D then 7

Truth table

	Disjunctive	Conditional	Truth Value
D7	TT	FT	T
D3	TF	FF	T
G7	FT	TT	T
H6	FF	TF	F

Either p or q (but not both) ⟷ *If and only if not p then q*

E.g.   Either T or 2 but not both
        If and only if not T then 2

Truth table

	Disjunctive	Conditional	Truth Value
T2	TT	FT	F
T6	TF	FF	T
B2	FT	TT	T
J7	FF	FF	F

seem also to distinguish equivalence from implication readings of the conditional. In the last two examples, conditionals of the form *If p then q* are replaced by disjunctives of the form *Either not p or q*. In this case the negative disjunctive does *not* appear to be acceptable as an alternative formulation of the affirmative conditional. Whilst it is possible to interpret a sentence such as 'Either it is not a dog or it is an animal', it hardly strikes one as a likely statement to occur in natural language.

Evans (1972a) claimed that disjunctives, unlike conditionals, are rarely formulated in natural language with negative components. This leads to a prediction of interpretational difficulty with such sentences, a hypothesis that will be borne in mind in the following review of experimental work. Let us, however, return to the acceptable alternatives of affirmative disjunction/negative conditional. Are there subtle contextual cues that might determine preference of usage in natural language? We saw in Chapter 2 that subjects

TABLE 10.2   *Natural uses of conditionals and disjunctives and their logical equivalents*

Natural form	Logical equivalent
Exclusive disjunctive A candidate for election to parliament must either poll more than 15 per cent of the vote or lose his deposit.	If (and only if) a candidate for election to parliament does not poll more than 15 per cent of the vote then he must lose his deposit.
Inclusive disjunction Students on the MSc programme must either hold a good honours degree or an equivalent professional qualification.	If students on the MSc programme do not hold a good honours degree then they must have an equivalent professional qualification.
Conditional equivalence If a person has a Y chromosome then that person is male	Either a person does not have a Y chromosome or that person is male (but not both).
Conditional implication If it is a dog then it is an animal.	Either it is not a dog or it is an animal.

regard the conditional as *directional*. Given *If p then q* they tend to reason from the supposition of *p* to the conclusion of *q*, and to regard the rule as 'irrelevant' to situations in which the antecedent condition is not fulfilled. In the disjunctive formulation *Either p or q* there may be some extra emphasis on the item mentioned first, but the rule appears far more symmetrical than the conditional. Perhaps, then, the disjunctive formulation is preferred when there is no wish to emphasise a direction of inference.

Looking again at the first example in Table 10.2. we may feel that the conditional formulation is actually *more* natural here, since a temporal connection is envisaged. First a candidate fails to poll 15 per cent and *then* he loses his deposit. The conditional equivalent referring to the events in reverse order would not be acceptable. 'If a candidate for election to parliament does not lose his deposit then he does not poll more than 15 per cent of the vote'. The disjunctive here would also read oddly if reversed. Perhaps the 'Either . . . or. . .' form would be chosen in a situation where the relation between the events represented by *p* and *q* is quite symmetrical.

Consider 'People are eligible to vote if they are either residents of the city or rate-paying businessmen.' An equivalent conditional formulation would be 'If people who are eligible to vote are not residents of the city then they are rate-paying businessmen.' Although this formulation might be meaningful in some contexts, it seems an odd way to define eligibility of voters.

Just as people rarely use 'If and only if' to distinguish equivalence readings of conditionals in natural language, so it is unlikely that they will say 'or both' or 'but not both' to qualify a disjunctive, unless the context is unclear. Thus a disjunctive *Either p or q* presented in an abstract reasoning task, without context, will be ambiguous in just the same way as the conditional *If p then q* is (cf. Chapter 8).

These preliminary linguistic considerations lead to several hypotheses about disjunctive reasoning performance on artificial tasks:

(1)   Subjects will have difficulty interpreting negative disjunctive rules, with a consequent increase in logical errors.

(2)   Inferences associated with either component of a disjunctive will be relatively symmetrical compared with conditional inferences.

(3)   In the absence of context the sentence from *Either p or q* will be ambiguous with respect to inclusion/exclusion.

The comparison of disjunctive with conditional reasoning is also important with respect to the two-factor theory of reasoning (Evans, 1972a; 1977a) which has been used to interpret the conditional reasoning work reviewed in the last two chapters. In the original formulation (Evans, 1972a), it was claimed that the operational component (non-logical response biases) was independent of the linguistic formulation of the rule. This would seem to predict that effects such as negative conclusion bias, and matching bias, should be observed on disjunctives as well as conditionals; however, there is a complication. These 'response biases' have been demonstrated on conditionals by manipulating the presence of negative components. If, as predicted by hypothesis (1) above, this manipulation also disrupts the interpretational component where disjunctives are concerned, the effects of response bias will be confounded with interpretational shifts. Bearing this problem in mind, we will now look at the experimental work.

Disjunctive inference

The question of interpretational difficulties of the single negative disjunctive – *Either p or not q* or *Either not p or q* – was considered by Evans (1972d; see also Wason, 1977a). In one of the experiments of Evans (1972d) premises of this form were included as part of a test of *reductio ad absurdum* reasoning. The subjects reported great difficulty in making sense of such sentences. Similar observations were made by the subjects of Johnson-Laird and Tridgell (1972), whose subjects had problems of the form:

(1)   *Either p or else q, not q*, therefore?
(2)   *Either p or else not q, q*, therefore?

In either case the conclusion *p* is valid. Subjects make it significantly more often when the problem is expressed in form (1). Johnson-Laird and Tridgell suggest that this is due to the fact that a contradiction of an affirmative by a negative is easier to perceive than vice versa. Evans (1972a) argued that it could alternatively be due to the interpretational difficulty of the negative disjunctive used in the second form. This is substantiated by the observation that the contradiction effect is not observed in studies of conditional inference, for example on the modus tollens inference.

These sorts of distinction can only be sorted out by examination of a full range of inferences on rules with systematic permutation of negatives. The possible inferences, equivalent to MP, DA, AC, MT on the conditional, are shown in Table 10.3. There are two types of inference; T-F in which the truth of one component implies the falsity of the other, and F-T in which the falsity of one component implies the truth of the other. The direction of inference is distinguished in the table, e.g. T1-F2 denotes an inference from the truth of the first component to the falsity of the second. Now, regardless of direction, F-T inferences are valid for all disjunctives, but T-F inferences are valid only if *exclusive* disjunction is assumed.

Subjects' tendencies to make these inferences with abstract materials has been investigated in a series of experiments by Roberge (1974; 1976a; 1976b; 1978). We can assess the evidence for the hypotheses presented in the introduction to this chapter with respect to his data. First of all, we consider the effect of negative rule components on performance. Roberge's data are shown in Table

TABLE 10.3　*Possible inferences from disjunctive rules*

	Inference							
	T1–F2*		T2–F1*		F1–T2		F2–T1	
Rule	Given	Conclude	Given	Conclude	Given	Conclude	Given	Conclude
Either p or q	p	not q	q	not p	not p	q	not q	p
Either p or not q	p	q	not q	not p	not p	not q	q	p
Either not p or q	not p	not q	q	p	p	q	not q	not p
Either not p or not q	not p	q	not q	p	p	not q	q	not p

* Valid only if exclusive disjunction is assumed.

10.4. according to whether subjects are instructed to adopt exclusive or inclusive interpretation of the rules. It is clear that in either case the affirmative rule is easiest. However, the inclusive and exclusive problems reveal different patterns. On exclusive problems the double-negative rule, *Either not p or q*, is easier than the rules which have just one negative component. On inclusive problems the difficulty of the double-negative rules is similar to that of single-negative rules.

TABLE 10.4　*Percentage errors on different disjunctive rules on the Roberge studies*

Rule	Exclusive			Inclusive		
	2	3	4	1	2	4
Either p or q	16	13	7	39	31	16
Either p or not q	50	56	63	56	48	49
Either p or not q	63	55	52	59	57	53
Either not p or not q	24	31	36	51	51	59

Key　1 Roberge (1974)　2 Roberge (1976a)
　　　3 Roberge (1976b)　4 Roberge (1978)

The simplest interpretation of these results is as follows: (1) a disjunctive with one negative is linguistically unnatural, and consequently leads to interpretational confusion and high error rates, and (ii) the double-negative disjunctive tends to be converted into an affirmative form. That is, the subject given *Either not p or not q* drops the negatives, and treats it as though it were *Either p or q*.

The evidence for conversion of a double negative lies in its differential difficulty with inclusive and exclusive disjunctive instructions. Under exclusive disjunction the double negative is *logically equivalent* to the affirmative. If the rule is exclusive, all the inferences shown in Table 10.3 are valid. It will be seen that any inference made on the affirmative rule must also be made on the double-negative rule (e.g. Given *p*, Conclude *not q*). If instructions are given to interpret the rules inclusively, however, dropping the negatives would lead the subject into error. Hence, the subject can avoid the difficulty of the double negative by conversion, but only with exclusive instructions. There is no easy means of avoiding the difficulty of single negatives, in either condition.

Roberge's results are consistent with one of the hypotheses concerning the interpretational component of disjunctive reasoning. A second hypothesis was of symmetry. The frequency of T-F or F-T inferences should not be affected by the direction of inference between first and second components. Roberge (1976b) provides some relevant data for exclusive disjunction problems, on which both T-F and F-T inferences are valid. The direction of reasoning did, in fact, interact significantly with type of inference made. Over all rules the percentage of errors was: T1-F2 38 per cent; T2-F1, 44 per cent; F1-T2, 36 per cent; F2-T1, 40 per cent. Thus it seems that there is some advantage in reasoning forwards – from first to second component – particularly on T-F inferences. The difference is quite small, however, compared with the MP/MT difference on conditionals. The third interpretational hypothesis – ambiguity of inclusive/exclusive interpretation – cannot be assessed in Roberge's studies, since interpretation was instructed.

Let us now consider the evidence for response-bias effects in these tasks. Recall that on the equivalent conditional-reasoning tasks there is evidence for a bias to endorse inferences with negative conclusions (see Chapter 8). Inspection of Table 10.3 reveals that each logical inference is associated sometimes with an affirmative and sometimes with a negative conclusion. Roberge (1976b; 1978) has looked at the evidence for negative-conclusion bias. The analysis shown by Roberge (1976b) is potentially confusing since he presented the subjects with the *opposite* of correct conclusions on half the problems – to which a correct answer is a denial. However, if we look at problems where the subject is asked to evaluate the actual conclusion of the argument, which is similar to Evans's (1977a) method on conditionals, then there is a tendency to make more correct T-F inferences when the conclusion that must be endorsed is negative (69 per cent) rather than affirmative (49 per cent), but no effect on F-T inferences. Roberge (1978) argues that the claim by Evans (1977a) that there exists a bias to negative conclusions does not generalise to disjunctives, although he does find evidence for it on conditionals ('If – then' and 'only if'). However, in this experiment he looked only at F-T inferences on the disjunctives.

When the disjunctive data are taken into account the evidence of a general negative-conclusion bias is not very substantial. What *is* clear is the tendency to make more inferences which deny affirmative rather than negative components.

Consider the following valid inferences:

> *MT conditional*
> (1)   If the letter is not A then the number is 7
> (2)   the number is not 7
> Therefore, the letter is A
> *T-F disjunctive*
> (1)   Either the letter is not A or the number is 7
> (2)   the number is 7
> Therefore, the letter is A

Each of these has been found empirically hard for subjects, who tend to say that the conclusion does not follow. This could well arise from a double negative (cf. Chapter 8). In order to reach the affirmative conclusion 'The letter is A' the subject must first infer that 'not A' cannot be the case. This 'operational' difficulty could account for the preference for negative conclusions on inferences involving denial. The assertion that negative conclusions are preferred on *all* inferences (Evans, 1977a) was based on the analysis of AC inference rate. That finding could, perhaps, be explained as in interpretational effect, if subjects are more inclined to treat a conditional as an equivalence if it has a negative antecedent. This hypothesis receives some support from consideration of truth-table data as well (see Chapter 8).

The examination of disjunctive inference studies seems, then, to refine the analysis of response-bias tendencies on the conditional task. However, two cautionary notes must be sounded: (i) Pollard (1979a) has provided extensive analysis to support and extend the original conclusion biases claimed on conditionals; and (ii) it seems that the introduction of negatives into the disjunctive disrupts the interpretational component of performance, in addition to any effect that it may have on response biases. Further consideration about the nature of disjunctive inference should await the inspection of data from other reasoning paradigms.

Disjunctive selection task and truth-table task

Van Duyne (1973; 1974) has criticised the explanation of aspects of conditional reasoning performance in terms of 'matching bias', on the ground that this bias does not generalise to disjunctive reasoning problems. The evidence for his claim is a low frequency of p,q card selections when the Wason selection task is administered with a rule of the form *Either not p or q* (Van Duyne, 1974). However, matching bias has always been demonstrated as a statistical tend- ency when logical factors are held constant. One needs to compare rules in which the presence of negative components is varied.

The only selection-task experiment that provides any relevant data is that of Wason and Johnson-Laird (1969). They administered the task with an affirmative rule *Either p or q* and a negative rule *Either not p or q*, using appropriate abstract material; e.g. 'Every card either has a number which is (isn't) Roman on one side, or it has a letter which is capital on the other side.' The procedure contained some unusual features, such as a restriction on the num- ber of cards that could be selected, and a set to believe that the rule was true or false. Subjects were not specifically told to interpret the rule inclusively, although aspects of the procedure implied this. The authors assume an inclusive definition for purposes of deciding 'correct' responses. Under such a definition the subject should choose cards which *falsify* each component (since F-T is the only valid type of inference). Thus on the affirmative rule subjects should choose $\bar{p}$ and $\bar{q}$, and on the negative rule p and $\bar{q}$.

If, as on the conditional selection task, there was a bias to select p and q (the matching values), one might expect the negative rule to be easier. In fact only 52 per cent chose correctly on this rule as compared with 75 per cent on the affirmative. Whilst this result appears to provide evidence against matching bias, we must bear in mind the confounding of interpretational effects. As noted earlier, the introduction of a single negative appears to confuse, and was associated with considerably more logical errors in the Roberge inference tasks.

Matching bias has been demonstrated not only on the conditional selection task, but also on conditional truth-table tasks. The first experiment in which it was observed (Evans, 1972b) was a truth-table construction task which was described in Chapter 8. Subjects were asked to construct exhaustive examples of verifying and falsifying cases, so that unconstructed cases could be inferred to be 'irrelevant'. Such non-constructions were strongly associated with mismatches between the items in the instance and those in the rule. Evans and Newstead (1980, Experiment I) repeated this experiment with disjunctives in place of conditionals, and all four permutations of affirmative/negative components. (Subjects were not instructed on the interpretation of exclusion/inclusion.) The only other change was in the materials which involved letter-number combinations. It was thought that an examination of initial constructions would give a particularly powerful test of the presence of matching bias in disjunctive reasoning. Consider the following rule:

Either the letter is a D,
or the number is not a 6.

The subject asked to construct verifying examples of this rule should include a TF and an FT case, regardless of whether he interprets it inclusively or exclusively. TF is produced by matching both components, D6, whereas FT requires a double mismatch, e.g. L3. Thus one would expect that even if the subject were to construct both, he would tend to think of the matching case first. No such tendency was observed. A curious feature of this experiment was a large proportion of contradictory responses, that is constructing the same logical case on *both* verifying and falsifying task. Not a single case of such contradiction was observed in the equivalent conditional reasoning experiment, although self-contradictions are not unusual in other experiments (see Wason, 1977). The subjects' protocols suggested the cause of contradiction on the disjunctive task. They would often claim that the rule was true provided that at least one component was true on the verifying task – which is fair enough if you assume inclusive disjunction. Some would also claim on the falsifying task that the rule was false if at least one component was false. This generalisation is only accurate if you take the rule to be a *conjunctive* (*p and q*). Consequently, the cases

TF and FT were classified as both verifying and falsifying the rule by some subjects.

While the absence of matching bias requires explanation, we will first look at the Evans and Newstead data in terms of the interpretational hypotheses about disjunctive reasoning. This is aided by a second experiment in which a truth-table evaluation task was used with a forced choice between 'true' and 'false'. This procedure was felt to be justified since the 'irrelevant' responses of the first experiment were relatively infrequent and evenly distributed across logical cases. There is no 'defective' truth table for disjunctives, unlike conditionals, and a two-valued logic seems appropriate. An advantage of this procedure was that it facilitated the collection of response latencies, which were divided into comprehension time (CT) and verification time (VT) by a similar procedure to that used by Evans and Newstead (1977). Some of the Evans and Newstead's (1980) data is summarised in Table 10.5.

TABLE 10.5   *Results from the study of Evans and Newstead (1980)*

	% correct*		Mean latency (Experiment II) (seconds)	
Rule	Experiment I	Experiment II	CT	VT
Either p or q	69	89	3.88	4.18
Either p or not q	46	77	4.35	6.23
Either not p or q	36	73	4.55	6.17
Either not p or not q	49	77	4.59	6.06

* Excluding the TT case.

Since subjects were not instructed on how to interpret the rule, the ambiguous TT case was excluded from the analysis of percentage correct. Classifications of this case were taken as an indication of whether subjects preferred an inclusive or exclusive reading. In both experiments a significant majority of true over false classifications was observed, suggesting a preference for an inclusive reading. This accords with the results of Paris (1973) but not those of Manktelow (1980), who found the reverse preference. In each study the rule clearly is ambiguous with considerable support for both readings.

The data presented in Table 10.5 support the conclusions following the examination of Roberge's disjunctive inference studies (Table 10.4). Negatives cause particular difficulty, especially when *one* negative only is present. The presence of a negative in either component interacts significantly in the analysis of variance of both frequency correct and response latency. This latter result contrasts with the additive effect of negatives on a conditional truth-table task (Evans and Newstead, 1977). Evans and Newstead's (1980) analyses also suggest that subjects may be converting the double-negative rule into an affirmative form, which could account for its lack of increasing difficulty on both frequency and latency measures. There is thus an encouraging convergence between the conclusions of the inference and truth table studies. This convergence in itself suggests that the effect of negatives is primarily interpretational.

What, however, has happened to matching bias? The bias appears not to be independent of linguistic structure, as proposed by Evans (1972a). Does this put the whole two-factor theory in jeopardy? I think not. Evans and Newstead point to two facts: (1) subjects' errors on the negative rules are consistent with a tendency to ignore the presence of negatives on all rules, at least in Experiment I. They tend to respond *as if* all rules were affirmative, which leads to more error on the single-negative rules than on the double negative. (2) Subjects' performance on all rules is well above chance rate which, for example, is 50 per cent in the forced-choice task of Experiment II.

Ignoring negatives is clearly non-logical, but the second observation equally clearly reveals a logical component. Matching bias can also be regarded as a tendency to ignore negatives, if we can explain why the bias to p and q should be there on the affirmatives. Evans and Newstead account for the apparent linguistic dependence of the matching effect in terms of the associational theory put forward by Pollard and Evans (1981b, cf. Chapter 9). The conditional form *If p then q*, from its everyday use, induces a set to expect a positive association of p and q. This induces a non-logical bias to focus on these values on abstract conditional-reasoning tasks. The disjunctive *Either p or q*, however, induces a set for *negative* association. 'Either/or' leads to an expectation of p without q or vice versa. Evans and Newstead find a clear bias to choose $p\bar{q}$ or $\bar{p}q$ as verifying cases when data from all rules tested in their first experiment are combined. They summarise the argument as follows:

On both conditionals and disjunctives, subjects succeed

partially in taking account of the negatives and arriving at the correct answers. To the extent that they fail they respond not randomly, but systematically with associational biases. These are positive in the case of conditionals but negative in the case of disjunctives.

The examination of disjunctive reasoning on both inference and truth-table tasks has, then, supported the two-factor theory, in that it appears necessary to postulate both an interpretational (logical) component and non-logical factors to explain performance. In each case, some discrepancies with behaviour on equivalent conditional reasoning tasks has led to re-analysis of the nature of the proposed response mechanisms, and facilitated explanation of their origin.

Thematic disjunctives

A recurring theme of interest in this book has been the effect of task content on reasoning performance. We have seen that thematic content may facilitate performance, but may also induce non-logical biases, particularly where beliefs and attitudes are concerned. Naturally, we should see what evidence pertinent to this has arisen in the study of disjunctive reasoning. Unfortunately, there are few such studies available.

Two studies permit the assessment of possible facilitation effects. Van Duyne (1974) compared selection-task performance with abstract rules such as:

A card doesn't have a P on one side,
or it has a 2 on the other side.

with concrete rules such as:

A student doesn't study French,
or he is at London.

There was no evidence of facilitation, with 5/24 solving the abstract form and 4/24 solving the thematic form. Roberge (1978), testing T-F and F-T inferences, looked at abstract and thematic disjunctives with all combinations of negatives, and with exclusive and inclusive formulations. An example of an affirmative inclusive thematic rule is:

Either Joan is athletic or she is rich
(or both).

Abstract rules referred to letters and numbers. His results contradict Van Duyne's in that facilitation did occur on single-negative rules, although not on affirmative or double-negative rules. This finding actually supports the view that the high error rates normally observed on single negative disjunctives are due to special interpretational difficulty. Presumably, when thematic content facilitates, it does so by aiding the operation of the interpretational component. In view of the studies reviewed in the last chapter, however, it is rather surprising that Roberge found any facilitation at all. His 'thematic' rules are quite arbitrary and placed in no semantic context.

Roberge (1977) has also looked at belief-bias effects with thematic disjunctives. He tested T-F and F-T inferences on affirmative inclusive rules, and with three types of content. Two of these, abstract and compatible thematic, were as used in the 1978 study. The third incompatible thematics provided disjunctions between items that were opposite in meaning e.g.

Either John is intelligent or he is
stupid (or both).

Roberge found that abstract and compatible materials produced similar performance, about 80 per cent correct on both inferences. However, the incompatible group showed marked differences. On the valid F-T inference performance rose to about 90 per cent but on the fallacious T-F inference it dropped to about 40 per cent. Since the T-F inference would be valid if the rule were an exclusive disjunction, the results are quite easy to explain. The incompatibility of the terms evidently imposed a *semantic* exclusiveness, which overrode the syntactic modifier 'or both'.

Another aspect of thematic materials considered previously (see Chapter 8) relates to the influence of context upon sentence interpretation. Springston and Clark (1973) claimed that the disjunctive *Either p or q* tends to be interpreted exclusively when used as a *pseudoimperative* as in the following:

Flip the switch or the fan goes on.

They tested this by presenting subjects with T-F and F-T inferences, and claimed evidence for the hypothesis since all tended to be endorsed. Unfortunately, this conclusion is unwarranted due to poor methodology. For example, a T-F inference might be tested by presenting the information that the switch is flipped and asking if the fan has gone on. The correct answer is 'can't say' but subjects were not given this alternative – they had to make a forced choice Yes or No. Faced with such a choice the subject has no option but to interpret the rule exclusively so that he can make a determinate (No) response. A comparable methodological error has been discussed in Chapter 8, in Taplin's conditional reasoning studies. Springston and Clark also fail to compare the use of disjunctives as pseudoimperatives with their use in other contexts.

The few available studies of thematic disjunctives discussed above provide evidence reasonably compatible with that from the more thoroughly investigated syllogistic and conditional reasoning tasks. One recent study, however, has produced most unexpected results. Manktelow (1980) using a truth-table evaluation task, compared abstract and thematic disjunctives, including rules with negative components. Examples of his rules were:

Abstract
Either there is a T on one side
or a 3 on the other.

Thematic
Either I eat chicken or I drink brandy.

The instances were written on cards for the subject to evaluate. Hence a TF case would be T7 or chicken, wine. With abstract disjunctives, Manktelow found a pattern of results similar to those of Evans and Newstead (1980), except that subjects tended towards an exclusive interpretation. With thematics the patterns changed entirely. Subjects showed a massive tendency to classify all double mismatches $\bar{p}\bar{q}$ as irrelevant, regardless of the presence of negatives. In total contrast to abstract disjunctives, the thematics appear to have induced a strong matching bias, although Manktelow offers an interpretational explanation. Manktelow also looked at 'if . . . then', and ' . . . only if . . .' conditionals. In each case the extent of matching bias, observed in the abstract form, significantly increased with the food and drinks material.

These findings are some of the most dramatic reported on the effect of content on reasoning. One is tempted to speculate that 'matching bias' has a perceptual basis and is facilitated by the use of 'imageable' concrete content. However, there may be something peculiar about the food and drink context. It will be recalled from the last chapter that this particular content produced an unrepresentative lack of facilitation on the Wason selection task (Manktelow and Evans, 1979). It may be that subjects bring particular presuppositions about meals to bear in this task. Replication of Manktelow's results with a variety of other thematic content is necessary before too much importance is attached to these results.

The THOG problem

Before concluding this survey of disjunctive inference, we will look at some work on a problem recently devised by Wason, which involves the logic of exclusive disjunction (Wason, 1977a; 1978; Wason and Brooks, 1979). Like the selection task, 'THOG' is a metainference task, that requires the formulation and testing of hypotheses, in addition to an ability to understand logical relationships. The subject is shown four designs: a blue diamond, a red diamond, a blue circle, and a red circle (see Figure 10.1).

The instructions used by Wason and Brooks are as follows:

In front of you are four designs: Blue Diamond, Red Diamond, Blue Circle and Red Circle.

You are to assume that I have written down one of the colours (blue or red) and one of the shapes (diamond or circle). Now read the following rule carefully:

If, and only if, any of the designs includes either the colour I have written down, or the shape I have written down, but not both, then it is called a THOG.

I will tell you that the Blue Diamond is a THOG.

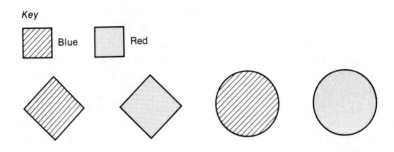

FIGURE 10.1   The four coloured shapes used in the THOG problem

Each of the designs can now be classified into one of the following
categories:
A) Definitely is a THOG.
B) Insufficient information to decide.
C) Definitely is not a THOG.

The correct answer is that red diamond and the blue circle cannot
be THOGS, and the red circle must be a THOG. As on the selection
task (i) the correct solution is infrequently found when student
populations are tested and (ii) there is a characteristic 'intuitive
error' which many subjects offer instead.

   In order to find the correct solution, one must first of all generate
the possible rules as hypotheses. Since the blue diamond is a THOG
the experimenter must have written down either its colour or its
shape but not both. Hence, he must have adopted one of the following two rules:

   R1   A THOG is either **BLUE** or **CIRCLE**,
        but not both.
   R2   A THOG is either **RED** or **DIAMOND**,
        but not both.

   Only these two rules would define blue diamond as a THOG.
The next step is to examine the remaining three designs and ask
how the rules R1 and R2 would classify them. Under R1, the red
diamond cannot be a THOG because it has neither named attribute, and the blue circle cannot be a THOG because it has both.

The red circle must, however, be a THOG because it has one attribute (shape). If we now follow R2, we are forced to the same classifications. Red diamond cannot be a THOG because it has both attributes, and blue circle cannot be a THOG because it has neither. Again the red circle *is* because it has one attribute (colour). So whichever rule the experimenter adopted the classifications are the same.

Most subjects do not succeed in finding this answer. Of the 56 tested by Wason and Brooks (1979), for example, only 17 solved it, despite the introduction of various procedures designed to aid its understanding. Why is it so difficult? It seems unlikely that it is due to a failure to appreciate the logic of exclusive disjunction, for two reasons. Firstly, subjects show a low error rate when asked to draw inferences from such a rule, provided, as in the THOG problem, it is expressed affirmatively (see Table 10.4). Secondly, Wason and Brooks asked subjects in one experiment to construct the truth table of an analogous rule before attempting the THOG problem. They had to devise a rule of the same sort – exclusive disjunctive – and indicate what patterns could or could not conform to it. All subjects were able to do this correctly, but performed no better on the subsequent THOG than a control group. There is a direct analogy here to the paradoxical findings on the selection task that subjects can all correctly evaluate the logical consequences of turning cards, but requiring them to do so exerts limited transfer on to a subsequent selection task (cf. Chapter 9). Wason and Brooks also tested the possibility that subjects are unable to complete the first step of the correct solution: generation of possible rules that the experimenter could be using. When asked to do this, 9 out of 14 were spontaneously correct and the others had to be coached. However, there was again no benefit of this procedure on a subsequent THOG problem, as compared with control.

As on the selection task, the combined requirement both to generate hypotheses and evaluate their logical consequences appears to defeat most subjects. On the selection task the 'intuitive error' is characterised as matching bias. What is the intuitive error on THOG? It consists of a tendency to say that red circle *cannot* be a THOG, whereas the red diamond, and blue circle are either indeterminate or else *are* THOGS. The characteristic error tends, then, to reverse the correct solution.

Wason's (1978) explanation of this characteristic error sounds very like matching bias. He states that, 'The basic conceptual difficulty with the THOG problem is that the person trying to solve it has to detach the notion of possible pairs of defining features away from the actual designs which exhibit those features.' The point is that if the hypothesised rule is say red or diamond, then the design containing both these features, the red diamond, 'counter-intuitively', *cannot* be a THOG. This might account for subjects' failure to state that the red diamond and blue circle cannot be THOGS. The failure to see that the red circle must be, and indeed to say that it *cannot* be a THOG, seems best explained in terms of what Bruner, Goodnow and Austin (1956) call the 'common element fallacy'. Bruner *et al.*, in a study of disjunctive concept attainment, found that subjects tended to assume that two members of the same category should have a common feature. This 'rule' obviously fails when the category is defined as exclusive disjunction. This explanation is also akin to matching bias.

The THOG problem is relatively new and little investigated. It is, however, useful to have an alternative structurally simple task which has so many characteristics in common with the selection task. It is worthy of further investigation, but if it is to gain equivalent success to the selection task conditions must be found under which subjects *can* achieve reasonable logical performance.

Conclusions

Studies of disjunctive reasoning have revealed a number of parallels to those of conditional reasoning. For example, reasoning performance is subject to the influence of similar content variables. There also appears to be a mixture of logical success and non-logical biases demonstrated on abstract tasks. However, the formulation of disjunctives with negative components does appear to be less linguistically natural than a similar treatment of conditionals. Thus the introduction of negative components leads to high logical error rates unless, as on double-negative exclusive rules, the subject can avoid the problem by conversion into an affirmative form.

The absence of matching bias on the abstract disjunctive truth-table tasks has led Evans and Newstead (1980) to postulate that the bias may be dependent on the linguistic content set by the conditional. However, there are some points on which to defend a more general concept of matching. Firstly, the technique by which matching is measured on conditionals – introduction of negative components – causes confusion of interpretation with disjunctives. When interpretation is aided by the use of thematic content, (Manktelow, 1979) matching returns with a vengeance. Secondly, when dealing with a disjunctive problem, THOG, which is analogous in its psychological complexity to the selection task, the characteristic intuitive error appears to result from a feature-matching tendency. More general theoretical arguments for retaining the notion of a general matching bias will be presented in the next chapter.

Part IV

Discussion

11 On explaining the results of reasoning experiments

We have now completed the main review of recent experimental research employing deductive reasoning paradigms. The task of this chapter is to draw together the various findings, consider explanations of the main factors that have emerged, and assess the usefulness of various general theoretical approaches. In Chapter 12, the dual process theory of reasoning, arising from work on the selection task (Chapter 9), will be examined in detail, together with its broader implications.

Let us start with a brief résumé of the material covered in the review. In part I, the focus was on relatively simple reasoning tasks in which response latency is the primary measure of interest. In both sentence verification (Chapter 3) and transitive inference tasks (Chapter 4) most authors agree on a general sequential model of reasoning, with a representation stage followed by a process stage. In both cases, much interest has been focused on linguistic factors which are thought to influence the representation of sentences used in the problems. The *format* of representation – propositional versus imagery-based – has also been an issue, particularly in transitive inference. However, in line with other fields of cognitive psychology, this debate has proved somewhat intractable, if not futile.

One important conclusion of the work reviewed in Part I was that, despite the importance of linguistic factors in the comprehension process, no satisfactory explanation of even simple reasoning tasks can be attempted without consideration of the processing requirements of the task itself. Such a conclusion will *a fortiori* apply to the more complex tasks involved in syllogistic (Part II) and propositional (Part III) reasoning. Two important differences exist between the types of study involved in these later sections and those

211

of Part I. One is behavioural. In the later experiments the nature of subjects' responses is much more varied, and becomes the dependent of variable of main interest. The other difference lies in the origin of the problems, and has had a profound influence on the construction of theories. For the experiments discussed in Parts II and III there is always a system of formal logic within which to describe the problem structure.

The dominant issue in Parts II and III has been the presence or absence of logical reasoning processes. It is perhaps a concern with *rationality* which has most distinguished the psychology of reasoning from other fields of cognitive psychology (with one important exception to be considered below). In general, cognitive psychology is concerned with the cognitive mechanisms underlying behaviour. The problem is to understand the organisation of the brain as an information-processing system. For example, in memory research people argue about how many types of memory store exist, how they are accessed, how they are connected to one another, etc. One does not assess the behaviour by some predefined normative system specifying what is rational. In a sense, rationality in the behaviour is implicitly assumed. Although the processes of perception, memory, etc. are constrained by the nature of the cognitive mechanisms available, such mechanisms have presumably evolved in an adaptive manner. There would be little survival value in mechanisms which produced a highly inaccurate representation of the real world.

This *pragmatic* notion of rationality is, however, very different from the *normative* type provided by logic, and it will be argued that the pragmatic notion is more appropriate also to the explanation of reasoning behaviour. Adaptive behaviour may, of course, arise from individual learning as well as from the evolution of mechanisms. The assumption that logicality corresponds to rationality in the pragmatic sense is highly disputable. There is not one but many alternative systems of formal logic. Even 'standard' logic is highly simplified compared with the subtle complexities of natural language. Also, there is no necessary reason why people should benefit from a logical assessment of arguments, and hence have learned to do it. The identification of formal logicality with rationality is, therefore, extremely dubious.

Many of the 'logical' theorists – including those influenced by Henle – postulate underlying mechanisms in the form of representation and process models. I would argue that the nature of the mechanisms proposed is motivated *not* primarily by a desire to explain the observed behaviour, but by a wish to see the subjects' behaviour as rationally determined (this motivation has been demonstrated repeatedly in Parts II and III of this book). If formal logic provides the criterion for rationality, then this exercise is unlikely to be very useful.

There is, of course, no argument about the fact that the observed *behaviour* on syllogistic and propositional reasoning tasks is frequently illogical. What is interesting, though, is the number of factors which appear to affect reasoning performance. These include the linguistic structure of the sentences used to express a logical relation, influences of context and content, and various apparently non-logical features of the tasks used. The theoretical task is to explain why people behave as they do on these tasks – regardless of logicality – and to infer something about the cognitive mechanisms and processes involved.

In the Introduction (Chapter 1) it was stated that one objective of the book was to place reasoning research in the general context of cognitive psychology. So far this has been attempted in detail only in Part I. In order to achieve this objective for the later work, we must forget the issue of logicality for the time being, and look at the structure of the tasks. There seem to be two alternative general frameworks into which these tasks could be placed – *problem-solving* and *decision-making*. A brief consideration of the main features of each approach is required in order to consider their applications to reasoning research.

Problem-solving or decision-making?

The most influential theory of problem-solving in contemporary psychology is that of Newell and Simon (1972; for recent developments see Simon, 1979). Their theory is derived from work in artificial intelligence, and in some cases they write actual computer programs to simulate the behaviours they are concerned with. Their approach is content-oriented in that they begin with a detailed *task analysis*, in order to specify how the problem may be represented internally, and what strategies may be appropriate to its solution. Psychological difficulty is seen to arise either through inadequate representation of the task environment or through the application of inappropriate strategies. An important concept in this approach is that of *problem space* (also called search space). This consists of an initial state, one or more goal states and a set of possible intermediate states. Problem-solving is thus defined as a search through the problem space for a solution path, leading from initial to goal states.

In order to illustrate the application of this approach to reasoning, let us consider the Wason selection task (cf. Chapter 9). Task analysis would indicate that the possible combinations of values on either side of the card should be considered, and their effect on the truth value of the rule evaluated in order to solve the problem. Unlike the problems studied by Newell and Simon (1972) the possibilities are very few, so an exhaustive construction and search of the problem space should be very easy. The full problem space is shown in Figure 11.1 (a). Each card is considered, together with either logical value that can appear on the back of it. Each of the eight paths is then evaluated for its effect on the truth value of the rule – in Figure 11.1 a defective truth table is assumed. If subjects understand the falsification principle, they should choose only those cards which have a path leading to 'false' evaluation – i.e. p and $\bar{q}$.

This much is task analysis. Now, how do we explain a common error pattern such as p, q? Wason (1966) proposed that subjects attempt to verify rather than falsify. If they search the correct problem space (Figure 11.1 (a)), but with this faulty principle, they will choose p and q since only these lead to a 'true' evaluation. An alternative cause of error is in the construction of the problem space. When Johnson-Laird and Wason (1970) claim that subjects without insight focus on the named values, they are in effect suggesting a restricted problem space as shown in Figure 11.1 (b). In this space subjects only search branches starting with the cards p and q. The two characteristic errors of subjects with 'no insight' are to choose p alone or else to choose p and q. Inspection of the problem space in Figure 11.1 (b) would favour the hypothesis that the former apply only a falsification principle, whereas the latter are looking for verifying and falsifying cards. Johnson-Laird and Wason – who did not refer to such a problem space explicitly – gave another explanation for the difference, which was internally inconsistent (see Chapter 9). Under partial insight or complete insight subjects are supposed to consider all cards, i.e. switch to the full search space. The difference between the two would again lie in the use of

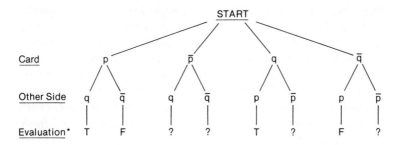

(a) Full problem space

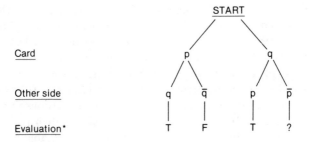

(b) Limited problem space

FIGURE 11.1   Possible problem spaces for the Wason selection task, for a rule of the form *If p then q*

*Assumes a defective truth table

verification and falsification principles – leading to p, q, $\bar{q}$, or the falsification principle alone – leading to p, $\bar{q}$.

The above analysis is not intended as a complete theoretical explanation of performance on the Wason selection task – indeed there are various aspects of the data for which it would not account. The point of the exercise is simply to illustrate the applicability of the problem-solving theory of Newell and Simon, and to show its main advantage – the distinction between errors of representation and errors of process or strategy.

The Henle hypothesis, which was evaluated in Parts II and III of this book, can be viewed within this framework. Essentially, the

Henle claim is that all reasoning errors arise during representation of the problem information, rather than in the execution of strategies. The latter are assumed always to accord with formal logic. This highly restrictive use of the representation-process distinction seems to lack *a priori* justification, other than a belief in man's inherent logicality. Newell and Simon (1972) certainly regard difficulties in the application of appropriate search methods, rather than problem representation, to be the major cause of problem-solving difficulty.

The problem-solving approach assumes that subjects are attempting to solve the problem as instructed – what Newell and Simon call 'intendedly rational behaviour'. One of the problems with reasoning experiments is that instructions presuppose a knowledge of logic in their subjects. Subjects will be asked to decide whether a conclusion 'necessarily follows', for example, and the explicit use of the term 'logic' is not uncommon. This contrasts markedly with Newell and Simon's own 'logic' problems, in which subjects are given an explicit set of rules for manipulating logical symbols, and then asked to prove theorems. In these experiments, subjects are never told that the symbols represent logical relationships. The reasoning experiments described in this book are then really tests of the extent to which subjects understand, and are able to apply, logical principles. Because so much of the problem-definition is implicit, and left to the subject's understanding, it is relatively difficult to discover what problem space people may actually be using. Also, these experiments have not generally used 'thinking aloud' techniques, favoured by Newell and Simon to trace thought processes in individuals (more of this in Chapter 12). Finally, Newell and Simon's theories are not meant to apply to group data, which is the usual form in which reasoning results are presented. For all these reasons, a detailed problem-solving analysis of reasoning experiments – as currently conducted – is not likely to be very easy.

All reasoning experiments require a decision to be made. The subject is asked to decide whether a rule is true or false, given certain evidence, whether or not a conclusion follows logically, whether or not a card need be turned over. It is worth considering, then, what general principles have been developed to account for decision-making in general. *Decision theory*, as developed by economists and mathematicians, has many applications in psychology (see Lee, 1971; Slovic, Fischhoff and Lichtenstein, 1977). This is the other field in which rationality is a dominant issue. Here rationalism is defined not by logicality but by the principle of maximisation of utility (personal subjective gain). 'Rational man' is a fundamental concept in economic theory. Rational man considers the consequences of his possible lines of action, evaluates the chances and costs of various outcomes, and chooses in a manner maximally beneficial to himself. Various decision rules or strategies may be applied according to the situation. In risky choice – such as gambling – rational man maximises expected utility (i.e. chooses the outcome that would, on average, yield the largest gain). Under rational competition with another player, he may choose so as to minimise his maximum loss. For example, in a game of chess you should choose the move that gains you most on the assumption that your opponent chooses the best possible reply from his point of view.

The notion of rational choice is as easy – and as hard! – to dismiss as that of logical reasoning. Just as one can easily demonstrate that people reason illogically, so one can demonstrate that they choose gambles with objectively expected losses. The decision-making equivalent of the Henle hypothesis, however, postulates that people choose rationally, given their subjective interpretation of the world. For example, it is rational to bet on the football pools, if you either overestimate the chance of winning, or overvalue the prize money relative to the stake. For this reason, much interest has focused on the subjective understanding of chance and probability, which are distorted in many respects. In this area a theoretical approach based on non-rationalist principles has been developed, and this is of considerable relevance to reasoning research.

The important work is that initiated by Kahneman and Tversky (1972). They proposed that subjects' assessments of probability are based, not on an understanding of the mathematics of probability, but on certain 'heuristics' or short-cuts devices, which may lead to considerable inaccuracies. For example, if subjects are asked to assess the likelihood of a given set of statistical data, they are assumed to use a heuristic called *representativeness*. That is, they examine the degree to which salient characteristics of the sample, such as mean or proportion, match the corresponding characteristics of the parent population. In the process they ignore statistically relevant factors such as sample size. Another proposal is that subjective likelihood is related to the *availability* of items for retrieval from memory (Tversky and Kahneman, 1973). For example, the finding that people overestimate the likelihood of sensational causes of death, e.g. from aeroplane crashes (Lichtenstein *et al.*, 1978), could be due to disproportionate coverage of such events in the media, compared with common causes of death such as strokes.

If reasoning experiments are looked at in terms of decision theory, we need to ask what the utilities are for the decisions made. Anyone who has run such experiments knows that however subjects may be instructed to the contrary, they regard such experiments as tests of intelligence, and are frequently very concerned about how well they have performed. It is a fair assumption, then, that subjects choose in order to maximise their chance of being 'right'. The fact that they so frequently fail to do so must be attributed to an inability to understand the problem or to base their responses on a rational, i.e. logical, base. The two important questions arising are as follows: (i) why is subjects' logical competence apparently so limited and situation-dependent and (ii) if subjects' choices are not based on logic, on what are they based? The answer to the second question may well lie in the application of more or less appropriate heuristics, intended to maximise chances of success. Firstly, however, we consider the general notion of logical competence.

Logical competence

There are two ways of defining competence. The easy but uninteresting way is task-specific. People's competence to solve a given logical task can easily be assessed. However, the term 'logical competence' is normally used to define something much more abstract. It refers to a hypothetical system of logic which the individual 'possesses'. It implies a potential capability to perform any task whose logical structure is amenable to solution by the system. This does not mean that all such problems will be solved, however. The translation of competence into performance is subject to the operation of a performance system.

The competence/performance distinction was developed by Chomsky in his linguistic theories (see Chapter 2). In that case, a grammatical theory was seen as a description of the language user's competence. Production or understanding of language would however be subject to performance limitations such as memory capacity, which could cause, for example, ungrammatical (incompetent) utterances. The application of this distinction to logic and reasoning raises various problems. As in the linguistic context, the competence model does not constitute an empirically testable theory, unless the performance component is also fully specified. Since performance factors are liable to be task specific, they may not be easy to define *a priori*. There is also the question of the competence system itself: should it be based on formal logic, or on alternative 'natural' logic (see, for example, Braine, 1978)?

If formal logic is taken as the basis of the competence system, then this approach might be seen as another attempt to preserve the notion of logicality in the face of overtly illogical behaviour. In this case, the deviations are attributed to 'performance factors'. The latter might include various non-logical biases discussed in this book, e.g. a preference for negative conclusions (Chapter 8) or a bias to accept arguments whose conclusions you believe (Chapter 6).

The Evans two-factor reasoning theory could be interpreted in this framework *if* it were assumed that the logical component was task-independent; and the stochastic reasoning model (cf. Evans, 1977b; and Chapter 9) could be seen as a description of the way in which logical tendencies arising from competence combine with task-specific performance factors. Evidently, then, the preservation of logicality by this device is rather different from the much maligned (in this book) Henle approach. Although Henle did indeed assume that subjects possess a competence based on formal logic, she unnecessarily restricted the source of performance errors to the interpretational stage.

The important point about logical competence, whether formally or naturally based, is its independence of task content. This means that competence can never be assessed with reference to a given situation unless one knows *a priori* the nature and effect of all performance factors. The observation that a subject fails to give a correct answer to a modus tollens (MT) problem, for example, does not entitle one to say that this subject does not possess the competence to make MT. What is less often recognised is that giving the correct answer does not imply that the subject has the competence either; he may have guessed, or been induced to give a spuriously correct answer by a non-logical strategy, such as the alleged atmosphere effect in syllogistic reasoning (Chapter 6). As Pollard (1979a) correctly points out, we are obliged to explain why people get problems *right*, and not simply to explain logical errors.

All of this means that the process of inferring competence from performance is extremely tricky. For example, it was shown in Chapter 8 that most people can make MT with an abstract rule of the form *If p then q*, but not with a rule of the form *If not p then q*. The attribution of the logical failure in the second case to a difficulty in making a denial of a negative presupposes the existence of competence for MT – the affirmative form allows such competence to be expressed, and the negative suppresses it. However, it could equally be argued that we do *not* have competence for MT and that the negative form gives the 'true' picture; the inference is only apparently made on the affirmative rule, owing to a non-logical bias towards arguments with negative conclusions. This latter interpretation seems less attractive, but must be taken seriously in the light of recent results by Pollard and Evans (1980). They found no evidence of correlation between the ability to make MT inferences on syntactically distinct rules.

The most influential theory postulating the existence of a competence system based in formal logic is that of Piaget. An understanding of logic is seen as growing in the child through various cognitive stages, reaching completion in the adult stage of *formal operations*, which is described in detail by Inhelder and Piaget (1958). In the penultimate stage, the stage of *concrete operations*, the child learns to apply logical operations in particular contexts. This is then supposed to evolve into a general abstract system, in which the adult is capable of representing a given situation in a propositional manner, and applying formal logical rules to its solution.

Wason (1977b) has attacked the viability of Piaget's theory of formal operations on the basis of adult reasoning experiments, particularly those employing the Wason selection task. He claims that certain logical operations of which intelligent adults should be capable, such as the appreciation of reversibility, or the ability to apply a *combinatorial analysis* (exhaustive search of logical possibilities), are manifestly absent on these tasks. Wason also points to the fact that logical performance is highly dependent on the nature of the task content, and is only relatively 'good' when the material is thematic. Other recent critics of Piaget, such as Donaldson (1978) have also focused on the task-dependent nature of subjects' responses, but in a rather different way. The claim is that certain variations on the conventional Piagetian paradigms can produce performance *beyond* that of which young children are supposed to be capable.

The content-dependent nature of reasoning is itself a matter of great interest, and will be discussed later in the chapter. Can Piaget escape his critics, however, by reference to the competence/performance distinction? Its use in defence of Piaget is illustrated by Flavell and Wohlwill (1969), who use it to explain inconsistent performances on various tasks at certain stages (*horizontal décalage*). It is conceivable, perhaps, that the poor and content-dependent nature of reasoning responses could be attributed entirely to 'performance factors', but to do so on this scale greatly weakens the explanatory power of the original theory. Piaget himself did seem to move some way towards recognising the content-dependent nature of adult thought:

> In our investigations of formal thinking we used rather specific types of experimental situations which were of a physical and logical-mathematical nature . . . it is possible to question whether these situations were, fundamentally, very general and therefore applicable to any school or professional environment. Let us consider the example of apprentices to carpenters, locksmiths or mechanics . . . It is highly likely that they will know how to reason, in a hypothetical manner *in their speciality* . . . faced with our experimental situations, their lack of knowledge . . . would hinder them from reasoning in a formal way (Piaget, 1972, italics mine).

The suggestion that formal operational thought is restricted to general areas of knowledge, if not specific content, seems to be a major change of direction in Piaget's thinking, and is much less susceptible to Wason's criticisms than is Piaget's earlier theorising. In effect, Piaget is saying that, although we possess logical competence in the potential for formal thought and hypothetical reasoning, this is only likely to be manifested in reasoning performance when the content relates to the general fields of experience and interest of the subjects. If he is right, then abstract reasoning tasks such as the majority reviewed in this book will necessarily underestimate the actual competence of the subjects tested. Furthermore, the facilitation of reasoning by thematic content, which is fundamental in Wason's

(1977b) critique, is to be expected in this revised theory of formal operations.

In general, however, the notion that formal logic may form the basis for a competence system has been criticised by various authors, since it does not correspond well to our use of natural language (see Wason and Johnson-Laird, 1972; Osherson, 1975; Johnson-Laird, 1975; Braine, 1978). Normally, the logic referred to is of the 'standard' propositional form, the elements of which were described in Chapter 7. The argument here defines competence in a manner analogous to Chomsky's linguistic use, in which the language user is supposed to have an intuitive ability to decide whether or not an utterance is grammatical. Thus it is argued that various features of formal logic are intuitively unacceptable. For example, in formal logic an implication $p \supset q$ is always true if its antecedent is false or its consequent true. There is no real linguistic equivalent which has this property. Consider the following 'If . . . then . . .' sentence:

If $2 + 2 = 5$ then the world is square

If this were a material implication, then the sentence would have to be deemed 'true'. Linguistically it is meaningless. Similarly, how many people would consider this to be a 'logical' argument:

England is the largest country in the world,
London is the capital of the largest country in the world,
Therefore, London is the capital of England.

This must be a logically valid argument since it can only be invalid when it is possible for the conclusion to be false, while all the premises are true.

The inability of 'standard' formal logic to account for people's understanding of linguistic relations is demonstrated by the need to postulate a third 'irrelevant' truth value, in order to explain people's comprehension of conditional statements (cf. Chapter 8). If formal logic is rejected as a competence model, then perhaps an alternative 'natural' logic might be proposed. For some recent attempts to do this the reader is referred to Johnson-Laird (1975), Ennis (1976) and Braine (1978). The problem with all such schemes is their testability. Unless detailed *a priori* performance assumptions are built in, it is not clear how any such theory will generate testable predictions. Braine, in particular, seems unaware of the number and magnitude of performance factors that would need to be taken into account, and fails to cite much of the relevant literature.

How does the competence/performance issue relate to the problem-solving and decision-making analyses? Newell and Simon (1972) claim that problem-solving processes are closely related to task content, and can be understood only after detailed task analysis. However, as was pointed out earlier, much of the task instruction in reasoning problems is implicit and rests on the subject's understanding of logic. Thus the potential capability to construct an appropriate problem space and search it correctly would rest upon the subject's competence. Performance deviations could be accounted for in terms either of the representational stage (à la Henle) or the processing stage. If, alternatively, we suppose that the subject is trying to maximise correct decisions, then his ability to do so can also be seen as reflecting competence/performance factors.

Since a subject's behaviour is not only frequently illogical, but also inconsistent across tasks, it is clear that much of this behaviour reflects performance factors. We will consequently take a closer look at some of the major variables which affect reasoning performance, and consider the explanation of their origin.

Linguistic factors

It was suggested earlier that the competence/performance distinction might relate to the distinction between logical and non-logical factors in reasoning. However, the 'logical' component does not necessarily imply logically *correct* behaviour. It merely refers to that part of the data which varies with the logically defined structure of the task. This component has been shown to be subject to the influence of linguistic factors, and indeed, in some contexts, it has been termed the *interpretational* component of performance.

Linguistic influences are themselves extra-logical factors in the determination of reasoning performance. Evidence for the importance of such factors can be found throughout this book. For example, in Chapter 3 it was observed that negation serves a linguistic function – that of denying presuppositions. Negatives used in a linguistically appropriate context are processed more easily. In Chapter 4, linguistic factors were seen to be important in influencing transitive inference. Clearly, problems containing lexically un-marked adjectives are easier to process than those using marked adjectives, whether or not we assume the use of imagery-based strategies. Such an effect must be explained by linguistic usage or organisation – there is no logical distinction involved.

There has been little investigation of syntactic factors in syllogistic reasoning (Chapter 6), although semantic content factors have been studied (see below). The propositional reasoning literature (Part III), however, provides various examples. Thus, conditional sen-tences have been shown to possess a directionality which is depen-dent upon their expression in the 'If . . . then . . .' or '. . . only if . . .' form. There is also evidence that the interpretation of such sentences is influenced by the use of contexts specifying temporal or causal connections. Disjunctive sentences, unlike conditionals, are treated relatively symmetrically, but prove very hard to interpret when negative components are introduced.

Clearly, then, the subject's knowledge of language influences his reasoning responses. The general principle seems to be that the normal linguistic usage of a particular syntactic form appears to influence its interpretation and use in an artificial experiment. In considering the role of *semantic* factors, however, we must consider the subject's knowledge of the world (semantic memory) as well as language, and consider non-linguistic influences on behaviour. For example, subjects may be applying learned strategies to optimise the role of making correct decisions. It is with this broader approach in mind that we now turn to a consideration of content and context effects.

Effects of content and context

The content-dependent nature of reasoning responses has been al-luded to earlier in the chapter. We look here at the specific types of effect that have arisen. Three general classes of effect have been claimed:

(i) In some circumstances it appears that thematic or 'realistic' content can facilitate logical performance. This was originally claimed by Wilkins (1928) in her early syllogistic reasoning experiments; recent confirmation comes mainly from work on the Wason selection task (Chapter 9).

(ii) Where subjects have beliefs about the truth or falsity of statements embedded in reasoning problems, their responses may be biased accordingly. A number of syllogistic reasoning experiments have demonstrated a bias to accept or reject the conclusion of an argument on the basis of *a priori* beliefs rather than logical validity (see Chapter 6). Recent selection-task experiments also show effects of the subjective truth status of the rule being tested (especially Pollard, 1979a; Pollard and Evans, 1981, discussed in Chapter 9).

(iii) The semantic context in which a sentence is used may affect its interpretation and consequently affect inferences associated with it; for example, conditionals are more likely to be interpreted as equivalences in causal or threat/promise contexts (Chapter 8).

Our concern here is to seek some general explanation of why such effects arise. We will consider the merits of the problem-solving and decision-making views of reasoning in turn.

It will be recalled that problem representation is an important concept in the problem-solving approach. A fundamental difference could arise in representing abstract and thematic problems. It was noted in Chapter 9 that thematic materials may only facilitate selection-task performance when they are also *realistic*, i.e. pertaining to likely areas of the subject's personal experience. In such cases subjects will have a pre-existing knowledge system or semantic memory, to which the problem relates. It is therefore possible that the representation of the problem is assisted by existing associations in semantic memory. In effect, the subject reasons with an augmented problem space, enriched by relevant personal experience. The dramatic 'facilitation' in the envelope and stamp version (Johnson-Laird, Legrenzi and Legrenzi, 1972) and its equally dramatic failure to transfer to a subsequent abstract task, is a good illustration. If failure on the abstract task arises from the failure to include the $\bar{q}$ card in the problem space, then the explanation is simple. In the realistic condition the subject knows from experience that an envelope with a low-valued stamp must be inspected, since it is only sometimes legal. He may also *exclude* the q card from the search space (commonly mistakenly selected in the abstract task) since an envelope with a high-valued stamp is *always* legal.

More difficult to explain is the use of 'towns and transport material' which apparently facilitate selections (Wason and Shapiro, 1971) although one recent study has failed to replicate this (Manktelow and Evans, 1979). It is highly improbable that subjects will have had any experience which relates specifically to a rule such as 'Every time I go to Manchester then I travel by train'. However, they will certainly have had more experience of travelling to destinations by various means of transport than of turning cards with letters and numbers on them. This may facilitate the imagination of alternative possibilities sufficiently to counteract the 'matching bias', characteristic of abstract selection tasks, and to permit inclusion of non-matching values in the search space.

The idea that the construction of problem spaces is influenced by existing associations in semantic memory is also applicable to context effects. Consider the 'invited inference' effects with threats and promises: 'If you mow the lawn then I'll give you five dollars' seems to imply that 'If you don't mow the lawn then I won't give you five dollars'. Experience will have taught us – from early childhood – to exclude certain logical possibilities in contexts involving threats and promises. If, consequently, the given sentence leads us to disregard the possibility of receiving five dollars for *not* mowing the lawn, then the inference naturally follows. It is not a formal truth table but a practical experience of possibilities that determines our responses.

It is entirely reasonable that we should think in problem spaces that are augmented or restricted by relevant previous experience. Perception, memory and thought are all shaped and directed by experience and expectations. It is, however, a mistaken simplification to suggest that, in general, realistic content *improves* our reasoning. Most evidence for facilitation by realistic content derives from work on the selection task, in which abstract performance provides an extraordinarily low logical base rate for comparison. The processes responsible for the abstract task performance will be discussed later. The point about realistic materials is that they induce responses that are *appropriate* to our experience, which may or may not correspond to a logical definition of validity.

The belief-bias effects are hardest to explain in this semi-rational problem-solving approach. To evaluate a conclusion on its *a priori* truth value seems to involve a 'failure to accept the logical task' (Henle, 1962). It is reasonably explicable if, like Pollard (1979a), we regard a 'rational' response as a tendency to maximise correct decisions. In effect, in a reasoning task one is asked to evaluate the truth of a statement (conclusion) on the basis of the evidence given (premises). If, however, one knows the answer *a priori* it is quite reasonable to ignore the evidence. This is certainly characteristic of much real-life behaviour. Why, for example, should one take the trouble to study the arguments of political opponents, when one already knows that their conclusions are wrong! This argument supposes little understanding of the concept of validity in subjects of these experiments. However, Pollard argues that an understanding of validity is of little practical use. It would only be of value in real life if one could evaluate the premises of an argument more easily than its conclusion. To put his argument into perspective, however, one must recall that belief-bias effects in syllogistic reasoning are relatively weak when compared with, say, atmosphere/conversion effects.

In a sense, the interpretation of content and context effects is fairly obvious and straightforward. Our thought is guided in ways appropriate to our previous experience, related to the material. However, this leaves a fundamental problem unsolved. Is all thought a function of specific experience? Is it no more than generalised learning, or is there truly an underlying system of reasoning competence, which is content independent, but modified by performance factors which are content dependent? The problem is that even the learning approach would lead one to expect a common factor of performance across situations. This is because certain logical inferences (e.g. modus ponens) will hold in all situations and thus will have been universally learned. Since all realistic reasoning tasks permit the suggestion that subjects are generalising learned responses, it can never be established that *reasoning*, in the philosophical sense, is occurring at all.

All of this leads to the view that it is most necessary to study and understand what happens in *abstract* reasoning tasks – a fortunate conclusion, perhaps, since most of the experiments in the literature fall into this category. Nevertheless, the conclusion is forced. If man has the capacity to reason, as opposed to make learned responses, then this must manifest itself in problem areas where he cannot make direct use of previous experience. It is, then, to a consideration of such abstract task performance that we now turn.

Abstract reasoning: non-logical biases

Several apparently non-logical biases appear to affect abstract reasoning performance, and it is obviously important to try to understand their origin. If we are to retain any notion of underlying logical competence, then these biases must be explained in one of two ways: either they are task-dependent 'performance' factors, or else an illusion created by the subjects' logical treatment of a mis-interpreted problem. This latter view, the Henle hypothesis, was considered and rejected as oversimplified in reviewing the work on syllogistic and propositional reasoning. We will therefore explore the former type of explanation.

A general tendency for subjects' thought to be influenced unduly by feature-matching processes has been observed. In the Wason selection task and in conditional truth-table tasks, subjects tend to focus attention on the items named in the problem sentences, regardless of their actual logical status. This 'matching bias' is normally demonstrated by manipulating the presence of negative components in the sentences. The tendency to focus on the named item, whether or not it is negated, can be related to some of the psychological studies of negation discussed in Chapter 3. Because negatives are normally used to deny presuppositions about affirmatives, a statement like 'The letter is not A' is still psychologically a statement about the letter A, rather than the letters B to Z. We are not accustomed to thinking in terms of negative classes or events. When task instructions force us to do so, then extra psychological difficulty is demonstrated (cf. Chapter 2).

Feature-matching tendencies, however, arise in other contexts, where they cannot be attributed to difficulties in understanding negatives. For example, the 'atmosphere effect' in syllogistic inference (Chapter 6) appears to demonstrate that subjects prefer to endorse conclusions which share common features with premises. Of course, the atmosphere effect, though well supported empirically, is highly controversial. Many authors attribute the results to illicit conversions, although this hypothesis does not fare too well on alternative paradigms. Further evidence for feature matching comes from work on Wason's new THOG problem (Chapter 10). It seems that intuitive errors in disjunctive reasoning can result from a fallacious expectation that members of the same category share common features.

One line of explanation for these effects lies in the development of Tversky and Kahneman's (1973) heuristic-bias 'availability' (see Pollard, 1979a for a detailed application to reasoning). Their use of this concept, as mentioned earlier, refers to the ease of retrieval of items from memory. Pollard (1979a) used it also in this sense when discussing biases affecting thematic reasoning. With abstract reasoning, where relevant areas of semantic memory are not stimulated, however, Pollard suggested that the primary determinant of the elements available to thought are features of the task itself. Thus the mention of particular letters and numbers in a conditional reasoning task increases their availability, resulting in matching bias. Similarly, the syntactic features of syllogistic premises determine the availability of alternative conclusions, producing an 'atmosphere effect'. The fact that thought can be influenced in this way is supported by an experiment of Kubovy (1977) in which subjects had to generate digits between zero and nine. If subjects are asked to state the 'first one-digit number that comes to mind', far more choose 'one' than if asked to state the 'first digit that comes to mind'. The effect appears to be unconscious, however, in that if a particular number is given as an example of a digit between zero and nine, then significantly *fewer* choose that number. Matching bias could, then, be the result of an unconscious response-priming process. However, the fact that an item is made available to thought does not mean that it will necessarily be selected. What it does mean is that a *mis*matching item is less likely to be selected. This interpretation is quite consistent with the data, and in fact on truth-table tasks matching is normally measured by the increasing number of 'irrelevant' classifications (or non-selections) of unnamed items.

Pollard's (1979a) applications of the availability heuristic to other reasoning data are also worthy of attention. Consider, for example, the facilitation of selection-task performance on problems where the test sentence is believed to be false (Pollard, 1979a; Pollard and Evans, 1981; cf. Chapter 10). Since the TA-FC association is available from previous experience, while the TA-TC association is not, correct consequent selection is facilitated. With experimentally trained experience on an abstract task, Pollard (1979a) found that this bias competed with matching bias, and could only be demonstrated by manipulation of negative components to control the latter. He regards the learned association and the feature-matching tendencies as influences which combine in the determination of the availability of cards.

The figural bias observed on syllogistic reasoning tasks is rather different (Chapter 6). Here subjects do not *match* features of the task, but their thinking is nevertheless influenced by the manner in which the task information is presented. It appears that subjects' thinking moves in a direction determined by the order in which items are presented in the premises. All else being equal, a conclusion whose order of items is congruent with their appearance in the premises is likely to be preferred.

Another non-logical bias that has been demonstrated in conditional reasoning tasks is a preference for negative conclusions. The explanation offered by Pollard and Evans (1981) is in line with the general notion of heuristic biases. It will be recalled (see Chapter 8) that in their study subjects were asked to decide whether or not one conditional sentence was implied by another. With this technique, the equivalent of a negative-conclusion bias is a preference for endorsing a statement with a negative consequent. Pollard and Evans also found a preference for endorsing statements with affirmative antecedents. Thus, with logical validity controlled, there was an overall bias to say that statements of the form *If p then not q* should be inferred from other statements, while statements of the form *If not p then q* were least likely to be endorsed. Pollard and Evans's explanation of this finding is analogous to the apparent explanation of belief-bias effects in thematic reasoning. That is, they supposed that, instead of making a validity judgment, subjects are attempting to evaluate the truth of the conclusion directly. The bias is, in fact, towards the least *falsifiable* statement. As Popper (1959) points out, a conditional is more falsifiable, the more general its antecedent and the more specific its consequent. Thus, the statement *If the letter is A then the number is not 4* can only be false with respect to one combination, A4. On the other hand the statement *If the letter is not D then the number is 7* is false if any except one letter is paired with any except one number. Thus Pollard and Evans suggested that subjects apply a caution heuristic, in which conclusions are regarded as safer if they cannot easily be falsified.

Having examined some possible causes of non-logical biases, we now consider the evidence for logical influences on performance.

The logical component

The question we must now ask is whether, taking all these 'performance' factors into account, there is still evidence of some underlying logical competence. It would be surprising, not to say worrying, if there were not such evidence. The various studies conducted by the author and his colleagues have always found evidence of some consistent responding to the logical structure of the task, when features eliciting non-logical biases are balanced – the so-called 'logical' or interpretational component. It is also suggested that the logical and non-logical components combine in an additive statistical manner. The formal model of Evans (1977b) has been applied only to selection-task data (see Chapter 9), although its general structure is assumed to underlie performance on other conditional reasoning tasks (see Figure 9.1). The apparently *parallel* nature of the two components will be considered in Chapter 12. Our concern here is to try to see whether this logical component reveals the basis of a possible competence system.

In Chapter 8, the evidence for a common logical component underlying inference and truth-table tasks was assessed. There was evidence on both tasks of a tendency for subjects to treat abstract conditionals as equivalences. There also appeared to be a competence to perform MP and to judge correctly that TT verifies and TF falsifies the rule. The assumption that many subjects treat the conditional as an equivalence explains the relatively high rate of AC inference and FT 'false' classifications. What this competence amounts to is simply an ability to suppose the antecedent and see that the consequent is a necessary consequence. Evidence of ability to make MT (or DA for the converse rule), which requires similar reasoning, is none too good.

The 'logical' component of selection-task performance (Chapter 10) ties in well with these conclusions. Following Pollard's (1979b) reanalysis of the Evans (1977b) parameters, it becomes clear that subjects are competent only in reasoning from antecedent to consequent and not vice versa. Overall, abstract conditional reasoning performance indicates no more than a superficial understanding of the sentence *If p then q*, and little evidence of any depth of reasoning.

With disjunctive reasoning, error rates are very high on inference tasks involving negative components (Table 10.4), although subjects are generally above chance on truth-table evaluation (Table 10.5).

The apparent competence demonstrated with affirmative disjunctives is not manifest on Wason's THOG problem, but arguably this is probably due to the failure to generate an appropriate hypothesis-testing strategy, rather than a misunderstanding of disjunctive logic *per se*.

The evidence for logical competence on syllogistic tasks is not good either. Subjects do perform quite well on *valid* syllogisms but not necessarily for the right reasons. Pollard (1979a) has pointed out that the great majority of valid syllogisms would be endorsed on the basis of atmosphere bias. He suggests in fact that the efficacy of the bias on valid problems may be a cause of its inappropriate application on fallacious problems. So far as the fallacious syllogisms are concerned, a substantial logical component can be inferred only if the conversion hypothesis is accepted. As we saw in Chapter 8, however, this hypothesis does not generalise across paradigms.

Only in Part I of the book have the problems appeared to lie generally within subjects' competence, although error rates can be quite high even on transitive inference (see, for example, De Soto, London and Handel, 1965). The tasks involved do not require subjects to understand formal logic. In Chapter 3, we looked at problems where affirmative and negative statements needed to be evaluated against evidence. In Chapter 4 we examined people's ability to arrange items along transitive scales. In such studies it appears that subjects are able to formulate successful strategies, although some problems take consistently longer to solve than others. In common with the more complex reasoning problems, difficulty is influenced by task-specific features, content and context. The effects are principally upon speed, rather than accuracy, however. We will now move to some general conclusions.

Conclusions

In this chapter, we have been concerned with the explanation of reasoning-task performance. It was argued that such tasks should be regarded as problem-solving or decision-making tasks, and viewed in the context of the general framework of such approaches. Certainly, the idea that subjects construct and search a problem space is applicable to some of this work, although it is difficult to identify subjects' representations. The decision-making approach has also proved useful, especially in the notion that decisions may be influenced by heuristic biases.

In examining reasoning performance, we inevitably need to be aware of the issue of logicality and the views of many, including Piaget, that intelligent adults possess a competence for formal logical reasoning. Such competence, on the basis of evidence from reasoning experiments, is surprisingly – no doubt to some – depressingly lacking. All the evidence points to content-dependent thought processes on these tasks. With thematic content, prior prejudice and belief influences judgment; logical behaviour is enhanced *or* inhibited according to context. Abstract-reasoning task performance is marked by the influence of task features, in a manner which is independent of their logical significance. Both the content and direction of thought processes appears to be highly stimulus-bound.

The rationalist approach to reasoning research appears to arise from *a priori* beliefs about man's rationality. It is argued that we could not have evolved our civilisation without our ability to reason. Our intelligence is demonstrably proven. When I started my research into reasoning, my own views were similar. What changed my mind, from the earliest evidence of response biases in my own experiments, was the sheer weight of evidence. I still believe man to be a highly intelligent, adaptive species, so how should the paradox be resolved? I must here agree with the views of Allport (1980a; 1980b) who believes that the search for general purpose mechanisms by cognitive psychologists is misconceived. It is in the very nature of cognitive processes, he argues, to be content specific. Certainly Allport's radical suggestions are fully supported by this review of reasoning research.

The positive aspect of the work on reasoning is that it has provided considerable evidence about the nature of thought processes. In the next and final chapter, we will consider the broader implications of the research for the psychology of thinking, with particular reference to the possibility of dual mechanisms of thought.

12 Dual processes and beyond

In Chapter 9, the suggestion was made that two distinct types of thought might be involved in selection-task experiments. From early 'therapy' studies, it appeared that there was a remarkable degree of independence between the process of selecting cards and the verbal evaluations of possible selections offered by the subjects. Similarly, Wason and Evans (1975), and Evans and Wason (1976), found that verbal justifications of selections were *rationalisations*, rather than accurate explanations of selection performance. This led to a theory of dual thought processes which has broad implications, not only for the psychology of reasoning, but for cognitive theory in general. The application of the theory to reasoning data has been revised recently (Evans, 1980a; 1980b), but we will first consider the original Wason and Evans (1975) version.

The Wason and Evans theory of dual processes

Wason and Evans (1975) proposed that card selections – and more generally reasoning *responses* – are unconsciously determined. The processes responsible are labelled 'Type 1' by Evans and Wason (1976). When a subject is asked to 'introspect' and gives a verbal explanation of his performance, then a 'Type 2', verbal justification is involved. The theory, as stated, was principally concerned with the explanation of discrepance between performance and introspection. Thus, it was assumed:

(1) The processes underlying the reasoning performance, e.g. matching bias, are not generally available for introspective report.

(2) Introspective reports of performance reflect a tendency for the subject to *construct* a justification of his own behaviour consistent with his knowledge of the situation.

Wason and Evans are arguing here for a reversal of common-sense thinking in which introspections are assumed to reveal the causes of behaviour. They argue that it is the behaviour which determines the nature of the introspection. The subject, in effect, is answering the question 'Given what I did, and the nature of the task and instructions, what is the best explanation of my behaviour?' In labelling this 'rationalisation' we seem to have been misunderstood as denigrating our subjects (see, e.g. Fellows, 1976). In fact, these verbalisations provide the best evidence of ability to *reason* which has been observed on reasoning tasks. Inspection of the protocols quoted in Chapter 9 reveals distinctly logical thought. If, on a given task, the subjects' behaviour is logically consistent with falsifying the rule, then they explain it in such terms. If it is consistent with verification, they explain it likewise. The puzzle is that if subjects possess such capacity for logical reasoning, why do they not use it to make the correct responses in the first place? We shall return to this point in due course.

If the Wason/Evans view of introspection can be generalized, then it has important implications. Much research in social science is based on the common-sense assumption that people can identify causes of their own behaviour. Is it, in fact, valid to ask people *why* they made certain decisions, such as to vote for a political party, or to live in a particular district? Is there any reason to suppose, in general, that we are not aware of the basis of our decision-making, but are adept in constructing *post hoc* explanations?

The problems of interpreting introspective reports have already been mentioned in the context of visual imagery (Chapter 2; see also Evans, 1980b). It is pertinent to this discussion, however, to look beyond the boundaries of cognitive psychology. Nisbett and Wilson (1977; see also Nisbett and Ross, 1980) have launched a major theoretical attack on the use of introspective reports by cognitive social psychologists. Their arguments parallel those of Wason and Evans in two respects: (i) they look at subjects' reports on tasks where the actual causal factors have been determined experimentally, and conclude that the subjects are not aware of them, (ii) they argue that the report produced is a consequence of the subjects' attempt to explain their own behaviour. They suggest that the subject is theorising about his behaviour, in a similar manner to the experimenter. He *may* give the correct explanation, if he has the right theory, but *not* because he has what Ryle (1949) termed 'privileged access' to private mental processes.

It is appropriate in this context to reply to a criticism of my own, very similar, position offered by Fellows (1976). He claimed that 'If Evans dismisses the subject's reports as rationalisations, then logically he must also dismiss his own explanations in the same way.' He is quite right to infer that one must engage in Type 2 thinking in order to write the discussion of an experimental paper. In a sense it *is* a rationalisation, in that one is trying to construct an explanation to make sense of the results. The reason that the author is more likely to get it right than the subject is that he has access to information that the subject does not. The subject does not have a training in experimental psychology, a knowledge of the relevant literature or an understanding of the nature and purpose of the experimental design. In this context it is the experimenter, not the subject, who enjoys privileged access.

Smith and Miller (1978) criticise Nisbett and Wilson (1977) on the grounds that the subjects were denied access to information they would need to assess the cause of their behaviour, e.g. the experimental treatment offered to other subjects. In view of the above points this criticism is sound, if the question one is interested in is whether people normally know the cause of their behaviour. It does not, of course, affect the argument that subjects have no direct access to their mental processes. The view taken here, and by Nisbett and Wilson, is similar to that expressed by Ryle (1949), 'our knowledge of other people and ourselves depends upon noticing how they and we behave.'

In my view it is important to distinguish two types of introspective report. I believe that subjects are able, to some extent, to make *phenomenal reports*, i.e. to report what they are experiencing. What they cannot do is to report the *process* or strategy underlying their behaviour. Take, for example, the phenomenon of size constancy. Unless they have studied experimental psychology, people will not be aware of the fact that objects are phenomenally enlarged to compensate for their distance. What they *are* aware of, and can report, is how big they look. It is the *product*, rather than the process, of size constancy that is available to introspection.

Nisbett and Wilson make a similar distinction which is disputed by Smith and Miller (1978), who cite as an example Newell and Simon's (1972) cryptarithmetic problems, in which subjects' verbal reports appear to reveal the process of thought being used. I would argue with this example, however, since I do not believe that the 'thinking aloud' protocols used by Newell and Simon are the same thing as introspective reports (see also Byrne, 1977). Newell and Simon's task is as follows:

$$\begin{array}{r} \text{DONALD} \\ + \text{GERALD} \\ \hline \text{ROBERT} \end{array} \qquad D = 5$$

The subject has to decide which digit is represented by each letter in order to make a legal sum. Now, it is true that the subject 'thinking aloud' does trace a fairly clear pattern of his thought process. However, this is not introspection. The point about a problem like this is that it breaks down into a series of sub-problems, each of which is solved by a sub-process. For example, processing the last column, with the information that $D = 5$, will quickly lead to the conclusion $T = 0$. The fact that the subject can say this is hardly remarkable – many problem-solving processes produce a verbal output. It is like asking someone to state the solution of an anagram. It is *not*, however, like asking them to explain how they solved the anagram. That, if it were possible, would be introspection.

In brief, problems of the sort studied by Newell and Simon are amenable to study by thinking aloud protocols, since they are composed of a number of sub-problems which have verbal outputs. Recording the outputs of such intermediate stages facilitates the construction of an overall picture of the problem-solving process. If, however, a thought process has no intermediate stages which produce verbal outputs, then the technique will not be helpful. I strongly suspect that selection-task responses come into this category. I once ran an experiment in which subjects were asked to think aloud prior to making their choices on the Wason selection task. The experiment had to be abandoned, since subjects simply could not comply with the instruction!

The discussion to date has focused mainly on the issue of introspective access to cognitive processes. If people do not have such access, *why* do they produce a rationalisation (Wason and Evans) or apply a causal theory to their own behaviour (Nisbett and Wilson)? Why do subjects not simply state that they do not know? Wason and Evans imply that subjects are motivated to create an illusion of rationality. Subjects convince themselves that they are in control of their behaviour and know why they have done things. Perhaps people have a need to explain their own behaviour. The 'cognitive consistency' theories of social psychologists would support such a view, in that people are seen to be motivated to generate internally consistent explanations of the world, including their own behaviour in it (see Zajonc, 1968). However, in the more recently fashionable attribution theory, motivational concepts are de-emphasised (e.g. Kelly, 1967; 1972). It could be that subjects construct explanations (or make causal attributions) to explain their behaviour, simply because the experimenter has required them to do so. The fact that one asks the subject to explain this behaviour implies that he ought to be able to do this. It would be a brave subject who refused to comply.

The Wason and Evans dual process theory is not, however, intended simply as a critique of introspection. The suggestion is that the thought processes underlying decision (Type 1) are qualitatively distinct from those generating verbal accounts (Type 2). Type 2 processes do not simply generate introspective reports. They are also seen as responsible for verbal evaluations of the consequences of selections. Further evidence for dual processes is found in an inductive reasoning task originally formulated by Wason (1960). Subjects are told that the experimenter has a rule in mind which classifies triads of digits. They are told that 2 4 6 complies with the rule, and asked to generate other triads in order to discover what the rule is, and only to announce the rule when they are sure of being right. The experimenter simply tells the subject if each triad conforms to the rule or not. If the subject announces a wrong rule, he is asked to continue.

The actual rule is 'any ascending sequence'. The example given 2 4 6, deliberately creates a misleading set to expect a more specific rule. Since subjects tend to examine only positive examples of their current hypotheses, they find it hard to eliminate them (see Wason, 1968; and for the most recent study Tweney *et al.*, 1980). The interesting aspect from our point of view is that many subjects persist in generating instances from the same rule, despite being told that their verbal announcement is wrong. They then announce 'other' rules that are actually reformulations of the same one.

For example, one of Wason's (1960) subjects generated triads such as 2 6 10 and 1 50 99 and announced the rule:

> *The rule is that the middle number is the arithmetic mean of the other two.*

On being told that this was wrong, she generated 3 10 17 and then announced:

> *The rule is that the difference between two numbers next to each other is the same.*

On being told that this was wrong, she tested a further triad and then announced:

> *The rule is on adding a number, always the same one, to form the next number.*

The frequent occurrence of such cases gives evidence for dual processes. It is supposed that the generation of triads is controlled by a Type 1 process, and the verbal formulation of rules by a Type 2 process. There is a close analogy here to the selection/evaluation-process distinction on the selection task. There is also a clear element of rationalisation in the rule formulations. The subjects do not seem to be aware that they are persisting with the same rule, and the alternative formulations would seem to maintain the self-deception.

The general conclusion would seem to be that Type 2 processes arise whenever a verbal explanation is required, whether or not such an account would be intended as an introspective report. Actual responses or decisions are, however, seen as determined by Type 1 processes. The two processes are independent, although the behavioural consequences of a Type 1 process may form an input to the Type 2 process.

The revised dual process theory

In recent publications, Evans (1980a; 1980b) has revised and extended the dual process theory somewhat. Firstly, the reference to Type 1 processes as unconscious and Type 2 processes as conscious has been rejected. If by 'unconscious' one means non-introspectible, then both processes are unconscious. Type 2 processes underlie so-called introspective reports, but they are not, themselves, reportable. Instead, Type 2 processes have been characterised as *verbal* and Type 1 as *non-verbal*. This does not mean that Type 2 processes consist of words, but merely that their function is to generate verbal responses. Because such verbalizations appear to be independent of aspects of decision processes, it is assumed that the Type 1 processes are non-verbal. The distinction implies that there may be discrete cognitive systems or mechanisms from which Type 1 and Type 2 processes originate.

This distinction is complicated by the second revision of the theory. In the Wason/Evans version, *all* reasoning responses were attributed to Type 1 processes. In the revised version, the dual processes are linked to the Evans two-factor theory of reasoning. Hence, Type 1 processes are considered to underlie the non-logical response processes, such as matching bias, but are *not* seen as responsible for the logical/interpretational component of performance. This is attributed instead to Type 2 processes.

In essence, the revised theory envisages Type 2 processes as arising from a verbal-rational system of thought. On abstract reasoning tasks, this system has only partial control of behaviour – generating the 'logical' component – and must compete with non-verbal Type 1 processes which generate the non-logical component. The mathematical model of Evans (1977b) can be seen as a formal description of two parallel, competing processes (see Figure 9.2). The weighting factor α, indicates the balance between the two processes. If α is increased, for example, by use of realistic materials, then it is possible for performance to come mainly under the control of verbal-rational (Type 2) processes. An advantage of this reformulation of the theory is the ability to explain people's ability to reason competently, when dealing with problem areas within their normal experience.

In the revised version, verbalisations are still seen as primarily arising from Type 2 processes. There is some influence of Type 1 thinking as well, though as evidenced by the 'secondary matching bias' observed on the Wason selection task (cf. Chapter 9).

Dual processes: the broader context

In the next section we will consider some research designed to give experimental test of the revised dual process theory. First, though, we look at some other ideas and work in the psychology of cognition which relate to the theory. These studies suggest some additional hypotheses about the nature of the dual processes which can also be examined.

The literature in the psychology of thinking is littered with dichotomies. One of the most fundamental is the Freudian distinction between the primary and secondary process. Primary-process thought is free associative, laden with imagery and characteristic of dreams and fantasies. The secondary process is reality-based, goal-directed, problem-solving thought. This type of distinction arises earlier (in philosophy) and later, in various guises. Artistic thinking is contrasted with scientific, creative thinking with problem-solving, divergent with convergent, insight with trial-and-error, etc, etc. The mere proliferation of such dichotomies does not establish the case for discrete mechanisms, but there may be some fire beneath all this smoke.

Two modern theories of thinking worthy of attention are those of Neisser (1963) and Paivio (1975). Neisser reviewed various dichotomous classifications of thought, such as those mentioned above, and concludes, 'The common core of all these theoretical dichotomies seems to be the distinction between a relatively well-ordered, easily describable, and efficient thought process on one side, and superficially confused profusion of activity on the other.' He went on to develop a theory of thinking based on the analogy to information-processing systems – a relatively novel procedure at that date. In particular, he drew on the distinction between sequential and parallel processes. He described secondary-process thought as the *main sequence* but subject to the influence of parallel or multiple 'preconscious' processes. The multiple processes were seen as responsible for intuitive, creative and divergent thinking.

Neisser did not explicitly specify that the main sequence is *verbal* in nature, but rather associated it with consciousness. However, 'conscious' mental activities are often defined by association with language, and it may be that it is the potential for verbalisation that Neisser had in mind. This suspicion is supported by his assertion that the effect of 'thinking aloud' experiments (cf. Neisser, 1963) is to restrict thought to the main process.

Paivio (1975), in a development of his dual coding theory of memory (cf. Chapter 2), described two systems of thought with similar functional characteristics to those of Neisser's. However, he referred to verbal and imagery systems, rather than to conscious and preconscious systems. He defined the systems as follows:

> The imagery system is assumed to be specialized for processing nonverbal information in the form of images, that is memory representations corresponding rather directly to concrete things. . . . The verbal system, on the other hand is specialized for dealing with abstract linguistic units, which involve discrete, sequentially arranged informational units that are only indirectly and arbitrarily related to things, according to the conventions of language. Such functions distinguish the verbal system as an abstract, logical mode of thinking, compared to the concrete, analogical mode that apparently characterizes imagery.

The functional relation to Neisser's theory is seen in the following quotation, 'the imagery system is specialized for synchronous organization and parallel processing of non-verbal information whereas verbal processes involve sequential organization of linguistic units.' Paivio's verbal system does seem to relate the Wason and Evans Type 2 process. Consideration of Neisser's and Paivio's theories suggest two possible characteristics of Type 1 processes that we might look for – firstly they may be parallel (multiple, synchronous), and secondly may involve concrete visual thinking (imagery).

First, though, I would like to introduce a further idea into the discussion. There is an increasing interest in research into the differentiation of function between the two hemispheres of the brain. The left hemisphere (in right-handers) is of course specialised for language and speech. There is increasing evidence that cognitive processes of a verbal nature take place in the left hemisphere, and those of a non-verbal, including visual, nature in the right hemisphere. Such evidence derives from studies of patients with 'split brains', or less dramatically with localised brain damage, and from experimental studies of normal subjects (see Cohen, 1977). In the last category, it is often reported that performance on a cognitive task is dependent upon the hemisphere to which the problem is initially presented. Presentation to right ear, hand, or visual hemisphere goes to the left hemisphere, and vice versa. For recent examples in problem-solving and reasoning the reader is referred to Golding, Reich and Wason (1974), Van Duyne and Sass (1979) and Katz (1980). The evidence for discrete cognitive systems with such a clear anatomical basis is quite exciting and should not be ignored simply because the research is at such an early stage. The possibility that Paivio's imagery and verbal systems – and perhaps Type 1 and Type 2 processes – are located in the right and left hemispheres respectively, must be seriously considered.

The discussion in this section leads to the following general conclusions. The idea of two distinct types of thought is not novel to the Wason/Evans dual process theory (or its revision) but is common throughout the literature on thinking. Type 2 processes might be part of a system specialised for verbal, sequential thought and this might be localised in the left hemisphere. The non-verbal, Type 1, system may be multiple in nature, associated with imagery and, perhaps, located in the right hemisphere of the brain. We must now ask what evidence there is that the Type 1 and Type 2 processes, as defined in the reasoning context, might possess some of these other characteristics.

Evidence for dual mechanisms

One suggestion that has arisen is that Type 2 thought may be intrinsically sequential. This is supported to some extent by the review of elementary reasoning tasks (Part I). Since those tasks are within the subjects' competence, it would be assumed in the revised theory that they are entirely under the control of Type 2 processes. In such cases, we found that sequential stage models generally gave a good fit to the latency data. There is also evidence of parallel processing on tasks where behaviour is strongly influenced by non-logical factors (attributed to Type 1 processes). Both Evans (1977b) and Pollard (1979a) have found considerable evidence that responses on the abstract selection task are *statistically independent*.

For example, knowing that a subject has chosen TC does not help you to guess whether or not he has also chosen FC. Similarly, Pollard and Evans (1980) have found little evidence of correlation between subjects' performance on different tasks of related logical structure. The fact that responses appear to be probabilistic and independent (though *not* random) could well result from parallel processing by an intrinsically indeterminate system.

The second main hypothesis relates to the modality of the two processes. It has been proposed that Type 2 processes are verbal and Type 1 processes non-verbal in nature. Paivio's work further suggests that the Type 1 processes might be imagery-related, and hence visual in nature. Some recent experiments which the author has designed in collaboration with P. G. Brooks provide evidence relevant to both these hypotheses. Let us consider, first of all, the suggestion that Type 2 processes result from a verbal cognitive system. We hoped to disrupt selectively the 'logical' component of performance (attributed to Type 2 processes in the revised theory) by use of a competing task of a verbal nature. The interference task used – concurrent articulation of irrelevant verbal items – was suggested by the research of Hitch and Baddeley (1976). They set out to test the working memory model of Baddeley and Hitch (1974) which is composed of a central executive and an articulatory loop. If such a working memory is used in reasoning, they argued, then concurrent interference tasks which affect its function should disrupt reasoning performance. They used three conditions:

Control   No interference

Articulation   Subjects were instructed to speak aloud continuously either digits (1 2 3 4 5 6 repeated) or 'the the the. . .' while performing the reasoning task.

Memory   Subjects were presented with a different six digit number to repeat on each trial. This adds a short-term memory load to the concurrent articulation task.

According to Baddeley and Hitch, concurrent irrelevant articulation should suppress use of the articulatory loop. A short-term memory load should further interfere with the central executive.

Their reasoning task was a simple verification task, in which subjects had to make true/false judgments to problems such as:

A precedes B   B A

The interference tasks did not disrupt reasoning performance, but they did lead to increased latencies, with means in the order control less than articulation less than memory. However, their task was very simple, and both they and we might expect interference with performance on more complex conditional reasoning tasks. From the viewpoint of the revised dual process theory, the Hitch and Baddeley interference tasks, being of a verbal nature, should disrupt the logical component of performance. Response-bias effects – attributed to an independent non-verbal system – should not be disrupted. If anything such effects should have *increased* strength since they have less competition from the verbal system. (In terms of the Evans, 1977b, model this means a decrease in the weighting parameter, α.)

A series of conditional-reasoning experiments have been run by Evans and Brooks with groups of subjects treated under control, articulation and memory conditions. In all experiments rules were used with all possible permutations of negative components: *If p then q, If p then not q, If not p then q, If not p then not q*. This enables logical and non-logical components of performance to be separated (cf. Chapter 8). In Experiment I an inference task was used in which negative-conclusion bias is the prevailing non-logical tendency. Three further experiments employed truth-table evaluation tasks, in which matching bias is the main non-logical effect.

Experiment I is reported by Evans and Brooks (1981) and full reports of the others are in prepartion. The results presented here are selected for their relevance to the theme of this chapter (see Table 12.1). Although the frequency data have been analysed in terms of both logical and non-logical components, the data shown in Table 12.1 (i) relate to the former analysis only. The prediction was that this logical performance would be inhibited by competing verbal tasks. In Experiment I, the type of inference (MP, DA, AC, MT) produced a significant main effect, similar to that observed in previous studies. It did *not*, however, significantly interact with groups. Thus there is no evidence here that competing verbal tasks interfere with logical performance.

TABLE 12.1   *Results of the Evans and Brooks interference experiments*

(i) Response frequencies
All data are averaged across four conditional rules in which the presence and absence of negated components is permuted.

Inference rate (% of arguments accepted)

Experiment I		MP	DA	AC	MT
	C	97	55	81	55
	A	92	57	69	51
	M	87	63	85	68
		92	58	79	59

Truth table evaluation (% correct responses)

Experiment II		Instance		
TT as 'true'		Verbal	Pictorial	
	C	93	97	95
	A	79	82	81
	M	83	90	87
		85	90	
TF as 'false'		Verbal	Pictorial	
	C	88	91	90
	A	68	90	79
	M	71	82	77
		76	87	

Experiment III		Instance			
			Verbal	Pictorial	
		Congruent	Incongruent		
TT as 'true'	C	81	83	92	85
	A	79	85	83	82
		80	84	88	
			Verbal	Pictorial	
		Congruent	Incongruent		
TT as 'false'	C	73	77	92	81
	A	60	73	88	74
		67	75	90	

Experiment IV		
	TT as 'true'	TF as 'false'
C	86	80
A	89	81
M	81	78

(ii)   Response latencies (seconds)

	C	A	M
Experiment I	8.58	6.13	11.62
Experiment II	8.38	6.96	9.05
Experiment III	7.11	6.59	–
Experiment IV	11.11	9.32	12.03

Key   C – Control – no interference
A – Concurrent articulation
M – Concurrent articulation with memory load

These conditions were administered to separate groups in all experiments.

In the other three experiments, the frequency of correct classifications of TT as 'true' and TF as 'false' were analysed separately. In Experiment II it can be seen that performance did drop under both articulation and memory conditions, and the effect was significant in both analyses. In Experiment III when no memory group was run, performance dropped under articulation in both analyses, but not significantly so. There was no evidence of interference in Experiment IV. The significance of the verbal/pictorial distinction in Table 12.1 (i) will be explained later. So far as the verbal interference tasks are concerned, the overall evidence suggests that logical performance may be affected, but the effect is relatively weak and unreliable. In general, the usual non-logical biases were observed and, with the exception of one odd result, were not affected by the presence of competing tasks. The lack of interference with response biases accords with the dual process predictions.

Following Hitch and Baddeley (1976) we might, then, expect to find interference reflected in the latency of responding. These results, summarised in Table 12.1 (ii), were most surprising. In Experiments I and II, there was a significant main effect of groups but the order was articulation faster than control faster than memory. Breakdown analysis confirmed that the unexpected acceleration of solution times under articulation was significant relative to control. Although the groups factor was not significant in Experiments III and IV, the means were in the same direction, and consistently so when broken down by various conditions not shown in Tables 12.1 (ii).

The Evans and Brooks experiments cause problems for various theories, not least for the working-memory model of Baddeley and Hitch. Additional variables were introduced into Experiment IV and other experiments to test the implications for their model, but it would be an unjustifiable diversion to discuss that work in this context. The relative lack of interference with logical performance under articulatory suppression seems also to cause problems for the theory that adult thought is based on internalised speech (Vygotsky, 1962). What the accelerated solution times suggest is that we are in the habit of sub-vocalising on such problems, but that this has little functional value and tends to slow us down. When implicit articulation is suppressed, we speed up with little loss of accuracy. It may well be that the effect is restricted to verbal problems of the sort involved in conditional reasoning. No evidence of facilitation under articulatory suppression was found in anagram-solving in a further experiment by Brooks. On the anagram task a much smaller proportion of solution time is devoted to reading and processing verbal material.

Where does this leave the revised dual process theory? There is some evidence of a tendency for the logical component to be affected relative to the non-logical component, but the evidence is far from conclusive. In particular, the speeding up of solution under concurrent articulation suggests that whatever it 'suppresses' is not vital to the reasoning process. We cannot dismiss the theory on the basis of this evidence, however. It may be that the verbal system – or that part of it connected with reasoning – is independent of articulatory processes *per se*.

What of the suggestion that Type 1 processes may be related to an imagery system? The role of imagery in reasoning has only received systematic study in the study of transitive inference. The conclusion of Chapter 4 was that there was little good evidence that imagery, in the sense of a visual information-processing system, was involved. Perhaps this is just as well if we are to attribute the *competent* reasoning which occurs on such problems to the Type 2 system. By the same token, however, we might expect some of the non-logical factors found on other tasks to be imaginal or perceptual in nature. It was noted in the previous chapter that one of the most fundamental aspects of non-logical behaviour is the undue influence of specific features of the task. In this category, 'matching bias', in particular, seems related to concrete, perceptually based thought. The tendency for thought to be fixated on the items named certainly fits well with Paivio's distinction, and more generally to the idea that behaviour is under the influence of a concrete rather than abstract thought process.

If we ask whether or not imagery is involved in syllogistic or propositional reasoning, the simple answer is that we do not know, because no experiments have been conducted to find out. The fact that thematic materials may facilitate reasoning (cf. Chapter 9) is hard to interpret in this context. So-called 'abstract' materials are in a sense quite concrete. For example, in Wason's (1969a) selection-task experiment, the rules referred to coloured shapes drawn on cards, which might be regarded as highly imageable. The only work that has deliberately manipulated a factor related to the visual/verbal is that of Evans and Brooks. In two of the truth table experiments (II and III) they varied the form in which the instance was presented. Thus, given the rule:

If it is not a triangle, then it is red,

the FT case was represented to the verbal group by the words 'red triangle' and to the pictorial group by a coloured drawing depicting a red triangle. The idea was that the use of pictorial representation might encourage the use of a visual or imagery code as opposed to the use of a verbal code. This relates to Paivio's (1971) earlier supposition of dual memory codes (see Chapter 2).

What predictions does this entail? According to the dual process theory (either version) matching is attributed to a Type 1 process. If such a process is related to Paivio's imagery system, then any factor encouraging use of this system should increase matching responses. As in other respects, the Evans and Brooks data were unexpected and surprising. The normal effects of matching bias were observed, but did not interact with the verbal-pictorial presentation as predicted. However, in Experiment II, logical performance was significantly *improved* when the instance was pictorial rather than verbal. It was thought that this result might be artifactual, since the order of reference to the shape and colour of the figure is incongruent between the sentence and instance in the verbal condition (see above example). Presumably, with pictorial presentation, the subject can extract the relevant features in an order determined by the sentence. Experiment III was designed to control for this possibility. It can be seen from Table 12.1 (i) that performance was again better in the pictorial condition than verbal, whether or not the latter was congruent. In the case of the TF analysis, the superiority of the pictorial condition was statistically significant.

These results contrast with those employing a similar technique on elementary sentence-verification tasks (cf. Chapter 3). In that context we noted that Seymour (1975) did not find evidence of dual coding, and favoured Clark and Chase's (1972) assumption of a common abstract propositional code underlying performance of such tasks. If our verbal and pictorial displays were encoded in such a common form, however, the differences we have observed should not have arisen. The only way that a Clark and Chase type model could account for our results is at the encoding stage itself. They would have to assume that more errors occur in coding a verbal description than a picture into its propositional representation. This explanation seems rather implausible, however, since the instances used – coloured shapes – are so simple that one would expect negligible coding errors in either form. On the other hand, if dual codes *are* assumed and the errors arise at the processing stage, then it must be admitted that direction of effect is wrong.

The final possibility to examine is that dual reasoning processes might relate to hemispheric specialisation. There is some evidence to support this hypothesis. Golding *et al.* (1974) found some suggestive evidence that evidence presented to the left hemisphere (via a right-hand tactile stimulus) was more effectively used in a reasoning task, than when it was presented to the right hemisphere. Much more impressive, however, are some recent results of Golding, in which the Wason selection task was administered to brain-damaged patients. In the first study she administered the task to patients with either left- or right- hemisphere lesions and to a control group (Golding, 1981). Whilst correct solutions were minimal in the left hemisphere and control groups, those with right-hemisphere damage performed significantly *better*. For example, selection of the FC cards was made by 50 per cent of this group, as compared with 0 per cent of controls. 50 per cent is well above the normal base rate in experiments using healthy intelligent adults. In a second study (Golding, 1980), she showed that patients who have the function of the non-dominant (normally right) hemisphere temporarily inhibited by ECT also show a dramatically higher solution rate than controls.

These results obviously invite the inference that logical performance on the selection task is normally inhibited by competing influences from the right hemisphere – a conclusion most happily in line with the revised dual process theory. Furthermore, Golding (1981) found that patients choosing correctly in the right-damaged group were those who possessed a particular type of perceptual deficit. Golding, herself, suggests that the competing response that has been eliminated is matching bias. In view of these results Wason and I recently designed an experiment with Brooks, in order to see if similar results could be obtained with normal subjects. The task was a modified version of the selection task in which cards were presented individually to either hemisphere, and in which decisions were indicated by a key press with either left or right hand. Both variables affected responding with the most striking results arising from the latter. For example, when indicating choices with the left hand, subjects chose the incorrect TC card on 44 per cent of occasions and the correct FC on 46 per cent of occasions. With a forced choice (under time pressure) this could be regarded as random responding. With the right hand, however, subjects chose TC on 29 per cent and FC on 68 per cent of occasions – yielding a significant hand × card interaction. This looks like improved logical performance with right hand (controlled by left hemisphere). There was not, however, a corresponding improvement in antecedent selections, although again it was only the right hand that discriminated the logical significance of the cards. Responding was also significantly more related to the logical structure of the task when cards were presented to the left hemisphere (via the right visual hemifield). The experiment did not, however, provide any evidence that matching bias is mediated by the right hemisphere. Possibly due to the unusual presentation of the task, the normal matching response was not observed.

There is, then, some evidence that selection-task performance reflects competing processes arising from the two hemispheres of the brain. This is the best evidence reviewed in this section to support the idea that dual processes on reasoning tasks reflect the operation of distinct cognitive mechanisms. The connection with the verbal and imagery systems of Paivio (1975) lacks clear support in the Evans and Brooks study. However, experiments of this sort are not all that easy to interpret, and it would certainly be premature to dismiss such a connection without further research. To search for underlying mechanisms on such complex tasks is, perhaps, rather ambitious, but it is surely important to make the attempt. A final consideration is that the qualitative difference between Type 1 and Type 2 processes is established by the kind of evidence described at the beginning of the chapter. This evidence stands, even if the search for underlying mechanisms should ultimately fail. The distinction is directly analogous to that discussed in Part I; in the imagery versus propositions debate. For example, the structure of the imagery theory of transitive inference was supported, despite the lack of evidence for a visual mechanism of representation. Likewise, it is argued that it is not evidence for the *existence* of dual processes which is open to question, but rather the evidence relating to their nature and origin.

Overview and new directions

In this final section, I shall attempt to summarise the main conclusions of the book as a whole, and point to some directions in which future research might fruitfully develop. At the outset (Chapter 1) it was pointed out that although the book was intended to survey the current state of research using reasoning *tasks*, it was not simply about reasoning *processes*. In the first place, the issue of whether reasoning – in the sense of logical, deductive thought processes – actually occurs on such tasks was seen as an empirical question. Secondly, reasoning experiments were perceived as using cognitive tasks similar to problem-solving and decision-making talks, and liable to influence by the same kinds of factors. Reasoning research should, therefore, be viewed within the context of cognitive psychology as a whole.

The issue of rationality, and the search for some kind of logical competence, has been considered throughout the book, and discussed in detail in the last chapter. The general conclusion is that there is little evidence of any impressive competence, while a whole host of performance factors have been identified. Even on the elementary reasoning tasks discussed in Part I, which do lie within the subjects' competence, there are many such performance factors influencing the *latency* of responding. The theoretical models proposed to account for such effects tended to be highly paradigm-specific – a problem encountered also in later parts of the book. I believe that this reflects some general problems with cognitive experiments. Firstly, they are *reactive*, in that the act of measuring a cognitive process tends to exert a large influence on the process being 'measured'. The second problem is a lack of *ecological validity*. It is very hard to generalise from the results of any particular experiment.

It is for this very reason that it is important to survey a large range of related paradigms, as in the present book. Only in this way can one hope to abstract general features. For example, the sequential representation and process model of reasoning adopted with some success in Part I, cannot be applied to much of the data in Parts II and III. One cannot claim that, *in general*, people solve reasoning tasks by successive stages of representation of problem information into an abstract propositional code, followed by application of reasoning strategies. All one can say is that it is possible to model behaviour *on some tasks* with this kind of approach.

It has been suggested earlier that reasoning experiments assess people's intuitive understanding of logic, in that the concept of logical argument is not explained in the instructions. The experimental work on syllogistic (Part II) and propositional (Part III) reasoning, suggests either that people have little such intuitive understanding, or else that logical tendencies compete rather badly with various non-logical influences. People do not seem to be aware of the lack of rationality in their own behaviour, however, judging from the discussion of introspection in the early part of this chapter. Whether or not they delude themselves into believing their behaviour to be rationally determined, they do seem to have deceived the authors of many papers on reasoning into just such a belief. The evidence that undermines the rationalist position arises again from variations in the nature of the paradigms used. These demonstrate non-logical biases that cannot be explained by any rationalist sleight of hand, and inconsistencies in the personal 'interpretations' of sentences that are supposed to underlie performance. Even in the Evans two-factor approach, the logical/interpretational component that can be divined, with due allowance for non-logical factors, demonstrates (i) incomplete awareness of logical possibilities and inferences and (ii) susceptibility to extra-logical factors, particularly of a linguistic nature.

We are forced to the conclusion that people manifest little ability for general deductive reasoning in these experiments. Very little behaviour can be attributed to an *a priori* system that is independent of the particular task content and structure. This does not mean that people cannot reason correctly in contexts where they have relevant and appropriate experience – indeed some evidence suggests that they can. It does mean, however, that adults' reasoning ability is far more concrete and context-dependent than has been generally believed.

The positive aspects of reasoning research lie in the various performance factors that have been identified (see previous chapter). Of these, the most impressive are, perhaps, the linguistic and pragmatic influences. Reasoning experiments provide some of the most useful situations in which to study the relation between language and thought. We have seen a number of examples of syntactic and contextual factors which have influenced reasoning performance, and which are clearly interpretable within a psycholinguistic framework. It is the very context-specific nature of reasoning responses that both undermines the rationalist and gives such scope to the psycholinguist.

The prevalence of non-logical factors and response biases, particularly in abstract tasks, may be worrying to some readers. However, if behaviour is considerably influenced by irrelevant task features, then it is important to know this, lest the data be misinterpreted in terms of some more general factor. Personally, I feel that these biases are of considerable interest in their own right. In the previous chapter, it was pointed out that the psychology of decision-making and subjective probability has become increasingly concerned with judgmental biases, and the application of more or less appropriate heuristics. An attempt was made to view the non-logical biases observed on reasoning tasks in a similar light. The fact that reasoning – and decision-making – processes are often influenced by *inappropriate* heuristics leads to some interesting questions. For example, where do such heuristics originate; are they learned in a context where they are appropriate, and then transferred to one where they no longer work?

The final kind of issue to arise in this book has been the question of what cognitive mechanisms may underlie behaviour on these tasks. In Part I, we discussed evidence for the use of dual memory codes, with particular reference to visual imagery. In this chapter, the evidence for possible dual mechanisms underlying qualitatively distinct features of task behaviour has also been examined. In neither case has the evidence proved conclusive, but in each case sufficiently suggestive to encourage further research. This type of research is obviously ambitious, when one considers the difficulties encountered in deciding what mechanisms underlie much simpler cognitive phenomena, such as those of short-term memory. The methodology involved, e.g. interference tasks, also tends to be complex and gives rise to problems of interpretation.

Finally, then, how can research into the psychology of reasoning usefully develop? My suggestions are very much determined by the above conclusions. I see little purpose, for example, in pursuing the search for logical competence, or in attempting to explain performance in an entirely rationalistic manner. Once the non-rational and content-dependent nature of the behaviour is recognised, new directions of research are indicated. There is much that needs clarification, particularly the origin of non-logical biases, and the precise nature of content and contextual factors.

If we do abandon the search for competence, then the justification for the paradigm appears to diminish. Why give someone a task of a given logical structure if one can make no general conclusions about people's ability to understand it? According to this discussion, there is little evidence of a general competence to perform any given inference. One may or may not be able to do so depending upon the linguistic form, the context, the nature of prevailing response biases, etc. If reasoning experiments do not elicit reasoning, in an *a priori* sense, then why bother to do them at all?

I would answer these points as follows. First of all, it has been necessary to engage in such research in order to show that one *cannot* deduce logical ability. When a field of research becomes dominated by false assumptions, then it is important that this be demonstrated. Secondly, these experiments have proved useful and interesting in other respects. As stated earlier, the paradigms have proved well suited to the investigation of linguistic and pragmatic factors. Also, certain reasoning tasks, notably the Wason selection task, have proved to be very conducive to the study of thought processes. I see no reason why such research should not continue and develop, *provided* that the experimenters recognise the tasks for what they are – specialised problem-solving or decision-making tasks.

Such recognition, however, has implications that go beyond the decline of rationalism. If reasoning experiments are specialised cognitive tasks, then their results should be related theoretically to those from other cognitive paradigms. Also, any general hypotheses about cognitive processes or mechanisms should be assessed on other tasks, which need not be defined as deductive reasoning experiments. In other words, we should be less concerned with explaining performance on particular paradigms, and more concerned with understanding the nature of the cognitive mechanisms and processes that underlie them. For example, cognitive psychologists interested in judgmental processes should look at a variety of different paradigms, including those used by cognitive social psychologists (see Nisbett and Ross, 1980). The disadvantages of limiting oneself to a particular paradigm – or class of paradigms – are two-fold. Firstly, one is denied access to the knowledge accumulated by other researchers studying the same processes by different means. Secondly, it is very difficult to tell which aspects of the data are paradigm-specific, and which indicative of more general features of the cognitive system under study. My recommendations in this respect have implications for theory construction, also. The current vogue for constructing very precise models to fit the data of specified paradigms (e.g. Clark and Chase, 1972) is not seen as very productive. This exercise tells us more about the tasks than the people who perform them. At the risk of condemning my own efforts (cf. Evans, 1977b), I must say that the construction of precise models is premature, when we do not have a clear, general picture of the organisation and function of cognitive systems. Model building may even be counter-productive, in that the elegance of the explanation distracts us from the all too severe limitations of that which is being explained.

In essence, the psychology of reasoning involves the study of processes derived from the same cognitive systems that underlie the results of other cognitive research. The concern with logic and rationalism has created an illusory isolation of the field. It is now time to perceive and pursue reasoning research in its correct context, and to recognise that the objectives, methods, and indeed fundamental difficulties, are not peculiar to the field, but are shared by all psychologists who seek to understand cognition.

References

Adams, M. J. (1978), 'Logical competence and transitive inference in young children', *Journal of Experimental Child Psychology*, 25, pp. 477–89.

Allport, D. A. (1975), 'The state of cognitive psychology, a critical notice of W. G. Chase (ed.), *Visual Information Processing*', *Quarterly Journal of Experimental Psychology*, 27, pp. 141–52.

Allport, D. A. (1980a), 'Patterns and actions: cognitive mechanisms are content specific', in G. Claxton (ed.), *Cognitive Psychology: New Directions*, Routledge & Kegan Paul: London.

Allport, D. A. (1980b), 'Attention and performance', in G. Claxton (ed.), *Cognitive Psychology: New Directions*, Routledge & Kegan Paul: London.

Anderson, J. R. (1976), *Language, Memory and Thought*, Erlbaum: New Jersey.

Anderson, J. R. (1978), 'Arguments concerning representations for mental imagery', *Psychological Review*, 85, pp. 249–77.

Anderson, J. R. (1979), 'Further arguments concerning representations for mental imagery: a response to Hayes-Roth and Pylyshyn', *Psychological Review*, 86, pp. 395–406.

Anderson, J. R. and Bower, G. H. (1973), *Human Associative Memory*, Winston: Washington, D.C.

Atwood, G. (1971), 'An experimental study of visual imagination and memory', *Cognitive Psychology*, 2, pp. 290–9.

Baddeley, A. D. and Hitch, G. J. (1974), 'Working memory', in G. A. Bower (ed.), *The Psychology of Learning and Motivation*, Academic Press: New York, pp. 47–90.

Begg, I. and Denny, P. J. (1969), 'Empirical reconciliation of atmosphere and conversion interpretations of syllogistic reasoning errors', *Journal of Experimental Psychology*, 81, pp. 351–4.

Bracewell, R. J. and Hidi, S. E. (1974), 'The solution of an inferential problem as a function of the stimulus materials', *Quarterly Journal of Experimental Psychology*, 26, pp. 480–8.

Braine, M. D. S. (1978), 'On the relation between the natural logic of reasoning and standard logic', *Psychological Review*, 85, pp. 1–21.

Bree, D. S. (1973), 'The interpretation of implication', in A. Elithorn and

D. Jones (eds), *Artificial and Human Thinking*, Elsevier Scientific Publications: Amsterdam.

Bree, D. S. and Coppens, G. (1976), 'The difficulty of an implication task', *British Journal of Psychology*, 67, pp. 579–86.

Bree, D. S. and Coppens, G. (1978), 'A reply to Moshman', *British Journal of Psychology*, 69, pp. 373–4.

Brooks, L. R. (1967), 'The suppression of visualisation by reading', *Quarterly Journal of Experimental Psychology*, 19, pp. 289–99.

Brooks, L. R. (1968), 'Spatial and verbal components of the act of recall', *Canadian Journal of Psychology*, 22, pp. 349–68.

Bruner, J. S., Goodnow, J. J. and Austin, G. A. (1956), *A Study of Thinking*, Wiley: New York.

Bryant, P. E. and Trabasso, T. (1971), 'Transitive inferences and memory in young children', *Nature*, 232, pp. 456–8.

Bucci, W. (1978), 'The interpretation of universal affirmative propositions', *Cognition*, 6, pp. 55–77.

Byrne, R. (1977), 'Planning meals: problem solving with a real data base', *Cognition*, 5, pp. 287–332.

Campbell, A. C. (1965), 'On the solving of code items demanding the use of indirect procedures', *British Journal of Psychology*, 56, pp. 45–51.

Carpenter, P. A. and Just, M. A. (1975), 'Sentence comprehension: a psycholinguistic processing model of verification', *Psychological Review*, 82, pp. 45–73.

Carpenter, P. A. and Just, M. A. (1976), 'Models of sentence verification and linguistic comprehension', *Psychological Review*, 83, pp. 318–29.

Carr, T. H. and Bacharach, V. R. (1977), 'Encoding and performance in sentence verification under varying memory load', *Memory and Cognition*, 5, pp. 590–6.

Catlin, J. and Jones, N. K. (1976), 'Verifying positive and negative sentences', *Psychological Review*, 83, pp. 497–501.

Ceraso, J. and Provitera, A, (1971), 'Sources of error in syllogistic reasoning', *Cognitive Psychology*, 2, pp. 400–10.

Chapman, L. J. and Chapman, J. P. (1959), 'Atmosphere effect re-examined', *Journal of Experimental Psychology*, 58, pp. 220–6.

Chase, W. G. and Clark, H. H. (1971), 'Semantics in the perception of verticality', *British Journal of Psychology*, 62, pp. 311–16.

Chomsky, N. (1957), *Syntactic Structures*, Mouton: The Hague.

Chomsky, N. (1959), 'Review of Skinner's Verbal Behaviour', *Language*, 35, pp. 26–38.

Chomsky, N. (1965), *Aspects of the Theory of Syntax*, MIT Press: Cambridge, Mass.

Chomsky, N. (1968), *Language and Mind*, Harper & Row: New York.

Clark, H. H. (1969), 'Linguistic processes in deductive reasoning', *Psychological Review*, 76, pp. 387–404.

Clark, H. H. (1970), 'How we understand negation', Paper presented to the COBRE workshop on Cognitive Organisation and Psychological Processes, Huntingdon Beach, California.

Clark, H. H. (1971), 'More about "Adjectives, comparatives and syllogisms": a reply to Huttenlocher and Higgins', *Psychological Review*, 78, pp. 505–14.

Clark, H. H. (1972), 'On the evidence concerning J. Huttenlocher and E. T. Higgins' theory of reasoning: a second reply', *Psychological Review*, 79, pp. 428–32.

Clark, H. H. (1973), 'The language-as-fixed-effect fallacy: a critique of language statistics in psychological research', *Journal of Verbal Learning and Verbal Behavior*, 12, pp. 335–9.

Clark, H. H., Carpenter, P. A. and Just, M. A. (1973), 'On the meetings of semantics and perception', in W. G. Chase (ed.) *Visual Information Processing*, Academic Press: New York.

Clark, H. H. and Chase, W. G. (1972), 'On the process of comparing sentences against pictures', *Cognitive Psychology*, 3, pp. 472–517.

Clark, H. H. and Chase, W. G. (1974), 'Perceptual coding strategies in the formation and verification of descriptions', *Memory and Cognition*, 2, pp. 101–11.

Clark, H. H. and Clark, E. V. (1977), *Psychology and Language*, Harcourt: New York.

Cohen, G. (1977), *The Psychology of Cognition*, Academic Press: London.

Cooper, L. A. (1975), 'Mental rotation of random two-dimension shapes', *Cognitive Psychology*, 7, pp. 20–43.

Cooper, L. A. and Shepard, P. N. (1973), 'Chronometric studies of rotation of mental images', in Chase, W. G. (ed.), *Visual Information Processing*, Academic Press: New York.

Costermans, J. and Hupet, M. (1977), 'The other side of Johnson-Laird's interpretation of the passive voice', *British Journal of Psychology*, 68, pp. 107–11.

De Soto, L. B., London, M. and Handel, L. S. (1965), 'Social reasoning and spatial paralogic', *Journal of Personality and Social Psychology*, 2, pp. 513–21.

Dickstein, L. S. (1975), 'Effects of instructions and premise order on errors in syllogistic reasoning', *Journal of Experimental Psychology: Human Learning and Memory*, 104, pp. 376–84.

Dickstein, L. S. (1976), 'Differential difficulty of categorical syllogisms', *Bulletin of the Psychonomic Society*, 8, pp. 330–2.

Dickstein, L. S. (1978a), 'The effect of figure on syllogistic reasoning', *Memory and Cognition*, 6, pp. 76–83.

Dickstein, L. S. (1978b), 'Error processes in syllogistic reasoning', *Memory and Cognition*, 6, pp. 537–43.

Divesta, F. J., Ingersoll, G. and Sunshine, P. (1971), 'A factor analysis of imagery tests', *Journal of Verbal Learning and Verbal Behavior*, 10, pp. 471–97.

Donaldson, M. (1959), 'Positive and negative information in matching problems', *British Journal of Psychology*, 50, pp. 235–62.

Donaldson, M. (1978), *Children's Minds*, Fontana: Glasgow.

Eifermann, R. R. (1961), 'Negation as a linguistic variable', *Acta Psychologica*, 18, pp. 258–73.

Ennis, R. H. (1976), 'An alternative to Piaget's conceptualisation of logical competence', *Child Development*, 17, pp. 903–19.

Erikson, J. R. (1974), 'A set analysis theory of behaviour in formal syllogistic reasoning tasks', in R. L. Salso (ed.), *Theories of Cognitive Psychology*, Erlbaum: New Jersey.

Erikson, J. R. (1978), 'Research on syllogistic reasoning', in R. Revlin and R. E. Mayer, *Human Reasoning*, Wiley: New York.

Evans, J. St. B. T. (1972a), 'On the problems of interpreting reasoning data: logical and psychological approaches', *Cognition*, 1, pp. 373–84.

Evans, J. St. B. T. (1972b), 'Reasoning with negatives', *British Journal of Psychology*, 63, pp. 213–19.

Evans, J. St. B. T. (1972c), 'Interpretation and "matching bias" in a reasoning task', *Quarterly Journal of Experimental Psychology*, 24, pp. 193–9.

Evans, J. St. B. T. (1972d), 'Deductive reasoning and linguistic usage', Unpublished PhD. thesis, University of London.

Evans, J. St. B. T. (1975), 'On interpreting reasoning data: a reply to Van Duyne', *Cognition*, 3, pp. 387–90.

Evans, J. St. B. T. (1977a), 'Linguistic factors in reasoning', *Quarterly Journal of Experimental Psychology*, 29, pp. 297–306.

Evans, J. St. B. T. (1977b) 'Toward a statistical theory of reasoning', *Quarterly Journal of Experimental Psychology*, 29, pp. 621–35.

Evans, J. St. B. T. (1980a), 'Current issues in the psychology of reasoning', *British Journal of Psychology*, 71, pp. 227–39.

Evans, J. St. B. T. (1980b), 'Thinking: experiential and information processing approaches', in G. Claxton (ed.), *Cognitive Psychology: New Directions*, Routledge & Kegan Paul: London.

Evans, J. St. B. T. and Brooks, P. G. (1981), 'Competing with reasoning: a test of the working memory hypothesis', *Current Psychological Research*, 1, pp. 139–47.

Evans, J. St. B. T. and Lynch J. S. (1973), 'Matching bias in the selection task', *British Journal of Psychology*, 64, pp. 391–7.

Evans, J. St. B. T. and Newstead, S. E. (1977), 'Language and reasoning: a study of temporal factors', *Cognition*, 8, pp. 265–83.

Evans, J. St. B. T. and Newstead, S. E. (1980), 'A study of disjunctive reasoning', *Psychological Research*, 41, pp. 373–88.

Evans, J. St. B. T. and Wason, P. C. (1976), 'Rationalisation in a reasoning task', *British Journal of Psychology*, 63, pp. 205–12.

Falmagne, R. J. (ed.) (1975), *Reasoning: Representation and Process*, Wiley: New York.

Feather, N. T. (1964), 'Acceptance and rejection of arguments in relation to attitude strength, critical ability and intolerance of inconsistency', *Journal of Abnormal and Social Psychology*, 69, pp. 127–36.

Fellows, B. J. (1976), 'The role of introspection in problem solving research: a reply to Evans', *British Journal of Psychology*, 67, pp. 519–20.

Fillenbaum, S. (1966), 'Memory for gist: some relevant variables', *Language and Speech*, 9, pp. 217–27.

Fillenbaum, S. (1975), 'If: some uses', *Psychological Research*, 37, pp. 245–60.

Fillenbaum, S. (1976), 'Inducements: on phrasing and logic of conditional promises, threats and warnings', *Psychological Research*, 38, pp. 231–50.

Flavell, J. H. and Wohlwill, J. F. (1969), 'Formal and functional aspects of cognitive development', in D. Elklind and J. H. Flavell (eds), *Studies in Cognitive Development*, Oxford University Press: New York.

Frase, L. T. (1966), 'Validity judgments in relation to two sets of items', *Journal of Educational Psychology*, 57, pp. 539–45.

Frase, L. T. (1968), 'Effects of semantic incompatibility upon deductive reasoning', *Psychonomic Science*, 12, p. 64.

French, P. L. (1979), 'Linguistic marking, strategy and affect in syllogistic reasoning', *Journal of Psycholinguistic Research*, 8, pp. 425–49.

Galton, F. (1883), *Inquiries into Human Faculty*, Macmillan: London.

Geiss, M. C. and Zwicky, A. M. (1971), 'On invited inferences', *Linguistic Inquiry*, 2, pp. 561–6.

Gilhooly, K. J. and Falconer, W. A. (1974), 'Concrete and abstract terms and relations in testing a rule', *Quarterly Journal of Experimental Psychology*, 26, pp. 355–9.

Glushko, R. J. and Cooper, L. A. (1978), 'Spatial comprehension and comparison processes in verification tasks', *Cognitive Psychology*, 10, pp. 391–421.

Golding, E. (1980), 'Non-dominant hemisphere ECT and reasoning', Paper read to the British Psychology Society at Aberdeen.

Golding, E. (1981), 'The effect of unilateral brain lesions on reasoning', *Cortex* (in press).

Golding, E., Reich, S. S. and Wason, P. C. (1974), 'Interhemispheric differences in problem solving', *Perception*, 3, pp. 231–5.

Goldman-Eisler, F. and Cohen, M. (1970), 'Is N, P and PN difficulty a valid criterion of transformational operations?', *Journal of Verbal Learning and Verbal Behavior*, 9, pp. 161–6.

Goodwin, R. Q. and Wason, P. C. (1972), 'Degrees of Insight', *British Journal of Psychology*, 63, pp. 205–12.

Gorden, R. L. (1953), 'The effect of attitude towards Russia on logical reasoning', *Journal of Social Psychology*, 37, pp. 103–11.

Gough, P. B. (1965), 'Grammatical transformations and the speed of understanding', *Journal of Verbal Learning and Verbal Behavior*, 4, pp. 107–11.

Gough, P. B. (1966), 'The verification of sentences: the effect of delay of evidence and sentence length', *Journal of Verbal Learning and Verbal Behavior*, 5, pp. 492–6.

Greene, J. M. (1970a), 'The semantic function of negatives and passives', *British Journal of Psychology*, 61, pp. 17–22.

Greene, J. M. (1970b), 'Syntactic form and semantic function', *Quarterly Journal of Experimental Psychology*, 22, pp. 14–27.

Greene, J. M. (1972), *Psycholinguistics: Chomsky and Psychology*, Penguin: Harmondsworth.

Griggs, R. A. (1976), 'Logical processing of set inclusion relations in meaningful text', *Memory and Cognition*, 4, pp. 730–40.

Griggs, R. A. (1978), 'Drawing inferences from set inclusion information given in text', in R. Revlin and R. E. Mayer (eds), *Human Reasoning*, Wiley: New York.

Griggs, R. A. and Osterman, L. J. (1980), 'Processing artificial set inclusion relations', *Journal of Experimental Psychology: Human Learning and Memory*, 6, pp. 39–52.

Harris, R. J. and Monaco, G. E. (1978), 'Psychology of pragmatic implication: information processing between the lines', *Journal of Experimental Psychology: General*, 107, pp. 1–22.

Hayes-Roth, F. (1979), 'Distinguishing theories of representation: a critique of Anderson's "Arguments concerning mental imagery"', *Psychological Review*, 86, pp. 376–82.

Henle, M. (1962), 'On the relation between logic and thinking', *Psychological Review*, 69, pp. 366–78.

Henle, M. and Michael, M. (1956), 'The influence of attitudes on syllogistic reasoning', *Journal of Social Psychology*, 44, pp. 115–27.

Higgins, E. T. (1976), 'Effects of presuppositions on deductive reasoning', *Journal of Verbal Learning and Verbal Behavior*, 15, pp. 419–30.

Hitch, G. J. and Baddeley, A. D. (1976), 'Verbal reasoning and working memory', *Quarterly Journal of Experimental Psychology*, 28, pp. 603–21.

Hovland, C. I. and Weiss, W. (1953), 'Transmission of information concerning concepts through positive and negative instances', *Journal of Experimental Psychology*, 45, pp. 178–82.

Hunter, I. M. L. (1957), 'The solving of three-term series problems', *British Journal of Psychology*, 48, pp. 286–98.

Huttenlocher, J. (1968), 'Constructing spatial images: a strategy in reasoning', *Psychological Review*, 75, pp. 286–98.

Huttenlocher, J. and Higgins, E. T. (1971), 'Adjectives, comparatives and syllogisms', *Psychological Review*, 78, pp. 487–504.

Huttenlocher, J. and Higgins, E. T. (1972), 'On reasoning, congruence and other matters', *Psychological Review*, 79, pp. 420–7.

Huttenlocher, J., Higgins, E. T., Milligan, L. and Kaufman, B. (1970), 'The mystery of the negative equative construction', *Journal of Verbal Learning and Verbal Behavior*, 9, pp. 334–41.

Inhelder, B. and Piaget, J. (1958), *The Growth of Logical Thinking*, Basic Books: New York.

Janis, I. L. and Frick, F. (1943), 'The relationship between attitudes towards conclusions and errors in judging logical validity of syllogisms', *Journal of Experimental Psychology*, 33, pp. 73–7.

Johnson-Laird, P. N. (1968a), 'The interpretation of the passive voice', *Quarterly Journal of Experimental Psychology*, 20, pp. 69–73.

Johnson-Laird, P. N. (1968b), 'The choice of the passive voice in a communicative task', *British Journal of Psychology*, 59, pp. 7–15.

Johnson-Laird, P. N. (1972), 'The three-term series problem', *Cognition*, 1, pp. 57–82.

Johnson-Laird, P. N. (1975), 'Models of deduction', in R. J. Falmagne (ed.), *Reasoning: Representation and Process*, Wiley: New York.

Johnson-Laird, P. N. (1977), 'The passive paradox: a reply to Costermans and Hupet', *British Journal of Psychology*, 68, pp. 113–16.

Johnson-Laird, P. N. (1979), 'Mental models in cognitive science', La Jolla Conference on Cognitive Science, California.

Johnson-Laird, P. N., Legrenzi, P. and Legrenzi, M. S. (1972), 'Reasoning and a sense of reality', *British Journal of Psychology*, 63, pp. 395–400.

Johnson-Laird P. N. and Steedman, M. (1978), 'The psychology of syllogisms', *Cognitive Psychology*, 10, pp. 64–98.

Johnson-Laird, P. N. and Stevenson, R. (1970), 'Memory for syntax', *Nature*, 227, p. 1412.

Johnson-Laird, P. N. and Tagart, J. (1969), 'How implication is understood', *American Journal of Psychology*, 2, pp. 367–73.

Johnson-Laird, P. N. and Tridgell, J. M. (1972), 'When negation is easier than affirmation', *Quarterly Journal of Experimental Psychology*, 24, pp. 87–91.

Johnson-Laird, P. N. and Wason, P. C. (1970), 'A theoretical analysis of insight into a reasoning task', *Cognitive Psychology*, 1, pp. 134–48.

Johnson-Laird, P. N. and Wason, P. C. (1977) (eds), *Thinking: Readings in Cognitive Science*, Cambridge University Press: Cambridge.

Jones, S. (1966a), 'The effect of a negative qualifier in an instruction', *Journal of Verbal Learning and Verbal Behavior*, 5, pp. 497–501.

Jones, S. (1966b), 'Decoding a deceptive instruction', *British Journal of Psychology*, 57, pp. 405–11.

Jones, S. (1968), 'Instructions, self-instructions and performance', *Quarterly Journal of Experimental Psychology*, 20, pp. 74–8.

Jones, S. (1970), 'Visual and verbal processes in problem solving', *Cognitive Psychology*, 1, pp. 201–14.

Just, M. A. and Carpenter, P. A. (1971), 'Comprehension of a negative with quantification', *Journal of Verbal Learning and Verbal Behavior*, 10, pp. 244–53.

Just, M. A. and Carpenter, P. A. (1976a), 'The relation between comprehending and remembering complex sentences', *Memory and Cognition*, 4, pp. 318–22.

Just, M. A. and Carpenter, P. A. (1976b), 'Eye fixations and cognitive processes', *Cognitive Psychology*, 8, pp. 449–80.

Kahneman, D. and Tversky, A. (1972), 'Subjective probability: A judgment of representativeness', *Cognitive Psychology*, 3, pp. 430–54.

Katz, A. N. (1980), 'Cognitive arithmetic: evidence for right hemisphere mediation in an elementary component state', *Quarterly Journal of Experimental Psychology*, 32, pp. 69–84.

Kaufman, H. and Goldstein, S. (1967), 'The effect of emotional value of conclusions upon distortion in syllogistic reasoning', *Psychonomic Science*, 7, pp. 367–8.

Kelly, G. A. (1955), *The Psychology of Personal Constructs* (2 vols), Norton: New York.

Kelly, H. (1967), 'Attribution theory in social psychology', in D. Levine-(ed.), *Nebraska Symposium on Motivation*, University of Nebraska Press: Lincoln.

Kelly, H. (1972), 'Attribution theory in social interaction', in E. E. Jones (ed.), *Attribution: Perceiving the Causes of Behaviour*, General Learning Press: Morristown, N.J.

Kieras, D. (1978), 'Beyond pictures and words: alternative information processing models for imagery effects in verbal memory', *Psychological Bulletin*, 85, pp. 532–4.

Kintsch, W. (1974), *The Representation of Meaning in Memory*, Erlbaum: New Jersey.

Klahr, D. and Wallace, J. G. (1976), *Cognitive Development: An Information Processing View*, Erlbaum: New Jersey.

Kordoff, J. K. and Roberge, J. J. (1975), 'Developmental analysis of the conditional reasoning abilities of primary grade children', *Developmental Psychology*, 11, pp. 21–8.

Kosslyn, S. M. (1975), 'Information representation in visual images', *Cognitive Psychology*, 7, pp. 341–70.

Kosslyn, S. M. (1978), 'Measuring the visual angle of the mind's eye', *Cognitive Psychology*, 10, pp. 356–89.

Kosslyn, S. M. and Pomeranz, J. R. (1977), 'Imagery, propositions and the form of internal representations', *Cognitive Psychology*, 9, pp. 52–76.

Kosslyn, S. M. and Schwartz, S. P. (1977), 'A data driven simulation of visual imagery', *Cognitive Science*, 1, pp. 265–96.

Kubovy, M. (1977), 'Response availability and the apparent spontaneity of numerical choices', *Journal of Experimental Psychology: Human Perception and Performance*, 3, pp. 359–64.

Lee, W. (1971), *Decision Theory and Human Behaviour*, Wiley: New York.

Lefford, A. (1946), 'The influence of emotional subject matter on logical reasoning', *Journal of General Psychology*, 34, pp. 127–51.

Legrenzi, P. (1970), 'Relations between language and reasoning about deductive rules', in G. B. Flores D'Arcais and W. J. M. Levelt (eds), *Advances in Psycholinguistics*, North Holland: Amsterdam.

Lemmon, E. J. (1965), *Beginning Logic*, Nelson: London.

Lichtenstein, S., Slovic, P., Fischoff, B., Layman, M. and Combs, B. (1978), 'Judged frequency of lethal events', *Journal of Experimental Psychology: Human Learning and Memory*, 6, pp. 551–79.

Lunzer, E. A., Harrison, C. and Davey, M. (1972), 'The four card problem and the generality of formal reasoning', *Quarterley Journal of Experimental Psychology*, 24, pp. 326–39.

Manktelow, K. I. (1980), 'The role of content in reasoning', Unpublished PhD thesis, Plymouth Polytechnic.

Manktelow, K. I. and Evans, J. St. B. T. (1979), 'Facilitation of reasoning by realism: effect or non-effect?', *British Journal of Psychology*, 71, pp. 227–31.

Marcus, S. L. and Rips, L. J. (1979), 'Conditional reasoning', *Journal of Verbal Learning and Verbal Behavior*, 18, pp. 199–223.

Mehler, J. (1963), 'Some effects of grammatical transformations on the recall of English sentences', *Journal of Verbal Learning and Verbal Behavior*, 2, pp. 346–51.

Miller, G. A. (1962), 'Some psychological studies of grammar', *American Psychologist*, 17, pp. 748–62.

Miller, G. A. (1967), *The Psychology of Communication*, Basic Books: New York.

Miller, G. A., Galanter, E. and Pribram, K. H. (1960), *Plans and the Structure of Behavior*, Holt, Rinehart & Winston: New York.

Miller, G. A. and Johnson-Laird, P. N. (1976), *Language and Perception*, Harvard University Press: Cambridge, Mass.

Miller, G. A. and McKean, K. O. (1964), 'A chronometric study of some relations between sentences', *Quarterly Journal of Experimental Psychology*, 16, pp. 297–308.

Morgan, J. I. B. and Morton, J. T. (1944), 'The distortions of syllogistic reasoning produced by personal connections', *Journal of Social Psychology*, 20, pp. 39–59.

Mosenthal, P. (1977), 'Psycholinguistic properties of aural and visual comprehension as determined by children's ability to comprehend syllogisms', *Reading Research Quarterly*, 22, pp. 55–92.

Moshman, D. (1978), 'Some comments on Bree and Coppens' "The difficulty of an implication task" ', *British Journal of Psychology*, 69, pp. 371–2.

Moyer, R. S. (1973), 'Comparing objects in memory: evidence suggesting an internal psychophysics', *Perception and Psychophysics*, 13, pp. 180–4.

Mynatt, C. R., Doherty, M. E. and Tweney, R. D. (1977), 'Confirmation bias in a simulated research environment: an experimental study of scientific inference', *Quarterly Journal of Experimental Psychology*, 29, pp. 85–96.

Neilsen, G. and Smith, E. (1973), 'Imaginal and verbal representations in short-term recognition of visual forms', *Journal of Experimental Psychology*, 101, pp. 375–8.

Neimark, E. D. and Chapman R. A. (1975), 'Development of the comprehension of logical quantifiers', in R. J. Falmagne (ed.), *Reasoning: Representation and Process*, Wiley: New York.

Neisser, U. (1963), 'The multiplicity of thought', *British Journal of Psychology*, 54, pp. 1–14.

Neisser, U. (1967), *Cognitive Psychology*, Appleton-Century-Crofts: New York.

Neisser, U. (1976), *Cognition and Reality*, Freeman: San Francisco.

Newell, A. and Simon, H. A. (1972), *Human Problem Solving*, Prentice-Hall: Englewood Cliffs, N.J.

Nisbett, R. E. and Ross, L. (1980), *Human Inference: Strategies and Shortcomings of Social Judgment*, Prentice-Hall: Englewood Cliffs, N.J.

Nisbett, R. E. and Wilson, T. D. (1977), 'Telling more than we can know: verbal reports on mental processes', *Psychological Review*, 84, pp. 231–59.

O'Brien, T. C. and Shapiro, B. J. (1968), 'The development of logical thinking in children', *American Educational Research Journal*, 5, pp. 531–42.

Olson, D. R. and Filby, N. (1972), 'On the comprehension of active and passive sentences', *Cognitive Psychology*, 3, pp. 361–81.

Osherson, D. (1975), 'Logic and models of logical thinking', in R. J. Falmagne (ed.), *Reasoning: Representation and Process*, Wiley: New York.

Paivio, A. (1971), *Imagery and Verbal Processes*, Holt, Rinehart and Winston: New York.

Paivio, A. (1975), 'Imagery and synchronic thinking', *Canadian Psychological Review*, 16, pp. 147–63.

Paivio, A. (1976), 'Images, propositions and knowledge', in J. M. Nicholas (ed.), *Images, Perception and Knowledge*, Dordrecht: Reidel.

Paris, S. G. (1973), 'Comprehension of language connectives and propositional logical relationships', *Journal of Experimental Child Psychology*, 16, pp. 278–91.

Perky, C. W. (1910), 'An experimental study of imagination', *American Journal of Psychology*, 21, pp. 422–52.

Pezzoli, J. A. and Frase, L. T. (1968), 'Mediated facilitation of syllogistic reasoning', *Journal of Experimental Psychology*, 78, pp. 228–32.

Phillips, W. A. and Christie, D. F. M. (1977), 'Interference with visualisation', *Quarterly Journal of Experimental Psychology*, 29, pp. 637–50.

Piaget, J. (1972), 'Intellectual evolution from adolescence to adulthood', *Human Development*, 15, pp. 1–12.

Pollard, P. (1979a), 'Human reasoning: logical and non-logical explanations', Unpublished PhD Thesis, Plymouth Polytechnic.

Pollard, P. (1979b), 'Evans' stochastic reasoning model: a re-evaluation', Paper read to the joint scientific meeting of the British Psychological Society's Cognitive and Mathematical & Statistical sections on 'Cognitive Models' at City of London Polytechnic.

Pollard, P. (1981), 'The effect of thematic content on the Wason selection task', *Current Psychological Research*, 1, pp. 21–30.

Pollard, P. and Evans, J. St. B. T. (1980), 'The influence of logic on conditional reasoning performance', *Quarterly Journal of Experimental Psychology*, 32, pp. 605–24.

Pollard, P. and Evans J. St. B. T. (1981), 'The effect of prior beliefs in reasoning: an associational interpretation', *British Journal of Psychology*, 72, pp. 73–82.

Popper, K. (1959), *The Logic of Scientific Discovery*, Hutchinson: London.

Potts, G. R. (1972), 'Information-processing strategies of the encoding of linear ordering', *Journal of Verbal Learning and Verbal Behavior*, 11, pp. 727–40.

Potts, G. R. (1974), 'Storing and retrieving information about ordered relationships', *Journal of Experimental Psychology*, 103, pp. 431–9.

Potts, G. R. (1976), 'Artificial logical relationships and their relevance to semantic memory', *Journal of Experimental Psychology: Human Learning and Memory*, 2, pp. 746–58.

Potts, G. R. (1978), 'The role of inference in memory for real and artificial information', in R. Revlin and R. E. Mayer (eds), *Human Reasoning*, Wiley: New York.

Potts, G. R. and Scholtz, K. W. (1975), 'The internal representation of three-term series problems', *Journal of Verbal Learning and Verbal Behavior*, 14, pp. 439–52.

Pylyshyn, Z. W. (1973), 'What the mind's eye tells the mind's brain: a critique of mental imagery', *Psychological Bulletin*, 80, pp. 1–24.

Pylyshyn, Z. W. (1979), 'Validating computer models: a critique of Anderson's indeterminacy of representation'. *Psychological Review*, 86, pp. 383–94.

Quinton, G. and Fellows, S. B. J. (1975), ' "Perceptual" strategies in the solving of three-term series problems', *British Journal of Psychology*, 66, pp. 69–78.

Revlin, R. and Leirer, V. O. (1978), 'The effect of personal biases on syllogistic reasoning: rational decisions from personalized representations', in R. Revlin and R. E. Mayer (eds), *Human Reasoning*, Wiley: New York.

Revlin, R. and Mayer, R. E. (eds), (1978), *Human Reasoning*, Wiley: New York.

Revlis, R. (1975a), 'Two models of syllogistic reasoning: Feature Selection and Conversion', *Journal of Verbal Learning and Verbal Behavior*, 14, pp. 180–95.

Revlis, R. (1975b), 'Syllogistic reasoning: logical decisions from a complex data base', in R. J. Falmagne (ed.), *Reasoning: Representation and Process*, Wiley: New York.

Richardson, A. (1969), *Mental Imagery*, Springer: New York.

Richardson, A. (1977), 'The meaning and measurement of visual imagery', *British Journal of Psychology*, 68, pp. 29–43.

Richardson, J. T. E. (1978), 'Reported mediators and individual differences in mental imagery', *Memory and Cognition*, 6, pp. 376–8.

Rips, L. J. and Marcus, S. L. (1977), 'Suppositions and the analysis of conditional sentences', in M. A. Just and P. A. Carpenter (eds), *Cognitive Processes in Comprehension*, Wiley: New York.

Roberge, J. J. (1970), 'A study of children's ability to reason with basic principles in deductive reasoning', *American Educational Research Journal*, 7, pp. 583–96.

Roberge, J. J. (1971a), 'Further examination of mediated associations in deductive reasoning', *Journal of Experimental Psychology*, 87, pp. 127–9.

Roberge, J. J. (1971b), 'Some effects of negation on adults' conditional reasoning abilities', *Psychological Reports*, 29, pp. 839–44.

Roberge, J. J. (1974), 'Effects of negation on adults' comprehension of fallacious conditional and disjunctive arguments', *Journal of General Psychology*, 91, pp. 287–93.

Roberge, J. J. (1976a), 'Effects of negation on adults' disjunctive reasoning abilities', *Journal of General Psychology*, 94, pp. 23–8.

Roberge, J. J. (1976b), 'Reasoning with exclusive disjunctive arguments', *Quarterly Journal of Experimental Psychology*, 28, pp. 419–27.

Roberge, J. J. (1977), 'Effects of content on inclusive disjunctive reasoning', *Quarterly Journal of Experimental Psychology*, 29, pp. 669–76.

Roberge, J. J. (1978), 'Linguistic and psychometric factors in propositional reasoning', *Quarterly Journal of Experimental Psychology*, 30, pp. 705–16.

Roth, E. M. (1979), 'Facilitating insight into a reasoning task', *British Journal of Psychology*, 70, pp. 265–72.

Ryle, G. (1949), *The Concept of Mind*, Hutchinson: London.

Salthouse, T. A. (1974), 'Using selective interference to investigate spatial memory representations', *Memory and Cognition*, 2, pp. 749–57.

Salthouse, T. A. (1975), 'Simultaneous processing of verbal and spatial information', *Memory and Cognition*, 3, pp. 221–5.

Savin, A. B. and Perchoneck, E. (1965), 'Grammatical structure and the immediate recall of English sentences', *Journal of Verbal Learning and Verbal Behavior*, 4, pp. 348–53.

Scholtz, K. W. and Potts, G. R. (1974), 'Cognitive processing of linear orderings', *Journal of Experimental Psychology*, 102, pp. 323–6.

Segal, S. J. (1971), 'Processing of the stimulus in imagery and perception', in S. J. Segal (ed.), *Imagery: Current Cognitive Approaches*, Academic Press: New York.

Segal, S. J. and Fusella, V. (1969), 'Effects of imaging on signal to noise ratio and varying signal conditions', *British Journal of Psychology*, 60, pp. 494–64.

Segal, S. J. and Fusella, V. (1970), 'Influence of imaged pictures and sounds on detection of visual and auditory signals', *Journal of Experimental Psychology*, 83, pp. 458–64.

Sells, S. B. (1936), 'The atmosphere effect: an experimental study of reasoning', *Archives of Psychology*, no. 200.

Seymour, P. H. K. (1974), 'Pictorial coding of verbal descriptions', *Quarterly Journal of Experimental Psychology*, 26, pp. 39–51.

Seymour, P. H. K. (1975), 'Semantic equivalence of verbal and pictorial displays', in A. Kennedy and A. Wilkes (eds), *Studies in Long-term Memory*, Wiley: Chichester.

Shanck, R. C. (1972), 'Conceptual dependency: a theory of natural language understanding', *Cognitive Psychology*, 3, pp. 552–631.

Shaver, P., Pierson, L. and Lang, S. (1975), 'Converging evidence for the functional significance of imagery in problem solving, *Cognition*, 3, pp. 359–75.

Sheehan, P. W. and Neisser, U. (1969), 'Some variables affecting the vividness of imagery in recall', *British Journal of Psychology*, 60, pp. 71–80.

Shepard, R. N. and Metzler, J. (1971), 'Mental rotation of three-dimensional objects', *Science*, 171, pp. 701–3.

Shoben, E. J. (1978), 'Choosing a model of sentence-picture comparison: a reply to Catlin and Jones', *Psychological Review*, 85, pp. 131–7.

Simon, H. A. (1979), 'Information processing models of cognition', *Annual Review of Psychology*, 30, pp. 363–96.

Simpson, M. E. and Johnson, D. M. (1966), 'Atmosphere and conversion errors in syllogistic reasoning', *Journal of Experimental Psychology*, 72, pp. 197–200.

Singer, J. L. (1966), *Daydreaming*, Random House: New York.

Skinner, B. F. (1972), *Beyond Freedom and Dignity*, Cape: London.

Slobin, D. I. (1966), 'Grammatical transformations and sentence comprehension in childhood and adulthood', *Journal of Verbal Learning and Verbal Behavior*, 5, pp. 219–27.

Slovic, P., Fischhoff, B. and Lichtenstein, S. (1977), 'Behavioural decision theory', *Annual Review of Psychology*, 28, pp. 1–39.

Smalley, N. S. (1974), 'Evaluating a rule against possible instances', *British Journal of Psychology*, 65, pp. 293–304.

Smedslund, J. (1970), 'On the circular relation between logic and understanding', *Scandinavian Journal of Psychology*, 11, pp. 217–19.

Smith, E. R. and Miller, F. D. (1978), 'Limits on perception of cognitive processes: a reply to Nisbett and Wilson', *Psychological Review*, 85, pp. 355–62.

Smoke, K. L. (1932), 'An objective study of concept formation', *Psychological Monographs*, 42, no. 191.

Springston, F. J. and Clark, H. H. (1973), '*And* and *or* or the comprehension of pseudoimperatives', *Journal of Verbal Learning and Verbal Behavior*, 12, pp. 258–72.

Staudenmayer, H. (1975), 'Understanding conditional reasoning with meaningful propositions', in R. J. Falmagne (ed.) *Reasoning: Representation and Process*, Wiley: New York.

Staudenmayer, H. and Bourne, L. E. (1978), 'The nature of denied propositions in the conditional reasoning task: interpretation and learning', in R. Revlin and R. E. Mayer (eds), *Human Reasoning*, Wiley: New York.

Suppes, P. (1965), 'On the behavioral foundations of mathematical concepts', in L. N. Morrissett and J. Visonhaler (eds), *Mathematical Learning, Monographs of the Society for Research in Child Development*, 30, pp. 60–96.

Tanenhaus, M. K., Carroll, J. M. and Bever, T. G. (1976), 'Sentence-picture verification models as theories of sentence comprehension: a critique of Carpenter and Just', *Psychological Review*, 83, pp. 310–17.

Taplin, J. E. (1971), 'Reasoning with conditional sentences', *Journal of Verbal Learning and Verbal Behavior*, 10, pp. 219–25.

Taplin, J. E. and Staudenmayer, H. (1973), 'Interpretation of abstract conditional sentences in deductive reasoning', *Journal of Verbal Learning and Verbal Behavior*, 12, pp. 530–42.

Trabasso, T. (1970), 'Reasoning and the processing of negative information', Paper presented to the 78th Annual Convention of the American Psychological Association.

Trabasso, T. (1977), 'The role of memory as a system in making transitive inferences', in R. V. Kail and J. W. Hagen (eds), *Perspectives in the Development of Memory and Cognition*, Erlbaum: New Jersey.

Trabasso, T., Riley, C. A. and Wilson, E. G. (1975), 'The representation of linear order and spatial strategies in reasoning: a developmental study', in R. J. Falmagne (ed.), *Reasoning: Representation and Process*, Wiley: New York.

Trabasso, T., Rollins, H. and Shaughnessy, E. (1971), 'Storage and verification stages in processing concepts', *Cognitive Psychology*, 2, pp. 239–89.

Tversky, A. and Kahneman, D. (1973), 'Availability: a heuristic for judging frequency and probability', *Cognitive Psychology*, 5, pp. 207–32.

Tweney, R. D., Doherty, M. E., Warner, W. J., Pliske, D. B., Mynatt, C. R., Gross, K. A. and Arkkezin, D. L. (1980), 'Strategies of rule discovery in an inference task', *Quarterly Journal of Experimental Psychology*, 32, pp. 109–24.

Van Duyne, H. J. and Sass, E. (1979), 'Verbal logic and ear-assymetry in third and fifth grade males and females', *Cortex*, 15, pp. 173–82.

Van Duyne, P. C. (1973), 'A short note on Evans' criticism of reasoning experiments and his matching bias hypothesis', *Cognition*, 2, pp. 239–42.

Van Duyne, P. C. (1974), 'Realism and linguistic complexity in reasoning', *British Journal of Psychology*, 65, pp. 59–67.

Van Duyne, P. C. (1976), 'Necessity and contingency in reasoning', *Acta Psychologica*, 40, pp. 85–101.

Vygotsky, L. S. (1962), *Thought and Language*, MIT Press: Cambridge, Mass.

Wannamacher, J. T. (1976), 'Processing strategies in sentence comprehension', *Memory and Cognition*, 4, pp. 48–52.

Wason, P. C. (1959), 'The processing of positive and negative information', *Quarterly Journal of Experimental Psychology*, 21, pp. 92–107.

Wason, P. C. (1960), 'On the failure to eliminate hypotheses in a conceptual task', *Quarterly Journal of Experimental Psychology*, 12, pp. 129–40.

Wason, P. C. (1961), 'Response to affirmative and negative binary statements', *British Journal of Psychology*, 52, pp. 133–42.

Wason, P. C. (1965), 'The contexts of plausible denial', *Journal of Verbal Learning and Verbal Behavior*, 4, pp. 7–11.

Wason, P. C. (1966), 'Reasoning', in B. M. Foss (ed.), *New Horizons in Psychology I*, Penguin: Harmondsworth.

Wason, P. C. (1968), 'Reasoning about a rule', *Quarterly Journal of Experimental Psychology*, 20, pp. 273–81.

Wason, P. C. (1969a), 'Regression in reasoning', *British Journal of Psychology*, 60, pp. 471–80.

Wason, P. C. (1969b), 'Structural simplicity and psychological complexity: some thoughts on a novel problem', *Bulletin of the British Psychological Society*, 60, pp. 471–80.

Wason, P. C. (1972), 'In real life negatives are false', *Logique et Analyse*, 19, pp. 19–38.

Wason, P. C. (1977a), 'Self-contradictions', in P. N. Johnson-Laird and P. C. Wason (eds), *Thinking: Readings in Cognitive Science*, Cambridge University Press: Cambridge.

Wason, P. C. (1977b), 'The theory of formal operations: a critique', in B. Geber (ed.), *Piaget and Knowing*, Routledge & Kegan Paul: London.

Wason, P. C. (1978), 'Hypothesis testing and reasoning', Unit 25, Block 4, *Cognitive Psychology*, Open University Press: Milton Keynes.

Wason, P. C. (1980), 'The verification task and beyond', in D. R. Olson (ed.), *The Social Foundations of Language and Thought*, New York: Norton.

Wason, P. C. and Brooks, P. G. (1979), 'THOG: the anatomy of a problem', *Psychological Research*, 41, pp. 79–90.

Wason, P. C. and Evans, J. St. B. T. (1975), 'Dual processes in reasoning?', *Cognition*, 3, pp. 141–54.

Wason, P. C. and Golding, E. (1974), 'The language of inconsistency', *British Journal of Psychology*, 65, pp. 537–46.

Wason, P. C. and Johnson-Laird, P. N. (1969), 'Proving a disjunctive rule', *Quarterly Journal of Experimental Psychology*, 21, pp. 14–20.

Wason, P. C. and Johnson-Laird, P. N. (1970), 'A conflict between selecting and evaluating information in an inferential task', *British Journal of Psychology*, 61, pp. 509–15.

Wason, P. C. and Johnson-Laird, P. N. (1972), *Psychology of Reasoning: Structure and Content*, Batsford: London.

Wason, P. C. and Jones, S. (1963), 'Negatives: denotation and connotation', *British Journal of Psychology*, 54, pp. 299–307.

Wason, P. C. and Shapiro, D. (1971), 'Natural and contrived experience in a reasoning problem', *Quarterly Journal of Experimental Psychology*, 23, pp. 63–71.

Whitfield, J. W. (1951), 'An experiment in problem solving', *Quarterly Journal of Experimental Psychology*, 3, pp. 184–97.

Wilkins, M. C. (1928), 'The effect of changed material on the ability to do formal syllogistic reasoning', *Archives of Psychology*, New York, no. 102.

Williams, R. L. (1979), 'Imagery and linguistic factors affecting the solution of linear syllogisms', *Journal of Psycholinguistic Research*, 8, pp. 123–40.

Winograd, T. (1972), 'Understanding natural language', *Cognitive Psychology*, 3, pp. 1–191.

Woodworth, R. S. and Sells, S. B. (1935), 'An atmosphere effect in syllogistic reasoning', *Journal of Experimental Psychology*, 18, pp. 451–60.

Young, R. and Chase, W. G. (1971), 'Additive stages in the comparison of sentences and pictures', Paper presented to the Mid-western Psychological Association, Chicago.

Zajonc, A. B. (1968), 'Cognitive theories in social psychology', in G. Lindzey and E. Aronson (eds), *The Handbook of Social Psychology*, vol 1, Addison-Wesley: London.

Name index

Subject index